EMERGING DIMENSIONS IN DECENTRALISATION

By the Same Author

(1) *New Panchayati Raj System at Work : An Evaluation*
(2) *Grassroot Democracy in Indian Society*
(3) *Capacity Building for Local Leaders*
(4) *Dynamics of New Panchayati Raj System in India (Vol. I)*
(5) *Dynamics of New Panchayati Raj System in India (Vol. II)*
(6) *New Panchayati Raj in Tamil Nadu (With Act in Original)*
(7) *Rural Transformation and Peoples Entitlements*
(8) *Dynamics of New Panchayati Raj System in India (Vol. III)*
(9) *Dynamics of New Panchayati Raj System in India (Vol. IV)*

About the Author

Ganapathy Palanithurai, Professor in Rajiv Gandhi Chair, Gandhigram Rural Institute is an academic activist working with the people in rural areas for building the capacity of the leaders and people to reinvent sustainable grassroots democracy. He is heading the Department of Political Science and Development Administration, in Gandhigram Rural University, Tamil Nadu. His policy advocacy role at the governmental level is increasingly felt at present in all the three levels, namely, sub-regional, regional and national as he does more field work than theorization. He has been associating himself with State Planning Commission of Tamil Nadu, Centre Planning Commission Population Foundation of India, Rajiv Gandhi Foundation, CAPART, Ministry of Rural Areas and Employment and DANIDA (Danish-Indo Development Agency) in specific areas of activities in connection with empowerment of people. He is in the network of the Non-Governmental Organisations for Panchayat activities. He involves himself in capacity building exercise for local body leaders. He has evolved training module and manual for local body leaders. He has to his credit twenty-nine books, seventy-five articles in reputed journals, ten working papers, seven monographs, seven review articles on three major areas, namely, Legislative Behaviour, Ethnicity and Panchayati Raj System. He was a recipient of Fellowship from Sastri Indo-Canadian Institute, New Delhi and World Academy of Art and Science, USA. He has visited the US and Canada, on academic assignments. He was a visiting fellow in the MiGill University, Canada in 1989. He is a life member of Indian Institute of Public Administration, Indian Association of Public Administration, Indian Association of Political Science, Indian Association of American Studies, and Indian Association of Canadian Studies. He is a member of the expert committee constituted by the Government of Tamil Nadu, to monitor the training programme for local body leaders.

EMERGING DIMENSIONS IN DECENTRALISATION

G. Palanithurai
Professor and Head,
Department of Political Science and Development Administration
Gandhigram Rural Institute — Deemed University
Gandhigram-624 302
Tamil Nadu

CONCEPT PUBLISHING COMPANY, NEW DELHI-110 059

Cataloging in Publication Data—DK
Courtesy: D.K. Agencies (P) Ltd. <docinfo@dkagencies.com>

Palanithurai, G. (Ganapathy), 1953-
Emerging dimensions in decentralisation/ G. Palanithurai.
p. cm.
Includes bibliographical references (p.)
Includes index.
ISBN 818069173X

1. Decentralization in government—India—Tamil Nadu. 2. Panchayat—India—Tamil Nadu.
I. Title.

DDC 352.283 095 482 21

The views and opinions expressed in this book are those of the author and do not necessarily reflect the views of the organization to which he belongs.

IISBN-81-8069-173-X

First Published 2005

Published and Printed by
Ashok Kumar Mittal
Concept Publishing Company
A/15-16, Commercial Block, Mohan Garden
NEW DELHI-110059 (India)

Phones : 25351460, 25351794
Fax : +91-11-25357103
Email : publishing@conceptpub.com

To

The Divine Mother

PREFACE

Exactly ten years after the passing of the 73rd Amendment to the Constitution of India, everyone is asking to what extent the objectives enshrined in the 73rd Amendment have been realized through the Panchayati Raj System in its functioning. The success of any system depends on how best the new system is perceived and operationalized by the people who are at the helm of affairs. In a diverse social structure, one cannot expect conformity in terms of the functions of institutions and organizations. The devolution process is also not a simple and easy task and it has to pass through several barriers and obstacles. The present scenario of Panchayati Raj facilitates a wide variety of changes in terms of the functions and their implications. There are success cases, failures and struggles in the Panchayats. The scenario varies from State to State. The implications of devolution vary from even district to district.

But, in Tamil Nadu, paradoxical situations are visible in the Panchayati Raj System. The devolution process is painful. Limited powers have been devolved. More responsibilities have been devolved and a very little resources are allocated to the Panchayats. No functionary's has been transferred to Panchayats. Yet success stories are abundant. With the limited power and finance Gram Panchayat Presidents have made a unique contribution in the social development sector. The representatives have formed their own associations and excerted pressure on the Government to devolve powers. Instead of begging they have started demanding power. Further they have assumed certain powers and demonstrated their potential. This is the story of devolution in Tamil Nadu. A number of experiments have been conducted in many Panchayats and the whole process has been documented in this small book. A variety of new phenomena are emerging from this experience of devolution of powers in Tamil Nadu.

No doubt, no work is possible without the cooperation of colleagues and co-workers. Here, in the Rajiv Gandhi Chair for

Panchayati Raj Studies, we have a dedicated band of committed workers working for developing a movement for grassroots democracy without whose cooperation this would not have been possible. Decentralisation is not a concept alone, it is a principle at every level and for every individual. In the Rajiv Gandhi Chair for Panchayati Raj Studies all the project staff assisted me in performing my role in different capacities in the University. Each one has one's own orbit of action for which one has got autonomy. Decentralisation in the unit has stamped an indelible mark on our activities for which all individuals are responsible. My teacher colleagues have stood with me in taking the department from one level to another in terms of its functioning. Yet another unit is my family, including my two children who have helped me a lot by allowing me to do my work without making demands on my time and distracting me. Finally, the authorities of the Institute have always been positive towards me in providing needed autonomy and support to all my activities. I profusely thank everyone in our units of work, Department and family for their generous help to complete this task. Finally, to the Panchayat leaders and functionaries, who are my masters in learning about the Panchayati Raj System, I express my deep sense of gratitude.

Gandhigram **G. PALANITHURAI**

CONTENTS

1

INTRODUCTION

In the Indian context, the decentralization process was initiated through the 73rd and 74th Amendments to the Constitution of India and thereby activities were initiated at the state level by passing conformity legislations to decentralize powers to the institutions working below the State Government. Though the phenomenon of decentralization is global, the initiatives in India for decentralization opened avenues for the people to take up this exercise and their own initiatives in different ways as the activities are being undertaken in the community with a lot of variations since Indian society has a pluralistic character. In a democracy like India, devolution or decentralization of powers is not an easy affair and the process is also not smooth.

Ten years of devolution in India have raised a variety of questions in the minds of the academics and administrators. First, whether the basic objectives enshrined in the 73rd Amendment have been conformed to in the State Acts; secondly, to what extent powers have been devolved to the three-tiers of the Panchayat system by law; thirdly, how far the provisions in the State Acts have been realized through rules and Government orders; fourthly, whether the powers conferred upon the Panchayat system are commensurate with the responsibilities fixed for the Panchayats; fifthly, whether needed resources (financial) and functionaries have been devolved to the Panchayats on par with the powers conferred upon the Panchayats; sixthly, whether the elected representatives and the officials have really enhanced their skills, capacities and capabilities to manage the Panchayat system as an institution of self-government and what steps the training institutions have taken for the same; seventhly, whether the government has evolved a training policy and training modules to train the

Panchayat leaders and functionaries; eighthly, to what extent the representatives of the people in the Panchayat system perform their roles and responsibilities; ninthly, to what extent people are being mobilized for the new dispensation; tenthly, how do traditional community organizations respond to the new framework for development activities; and, finally, how does the existing social structure respond to the new dispensation.

The above questions are crucial for an evaluation of the devolution of powers in any State in India. Tamil Nadu State is unique in many respects. The ethnic political parties, namely, the Dravida Munnetra Kazhagam (DMK) and the All India Anna Dravida Munnetra Kazhagam (AIADMK) are vociferous in voicing the grievances of the State. They gave a clarion call for State autonomy and clamour more powers to the State and removal of Article 356 of the Constitution. But when a new system was created below the State as the Panchayat system as an institution of self-governance, it was opposed by the two political parties. The two political parties, the DMK and the AIADMK, never concur on any issue in politics but they uniformly hold the view that they do not require a three-tier Panchayat system for Tamil Nadu. Hence they opposed the both bills, *i.e.,* 64th and 72nd Amendment Bills. The two political parties cited the reasons that the District Panchayat was abolished during the period of Shri K. Kamaraj as they were under the control of landlords and zamindars. But now, after 55 years of social transformation, no zamindar or landlord has such power over a District to control the system. MPs and MLAs are drawn not from among landlord and zamindar families. They are drawn from the middle class, the lower middle class and a few from subalterns. In such a context both the political parties bringing up this argument is academically and logically untenable. The real reason for their opposition is that they do not want any power centre below them as their supremacy will be diluted and they cannot hold sway over the Panchayats as they are institutions of self-government. Now the State wields power through the District Collector. This will be changed if a powerful District Panchayat system is created. Based on this assumption both the DMK and the AIADMK opposed the creation of the three-tier Panchayat system in this State.

In the thirty-five years of governance of the State by the ethnic political parties, namely the DMK and the AIADMK, power has been transferred from the upper caste and class to the middle class and the backward class communities and the current political struggle in Tamil Nadu is for transfer of power from the middle class and backward class to the subalterns, especially to the *Dalits*. Decentralization of power will enable the oppressed class to hold powers to decide their destiny. In this context, holding the view that the District Panchayat will enable the upper caste and class to capture power is untenable and illogical. Against this background the Government of Tamil Nadu, under the AIADMK rule, after one year of procrastination, passed a legislation in the year 1994 to satisfy the legal and Constitutional requirements without much discussion and debate either on the floor of or outside the Assembly. The act of sleeping over the Amendment by the State Government for a period of one year and placing a hastily prepared bill with many retrograde provisions and passing the same without giving time to go through the bill and hold discussion brings to light the level of seriousness of the State Government in devolving powers to the new dispensation.

From the passage of the new Act, till 1996, there was no effort on the part of the Government to conduct elections to the Local Bodies. The AIADMK Government which had passed the legislation did not conduct the election. It is a well known fact that Tamil Nadu is known for its failure in conducting elections to the Local Bodies. During the Assembly election in the year 1996 the Local Bodies issue figured as the DMK included as an issue in its manifesto that if the DMK came to power, it would conduct the Local Bodies election soon. Till the conduct of the general election, Gandhigram, through its outfit Tamil Nadu Campaign for Panchayati Raj (TCPR), conducted several programmes in many parts of the State with the cooperation and assistance of NGOs to create awareness among the people about the new Panchayati Raj System and its implications and thereby to exert pressure on the government to conduct elections to the Local Bodies. Further it was resolved among the NGOs that at least the political parties which contest in the election should make a declaration that they will support the cause of Panchayati

Raj. After the general election was over the new Government under the DMK initiated the process for conducting elections to the Local Bodies. Some of the provisions which acted as a barrier to conducting the election to the Local Bodies were removed and the election was conducted at one stroke, which was considered one of the most remarkable achievements of the State Election Commission of Tamil Nadu. Even before the conduct of the election the First State Finance Commission was constituted to make recommendations and suggestions so as to devolve finance to grassroots institutions. After the election a committee was constituted under the chairmanship of Shri L.C. Jain to work out modalities to entrust responsibilities to the three-tier Panchayats. In the meanwhile, the Government of Tamil Nadu decided to entrust the responsibilities of carrying out the programmes and schemes of both the State and the Central Government to the three-tiers of Panchayats. At this juncture, recommendations and suggestions were made to the Government based on the workshops and seminars conducted by various organizations to devolve appropriate powers as recommended by the 73rd Amendment to the Constitution of India. Before finalising the recommendations with regard to devolution of powers to the three-tiers, the First State Finance Commission submitted its recommendations. Subsequently the L.C. Jain Committee submitted its report on devolution of powers. Based on the reports of the State Finance Commission and the L.C. Jain Committee, the Tamil Nadu Legislative Assembly took a decision on devolution of powers and finance. The decisions were opposed and criticized by various organizations and political parties. In the meanwhile the Government of Tamil Nadu passed an order by which District Collector was made the Chairperson of the District Planning Committee Shri L.C. Jain resigned from the State Planning Commission to protest against this decision of the Government. Subsequently a volley of criticisms was levelled against the State Government for not having devolved adequate powers and finances to the Local Bodies. To overcome such criticisms, the Government of Tamil Nadu constituted another committee under the leadership of the Minister for Local Administration with representatives from the political parties as members of the committee.

The Local Body leaders of the three-tiers approached the committee and appraised them of the problems faced by them in Panchayat administration. This committee also submitted a report to the Government. Based on this report again certain decisions were taken. Even after taking such decisions only advisory and supervisory powers were given to the Panchayati institutions and not the power to take decisions. The powers that were given to the Panchayats were not through an Act but through orders of the Government. The whole process took nearly three years. In the three-year period, Local Body leaders were oriented only in implementing the policies and programmes of the Government and thereby the bureaucracy at the lower level established its supremacy over the elected representatives. The elected representatives who had a little bit orientation in governance found it difficult to manage the Panchayats.

Both the bureaucracy at lower levels and the elected representatives were in confusion for about three years in the absence of proper training and capacity building. From the beginning Gandhigram Rural Institute, through the Rajiv Gandhi Chair for Panchayati Raj Studies, pleaded and lobbied with the Government for proper training to the Local Body leaders. The Rajiv Gandhi Chair for Panchayati Raj Studies conducted such a training programme to a limited extent with the support of CAPART and a few other funding agencies. These training programmes could not be considered full-fledged training as there was no training policy, no training manual and no well trained master trainers. But certain things were made clear: the basic objectives of 73rd Amendment to the Constitution of India, and where they stood in Tamil Nadu, and, how to realize the objectives fixed by the Amendment. In the first period, the Panchayati leaders were oriented as contractors to carry out Government schemes. NGOs tried to change the mindset of the leaders of local bodies as change agents.

But the Panchayati leaders have now formed their own association to project their demands and exert pressure on the Government to devolve powers. Such associations are many. Gram Panchayat leaders have their own and likewise Block Panchayat leaders have formed their association. District Panchayat leaders have formed their own outfit too. Women

Panchayat leaders have organized their association exclusively to project their demands. *Dalit* leaders have also formed their own association. Periodically they convene meetings and project their demands.

In the last phase of the first period, the Government of Tamil Nadu has took the initiative to prepare a comprehensive training module to train the Panchayat leaders very effectively with the objective of building needed skills and capacity to manage the Panchayati institutions. Materials were prepared for circulation among the leaders and functionaries. These activities were carried out with the assistance of UNICEF but they were shelved as the general election to the Legislative Assembly was held and the tables were turned. In the meanwhile the Rajiv Gandhi Chair for Panchayati Raj Studies prepared a module for training with the assistance of the Ford Foundation. Modules were published and distributed among the NGOs involved in training Panchayat leaders. Further the information needed to Panchayats like updated Panchayat Act, rules, Government orders passed, schemes and programmes of the Government of India and the Government of Tamil Nadu were prepared in the form a manual for ready reference. This was published for wider circulation. To impart quality training a committed team of experts was organised and prepared as master trainers through a Training of Trainers programme. With the help of this team, nearly 3000 Gram Panchayat leaders were trained with the financial support of CAPART and The Hunger Project. Apart from the eight districts covered by the Rajiv Gandhi Chair for Panchayati Raj Studies, all the other districts have to be covered by the district administration through a training team developed by the District Panchayat. A Government order was issued in this regard. Needed information was circulated among the officials.

In the meanwhile several experiments were conducted in several Panchayats as pilot projects. A variety of research projects were carried out on the vital issues of the Panchayat system. The Second State Finance Commission submitted its report and that was accepted by the State Government. The seven years of Panchayat activities in the rural areas have given an idea to the people about the Panchayati Raj System. People have to be prepared for a new task in achieving development. So far the Government was regarded as a provider and the people as beneficiaries. The new dispensation has altered the paradigm of development and, in this new paradigm, the Government is not a provider but it is only a facilitator and the people are not beneficiaries or petitioners but stakeholders and development participants. The people will decide their destiny and the destiny of the nation provided opportunities are given to them to take initiatives and participate in the whole process of development. To bring the people to such a mindset awareness has to be created among the people.

Further while power was devolved in a highly fragmented and segmented society on a caste basis, organized groups could capture power. Power flows only through organizations and they are being captured in an organized way. The oppressed *Dalits* and women have assumed powers and responsibilities but they find it difficult to discharge their roles and responsibilities. The problems are multi-dimensional in nature. Still the traditional communities are holding on to power. The linkage between the community Panchayats and the formal Panchayats is crucial in the development process. Even now in Panchayats common property resource management is a tough job as the properties are being encroached upon by many. To remove encroachments the leaders have to face several encounters. Yet the Panchayats have done several innovations and thereby they demand more powers to the Panchayats. At this juncture it is necessary to evaluate the devolution process in the past seven years. When the whole electoral process is evaluated one finds that the community practices have been extended to the Local Body elections. Selections, nominations, elections, and other all kinds of practices have been adopted. The communities are closely wedded to the formal Panchayats.

This work is a collection of articles written at different times in the past five years based on the activities carried out by the Rajiv Gandhi Chair for Panchayati Raj Studies in the Panchayats. The second chapter is the result of a pre-election voters awareness campaign carried out by Gandhigram Rural Institute in association with a band of NGOs in Tamil Nadu. It gives the details of the activities carried out by the NGOs and their implications. The second chapter provides a very interesting analysis of the whole electoral process to the Local Bodies. A variety of options were exercised by the communities in the election. Communities have several practices by which leaders are being selected, nominated or elected. Auctioning of positions and selecting individuals for positions through lot are common practices in many places which are not challenged by the Government or the Election Commission. In most of the cases the Election Commission norms have been violated, yet both the State Election Commission and the State Government have not done anything. All the above practices have been explained in this chapter. The fourth chapter presents the achievements of ten Gram Panchayats with the support of the communities on social development issues. This is the result of an experiment carried out by Gandhigram Rural Institute with the support of the Population Foundation of India. The fifth chapter deals with the development initiatives of the Panchayats and the people. In the context of the role change on the part of the Government from provider to facilitator, the Panchayats, with the active support of the communities, have developed a perspective plan for the development of the villages. The changing roles of the Government and the Panchayats have been explained in this chapter.

In many places traditional Panchayats are vibrant and active in deciding things in the society. After the establishment of the new Panchayati Raj System, conflicts between traditional Panchayats and formal Panchayats are visible in many places. But there are a few Panchayats where both the traditional Panchayats and formal Panchayats have been absoluted integrated with each other. The sixth chapter portrays the linkages between the traditional Panchayats and the formal Panchayats in attending to community work and for effective delivery of services to the people. The seventh chapter brings to light the initiatives taken by the elected women representatives towards building a federation for themselves to represent their problems exclusively to the higher officials and the State Government. A series of problems have been tackled through their initiatives. Their achievements have been explained. The eighth chapter presents the process of capacity building exercises carried out in Gandhigram for Panchayat leaders. It provides details about the methodology, content and material provided in the training programme. It is more of a report of the whole exercise.

The ninth chapter analyses the performance of the *Dalit* Panchayat leaders in Tamil Nadu. It was a major accusation that the *Dalit* Panchayat leaders have not performed their role and responsibilities as effectively as others, because they are not permitted by others to perform their roles and responsibilities. A study was conducted to inquire about the performance of the *Dalit* leaders. The results have been explained in this chapter. The final chapter forms the conclusion.

2

VOTERS AWARENESS CAMPAIGN

I. INTRODUCTION

Panchayats are institutions of local self-governance in rural India. Here the people are organised into a system of self-governance, whereby according to the principles of democracy, they elect their own representatives to this form of governance. They in turn work to further the development of their area seeking the participation of the people within the said area. The Panchayats have been a feature of Indian political history. Since independence, many commissions have been appointed, studies conducted and recommendations made to make the Panchayats more viable and responsive people's bodies. Notable among them are the Ashok Mehta Commission (1997) and the Balwantrai Mehta Committee Report (1957). This led to the realisation of the need for drafting a Bill to give Constitutional Status to Panchayati Raj Institutions (PRIs). The Constitution had hitherto devoted not more than three to four lines to the matter of establishing village panchayats. (Article 40 of the Directive Principle of State Policy). The basis for the Bill had been the shortcoming of the Panchayat like the lack of regular election. Prolonged supersessions, inadequate representation of weaker sections, insufficient devolution of power, inadequate financial support and constitutional obligation on the party of State Government to empower PRIs.

Elections: Importance for Effective People's Participation

Governance for the last 50 years, has largely adopted a top-down approach, lacking transparency and accountability. This resulted in alienation of people, thus engendering and compelling the malaise of dependency in them. The problem of dependency can be challenged head on in participatory, democratic fora, rather than representative ones. The great potential for leadership amongst women, *Dalits* and other excluded constituencies, hitherto relegated to the periphery and forced into silence and invisibility. Lack of awareness of the function of PRI, lack of role clarity, inadequate funds and gender bias acts as large barrier to the achievement of 'democratic governance' in the true sense. The need of the hour was to usher in a process of change, initiated and controlled by the people. With the enactment of 73rd (Constitution Amendment) Act, 1992, Panchayats received formal constitutional recognition. Within it were incorporated certain mandatory rules to secure people's participation (both women and men) in PRIs the following are just a few:

- Elections to PRI are to be held regularly and at the village level they should be held on a non-party lines.
- One-third of the seats are to be reserved for women and persons belonging to Scheduled Castes and Scheduled Tribes (SC/ST) in the PRI at different levels.
- Conducting Gram Sabhas (people's forum) twice a year.
- Mandatory elections to PRI, after completing their five-year term.
- Direct elections of the members to the Panchayat.
- Conduct of local elections by State level Election Commission.

The underlined rational of this Amendment is based on several assumptions. These include:

1. Shared perception of justice, deprivation and oppression among the citizens.
2. Shared experience of marginalised *vis-à-vis* the power structure.
3. Collective empowerment through representation and democratic process (election) will give voice, feeling of solidarity and democratic politics.

4. With regular elections and constitutional mandated panchayats, permutations will change and issue oriented groupings or interest groups will emerge.
5. Affirmative action will build a critical mass of local leadership from such groups, who will be active participants in the strategic decision-making process.

Hence, elections to these bodies of governance were a stepping stone to the direction of good governance. It provided space for people's initiative, to elect a person of their choice that would represent, heed and strive to fulfil their needs and interest. Such an understanding of the significance of elections, which is stressed upon by the recommendation committees as well as the amendment, ensures participation of local people in governance processes. But it this true?

Ground Realities

In the last five years since the enactment of the Amendment, various studies, group discussions with the village, representatives at the local level, community based organisation as well as government functionaries reveals a different picture against the picture thought out. The follies were traced to one core cause – Lack of Participation.

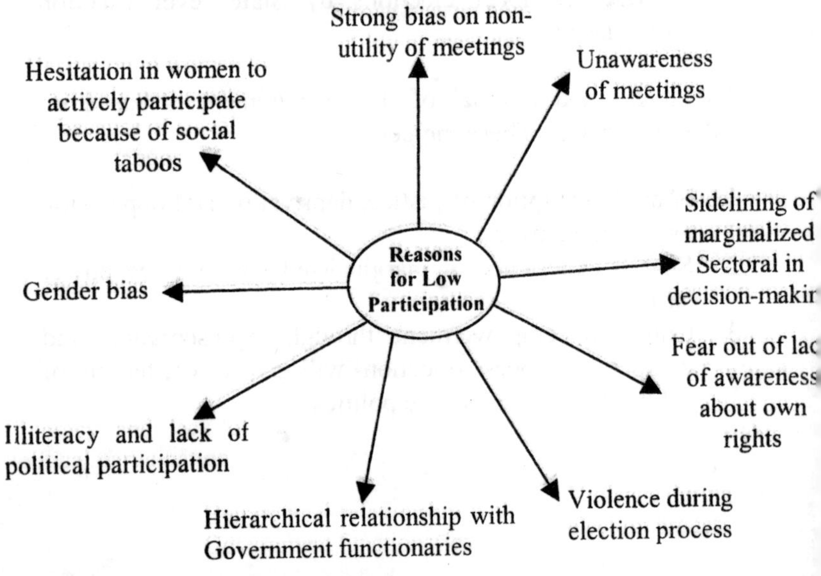

73rd Constitutional Amendment which sought to ensure the participation of women, men and marginalised group cannot break the traditional patterns of socio-economic and political structures in the villages and bring awareness to the marginalised groups overnight. There must be enabling conditions such as people's organisation, improving the confidence of women and marginalised group, building awareness, etc. PRIA along with its partner organisation took the opportunity provided as well as taking account of the local people, to spread awareness at the local level prior to the election processes. The aim of the campaign was to make the people aware of the value of their votes and how the votes help them in electing right candidates. With this regard, the following needs were identified :

(a) The common citizens need to be made aware of and informed about the PRIs.
(b) The citizens need to understand their rights and responsibilities.
(c) Citizens need to behave as active citizens in the family and community.
(d) Citizens need to participate in local associations and organisations to work on common public agenda.
(e) Citizens need to demonstrate assertive, caring and ethical leadership.
(f) Citizens need to be enabled and encouraged to engage and connect with public institutions, officials and leaders, on public concerns.
(g) Citizens need to show solidarity, generosity and mutual support towards fellow citizens.

Pre-Election Voter's Awareness Campaign (PEVAC)

Campaign are viewed, as a means for disseminating information. It aims at bringing about awareness among people, their agreement/disagreement and hence involve in the process. Today, campaigns need to be a structured event, with boundaries of time, money, place and human, for its effectiveness. So, the major questions that come to mind and need to be answered for an understanding of PEVAC are:

- What is PEVAC?
- Why PEVAC?
- PEVAC for whom?
- How PEVAC was conducted?

What is PEVAC?

Campaign, traditionally was a means through which people voiced their problems, impediments and wrong happening in society. It created a platform for people to speak and make their fellow citizens aware. It was an awareness building project. It was informal, based on local means and simple language. To some extent, it was interactive. But "effectivity" became the top priority and management (of the three major M's – man, money and material) was introduced into this field, planning became the major agenda before conducting any form of campaign. Identifying target groups, their need assessment, chalking out objectives, assumptions, proposing desired steps to be followed in conducting the campaign, are some of the desired activities that were followed.

Why PEVAC?

With planning being introduced, PEVAC seemed to not limit itself to transferring of ideas, information or equated with imparting knowledge. It is seen as a process of growth and discovery aimed not just at knowing more but at a behavioural shift. The focus is on building up people's critical consciousness, examining their current situations, ideals, value, attitudes, by inducing alternative ideologies. It aims at building a more questioning attitude, re-thinking and following "rational" or democratic ideology. It aims at building a common under-standing for common action towards a common goals. The objective of PEVAC revolved around people's need and participation.

A pre-election voter's awareness campaign was conducted in Haryana, Madhya Pradesh, Uttar Pradesh and Rajasthan, was found to be an effective means of communication in rural India.

The three main purposes expected out of this campaign. They were:

1. Make people aware and interested about current issues.
2. Inform them about the concern issues.
3. Persuade and motivate them to take action at both personal and community level.

INFORMATION → AWARENESS → MOTIVATION → ACTION

Conducting PEVAC for Whom?

The felt needs became the basis on which PEVAC's objective was shaped as activities carried out. The end result of PEVAC was to reach these objectives and get the messages across to the local people.

As it is strongly believed that development starts at the grassroots level and initiative, creativity and energies of the people can be utilised to improve their own lives using democratic processes and voluntary efforts. It implies that through consciousness raising, people at the grassroots level become awakened to realise their own potential. Hence for achieving this felt needs arising from the local people should be taken into consideration.

Note : If the issue, that any organisation or individual feels are critical and the target groups are not aware of the seriousness or have not recognised them as critical themselves, they (organisation or individual) will have to begin with a major awareness campaign to atleast make the people realise that the existing problems are critical to them personally and need their immediate attention.

Objectives of the Campaign

The objectives of the PEVAC are as follows:

1. To create an enabling environment for free and fair election at village level (fearless environment to contest, lesser use of money, alcohol, opium).
2. To reduce dummy candidature.
3. To enhance participation of women and weaker sections in the election process.

4. To sensitise the voter's about their rights.
5. To increase the polling at the Gram Panchayat level.

How PEVAC was Conducted ?

In ensures people's participation and proper co-ordination as well as helps monitoring the campaign planning for it is a must. It ensures optimal utilisation of resources, facilitates smooth implementation, reduces the risk factor and time wastage planning is crucial for effectivity of PEVAC. A plan to be effectively formulated must be systematic and clearly address the questions of what, where, when, why, how and for whom. In other words, a Plan for any campaign, should be able to answer the following questions clearly:

(a) What are the activities to be carried out by the campaign? Should cover all the methodologies that needed to disseminate the required information from the sender to the recipient.
(b) When is the campaign to be initiated? This should spell out the time frame or duration of intended campaign.
(c) Where is the activity going to take place? This should show the area of coverage within a geographical boundary, including extensive (breadth-wise) and intensive (in-depth) coverage.
(d) Why is this campaign taking place? What is the purpose of the intended campaign? What is the desired outcome that the organisation or the individual conducting the expecting ?
(e) Who will conduct the activity? The names of the organisations should be clearly mentioned for documentation purposes that are carrying out the campaign.
(f) How will the campaign be conducted? This should spell out the step-by-step process that would be taken in conducting the campaign.
(g) For whom is the campaign intended? This will show the target group for which the campaign was initiated in the first place.

Such a plan give a clear direction, a map for the organisation conducting the process of the ways and means on how to go about it.

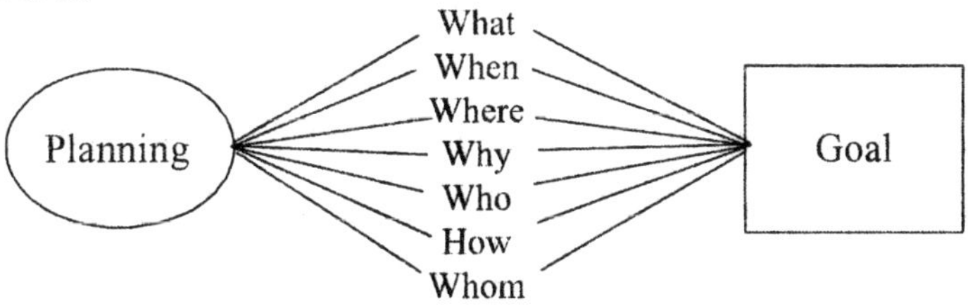

In PEVAC, planning must not be too rigid. Flexibility is the key to the success of this campaign. Flexibility ensures that any changes, required for the effectivity of the process, could be done on the spot. In answering the above question during the planning process, the steps adopted in conducting PEVAC falls into the following:

Strategy

- The village/intervened district were selected on the basis of the village composition in terms of minority groups (SC/ST), level of literacy and distance from the block office.
- New districts were also included on the criteria of close proximity to former intervened district.
- Observe neutrality. Have not affiliation to any party or leniency to any candidate desirous of contesting the elections.
- Sensitise the media in the approach of campaign and help in the coverage to reach areas that were not reachable.
- Choice of area selection was discussed with local/ community based organisations.
- Identification of NGO, Vas, CBOs, cultural teams who have been working or willing to work on issues concerning PRI, awareness, women and education.
- Workshops in order to bring the multitude of people to a common platform to open dialogue on issues of an Awareness Campaign.
- Conducting a SWOT on organisational strength and capacity with reference to the three essential M's

(manpower, money and material) of both illiterate and literate population of the local community.

- Emphasising the need of women in the campaign group as agents that could get accessibility to village women.
- Acquisition of relevant data from the block office regarding election process, procedures, list of voter's time frame, rules and regulation.
- Gram Panchayat Level information centres to provide related information filling and filing of nomination forms and meetings with candidates.

Method Used

Methodology	Description
(a) Slogan writing/ *'Nara lekhan'*	*'Nara lekhan'* involves mainly the writing of slogans on the walls in public places. Walls of public buildings, compounds etc., are considered for this purpose. Even the walls of some of the private buildings that were located in appropriate positions were included in the process of writing slogans. Writing was done either by professional painters or amateurs. The colours used are brick red or deep blue. The major tool used for writing is a either a paint brush or a *neem* stick with the tip smashed to form a 'brush'.
(b) Bicycle rally	Mostly volunteer with their bicycle attached with a tape-recorder went around the villages distributing pamphlets regarding information about voter's as well as playing awareness songs.
(c) *Padyatra*	*'Padyatra'* involves the marching of a group of people holding banners and playcards, which display the messages/slogans of the campaign.

(Contd.)

Methodology	Description
(d) *'Nukad Natak'/ 'Kala Jatha'*	*Kala Jatha* is art form based on dance and music through which the messages are conveyed to the people. This is a popular folk art in Rajasthan.
(e) Puppet show/ *'Katputli'* and *'Hasthtputli'*	Puppet show is traditional art form and is very popular in Rajasthan. There are two models of puppets that are commonly used. In one model, the puppets made of cloth and strings are played in front of a curtain and the movement of the puppets is controlled using the strings attached to them by the person standing behind the curtain. Here the puppets play at the ground level. In the other model the puppets are made out of hard materials like wood. The movements of the puppets are controlled by the person from behind the curtain using the sticks attached to the puppets. Here the puppets play at a higher level, above the head level of the person behind.
(f) Small group meetings/Mahila Sammelan	Small group meetings are organized at the village level to facilitate the process of creating awareness among the voters particularly the women.
(g) Matadata Jagaruk Mandal	To provide information to the voters information centres were opened.
(h) Electronic media coverage	Inviting the attention of the media, including the newspapers, radio and the TV, to the developments related to PEVAC is the main activity. The media representatives are provided with necessary information regarding the activities of the PEVAC. The media coverage is expected to create wider public education and a favourable climate of opinion.

(Contd.)

Methodology	Description
(i) Poster fixing	Posters printed on paper are pasted on the walls in public places. Walls of public buildings, compounds etc. are considered for this purpose. Even the walls of some of the private buildings that are located in appropriate positions are considered for the purpose of pasting posters. Pasting is done either by amateurs. The raw material used for pasting the poster is a paste prepared by mixing wheat flour and warm water. Wheat flour is a locally available raw material, which is less expensive.
(j) Distribution of Audio Cassettes	The message of the PEVAC are recorded, in the form of songs, slogans and narration's on audio cassettes. Copies of these cassettes are then distributed to the appropriate individuals, shopkeepers including tea shops/ *'Dhabas'*, provision shops, bus crew operators etc. for the purpose of playing them in the cassette players.
(k) Pamphlets	Two pamphlets were prepared for the campaign. One was the yellow pamphlet that stated the importance of voting and the value of each and everyone vote. The second being informative. It informs the voters about the votes has to case in the three-tier elections.
(l) Volunteers orientation	These included the youth of the community that were willing to work for the campaign. Also the vehicle that was used, the driver also lent their support after being convinced about the intention of the campaign.

Highlights

Some of the field activity in States where the second round of election took place saw the following highlights. These were:

- Women were found to have contested from Unreserved Seats.
- Violence minimal during polling day.
- Increase of Unopposed Panchayats at the Gram Panchayat level.
- Increase in polling percentage of women in 2001, from 55 per cent to 65 per cent.
- Level of awareness regarding election processes seen.
- Less polling and interest in elections were seen where *Dalit* candidates contested for Sarpanch.
- Voter's list was not updated.
- Voices, especially of women, were raised against the distribution of alcohol.
- Concern was raised as to the number of polling booths in proportion to the number of voters.
- Name's of unmarried women, above the age of 18 years not included in the voter's list.
- Lack of women polling officers as well as polling agents.
- Women were seen conducting rallies for their own candidates.
- Caste played a significant role in election process.
- Voter's indifference to the whole PRI system in some areas due to loss of hope.
- At certain places nomination papers were not printed in adequate number, hence, some candidates were seen to be manually writing them down.

SWOT Analysis of PEVAC

Assessing PEVAC would give a clear picture of the use as well as the threats of such a process of creating awareness. Such an analysis would bring out the internal and external factors that may help or hinder the programme. Internal environment refers to organisational structures, such as resources or activities that will affect programme implementation. The word "resources" implies physical, material, institutional and human inputs for the achievement of the objectives of the campaign. External factors are not directly related to the campaign, such as social, political or economic issues, but which may still affect the campaign indirectly. For instance, in the PEVAC, the Rajasthan government employees were on a strike, was a consideration that was taken in as a impediment/threat. To overcome it an objective of "free and fair elections" was the top priority for this campaign.

PEVAC

Internal		External	
Strengths	Weakness	Opportunities	Threats
An issue that has lot of takers	Inadequate quality control	Push towards devolution and local self-governance in rural and urban areas	Wide-spread of poverty illiteracy
Good basis for networking	Outgoing learning material inadequate	Use of new information technology for promoting learning	Growing dependencies on public institutions
No hierarchy needed for the performance of this campaign	Lack of resources limited the outreach of PEVAC	Voicing for urgent reform of state instutions	Increased use of violence

(Contd.)

Internal		External	
Strengths	Weakness	Opportunities	Threats
Local resources could be used, that is cost-effective	Inter-unit communication and coordination not effective	Engaging business sector to pay attention to their role and contribution in society	Blind faith in free market solutions to societal problems
Growing need for "Awareness"		Rapport building	Increased use of alcohol by people decreased citizens participation
Rapport with Media and Government is built on such an issue (as citizen concern is mutual within this two institutions)		Increasing the knowledge base of the team members	Growing political interference in local Panchayat elections
No academic qualification needed to get involve in this process)	Local fund-raising weak	Provides space for all people to participate in the awareness campaign	Decline in 'aid'

On the basis of the SWOT analysis, in conducting PEVAC organisations or the individuals concern should go on to evaluate on the basis of the strengths and opportunity of such a process in order to overcome the weaknesses and threats to it.

Concerns : Need to be Dealt with

Concerns that came to light in the process of election process as well as during the Pre-Election vote's awareness campaign.

	Opportunities	Threats
Strengths	Clearly high in conducting this process. As it gives an opportunity to spread awareness and allow the possibility of the masses to critically analyse their given societal issues, closely. It allows for people's participation	Increase of security arrangement could be requested from the block office to reduce violence. Distribution of alcohol/sale could be suspended (if possible) Adequate nomination forms/volunteers could be trained.
Weakness	Social and cultural norms could be dealt with sensitively, if they are a threat. Women polling agents as well as staff from the government bodies during election process could be reuested from the block office	With the awareness could be decrease "damage control" of this section, where treats and weakness have to be done in mind. Precaution of all the other three could compensate.

Two Child Norm

Field experiences suggest that this rule goes against women. In the states of Haryana, Madhya Pradesh, Rajasthan and Himachal Pradesh, where this rule has come into force, the average age of women as Panchayat members were found to be between 35-40 years. It means that, in majority of the cases, the women aged 35 years and above are potential contestants for PRI elections in these states. In rural India a pattern of early childbearing has been observed across the States, with total fertility rate being more than four. That means, that by the age of 35, almost all women become mothers of, as many children as (often) desired by their husbands and in-laws. Consequently, a majority of these women (who are socially eligible to contest PRI elections, as present trends suggest) get automatically excluded from election arena because of the two-child norm. Then who is to be chosen for PRI seats? Naturally, either the younger generation (who do not fall pray to the two-child rule) or those who are above 35 years but do not have more than two kinds. The former are more susceptible to be proxy representatives because their social freedom is restricted, while the latter may be indifferent to politics. Thus, two-child norm whether it would be able to reduce population growth or not is a billion-dollar question, out this will certainly promote cases of proxy representatives.

Election Process

The responsibility and procedure for determining reservation requirements for SC/ST, women and backward classes differ from state to state. In states like Kerala, Maharashtra and West Bengal, the State Election Commission has this responsibility, whereas in Madhya Pradesh, Rajasthan, Andhra Pradesh and Uttar Pradesh, the responsibility lies with the State Government. The rotation of reserved matter was even raised in High Courts. In Haryana, Rajasthan and Madhya Pradesh a number of constituencies were reserved for SC/ST while there were no SC/ST population in those constituencies. Moreover, reservation of constituency for one term creates a sort of adhocism in the elected members. Many of women elected (from reserved seats) representatives in Madhya Pradesh, during informal conversations with the author, said that, "why should they worry about our performance, if the next time we cannot win against a man when our present constituency gets unreserved". These issues need to be resolved for healthy functioning of PRIs. The legislature can prescribe the principles and the government may provide clear and transparent guidelines, but the ultimate responsibility of managing these issues (rotation, reservation, qualification of candidates and election expenses) should be entrusted to the State Election Commission.

Regularity of Elections

As per Article 243E of the Constitution, every Panchayat, unless sooner dissolved under any law for the time being in force, shall continue for five years from the date appointed and no longer. So, any executive action delaying or deferring these elections violates the Constitution. Thus, states of Karnataka, Madhya Pradesh, Haryana, Andhra Pradesh, Uttar Pradesh and some other states have violated the Constitution by deferring and delaying elections to the local bodies. Article 257 (also the infamous Article 256) of the Constitution empowers Central Government to give directions to States to fulfil their Constitutional obligations. It implies that Centre too has failed in showing political will to direct States to hold Panchayat elections. The issues of revision of electoral rolls and delimitation of constituencies based on population size and geographical continuity can be undertaken regularly and well before Panchayat elections are due, as has been done in many states. The States and Central Governments have to be alive and sensitive to the constitutional mandate of holding elections to Panchayat on time.

Update of Voters List

Constant update of the voter's list must be made to ensure full participation of people in the Election processes. Women above the age of 18 years and over, whether married or unmarried must be registered. Usual reply, that villager give to justify their act for not recording their daughters name in the voters list is that, people would know that they are of marriageable age and not yet married or that their name will be registered only in their in-laws/husbands village. Tackling this problem needs consideration, as misuse or proxy voting could be curbed.

Women Polling Staff

The presence of women polling staff with the polling booth, would provide a security for women entering the polling station. It will also benefit not only in explaining the process of where the ballot paper need to be placed but also could be used to check the name with the fee, as most of the women are veiled *"ghunghats"*. Hence, men polling staff are apprehensive in checking women. Based on the principles strategies and methods adopted in other states in India for PEVAC, Gandhigram Rural Institute in collaboration with NGO network and government planned the strategies and methods for PEVAC and carried out the activities. Those details are presented in this report.

II. METHODOLOGY

Introduction

In the context of Globalization of Economy Decentralization of powers has twin functions at the grassroots, namely to protect the people from misery and to administer economic development and social justice. It is only after four decades of India's independence that an amendment was made in the Indian Constitution (73rd) and by which compulsorily reservation of seats are made for SC/ST and women for active and effective participation in governance at the grassroots. It paves way for all marginalised groups to contest in the election and to assert themselves as factors to reckon within governance. No doubt, this was possible only because of the amendment to the Constitution of India. Though in the previous election SC/ST and women took part and participated in governance at the grassroots from village panchayat to district level, their level of participation in election and performance in governance had both positive and negative trends which need attention and introspection.

Many attempts have been made in the past towards development of SC/ST and women of Tamil Nadu. Yet much could not be accomplished due a variety of reasons. Hence new initiatives are taken to empower them and through which development could be achieved. It is obvious that mere possession of political power without the basic knowledge and exposure to power and knowledge about the constitutional rights and responsibilities, would not bring much change as we expect. The 73rd Amendment is being considered as an instrument, to the marginalised to move from periphery to mainstream but the elected representatives at all levels have not used it positively or favourably. Even the marginalised section did not have the basic knowledge of filling the forms and filing the nomination and this led to rejection and disqualification of their candidatures. It was observed among the representatives from SC/ST and women from rural Tamil Nadu. Though there were constitutional rights and privileges, the elected representatives don't realise and utilize the full potentiality of it. It is mainly due to lack of orientation and training to the aspiring candidates before the election. Most of the occasions they were asked to contest in the election on behalf of someone else. As a result they got branded as proxy. To avoid such a name, attempts have been made to create awareness among the marginalised section about the power devolution and its implication in the development process. Since, the second Panchayat election was to take place in October, 2001, it was seriously thought of and fulfledged training and orientation to the aspiring candidates in rural areas were arranged. Other disheartening observation made in the process is that people dwelling both in the urban and rural areas roughly about half of the voters do not cast their votes for the reason unknown. In spite of the fact that government declares the day of general election a holiday the voting rate has gone down. The base for democratic structure, the Gram Sabha, was not given due importance as it deserves.

It was also witnessed till the recent election that in many places *Dalits*/women were restricted from casting their votes by saying that their votes have already been casted. Against this background how do we expect their participation in the election process. In many places where *Dalits* were living in minority, they were not allowed even to think of contesting in the election. At this juncture, PRIA, a Delhi based agency with the financial support of Ministry of Rural Development, Government of India intended to take some steps to motivate these suppressed and marginalised section of the society and to make them to contest in the election. Hence this project "Pre-Election Voters Awareness Campaign" (PEVAC).

PRIA – Objectives and Strategies for PEVAC

'PRIA' (Society for Participatory Research in Asia) a non-government organisation had already organised this type of campaign during panchayati raj election in Madhya Pradesh, Uttar Pradesh, Himachal Pradesh, Haryana, Kerala and Bihar.

The main objectives of this programme were:

- To create suitable environment for free and fair elections by sensitising the voters, particularly among women and SC/ST in rural area, about the rights and responsibilities in the electoral process.
- To reduce the number of proxy candidates from women and SC/ST.
- To increase the polling percentage at the village level.

The State Election Commission openly made a plea that the NGOs must involve themselves in creating awareness among the people about the importance of the local democracy and its implication in the life of the poor.

Strategies of PRIA

- PRIA wanted to cover the entire state of Tamil Nadu (29 districts).
- NGO network can be utilised for executing these activities.
- Strategies framed by the NGO network according to the local reality can be used.
- More number of organisations can be enlisted together for carrying out PEVAC activities.

PRIA wanted to conduct a one day state level workshop on PEVAC in Gandhigram in the first week of September to finalise the strategies and modalities to conduct PEVAC activities. It was conducted on 10th September, 2001. The report of the programme gives details regarding the various techniques and strategies to be followed by different NGOs in carrying out the PEVAC activities during the local bodies election.

State Level Workshop on PEVAC

On September 10th a state level workshop was conducted in Gandhigram Rural Institute. The Department of Political Science and Development Administration organised the same for which participants from different NGOs, NYKs of all the districts in Tamil Nadu, academic institutions and some social activists were invited. From PRIA, Ms. Shagun, Mr. Satinder Singh Sahni and Mr. Madhavan from Hunger Project have participated in this workshop. Representatives from PRIA have explained the success story of Andhra Pradesh where the local bodies election held recently. It was decided in the workshop that all the districts in Tamil Nadu may be covered except two, *i.e.* Sivaganga and Nilgiris which have already been taken up by Gandhigram Rural Institute under "The Hunger Project" for PEVAC activities. Among the participants there were four NGO networks, namely TCPR, SAM, RCPED and IFPAAW working in different districts. After a lengthy discussion with each networks representatives it was decided that all the NGO network could cover their respective districts where they are already working.

Finalisation of NGO Networks

There were four NGOs networks finalized as below:

1. TCPR — CHERU, Vellabommanpatty, Dindigul district
2. SAM — Dindigul
3. IFPAAW — Perambalur
4. CREA Net — Madurai

The details regarding the coverage of districts are enclosed. Later CREA Net due to some reasons changed its mind and withdrew from this PEVAC exercise. So, it was given to ROAD an NGO network based in Marthandam of Tamil Nadu.

Target Groups Proposed

It was decided that more emphasis should be given to only rural voters and among the rural voters, the ever socially suppressed and politically exploited sections of the society like women and *Dalits* should be focused much. Even among the women, the women belong to SC/ST community are to be concentrated specifically.

Strategies Framed by the NGO Networks

Each network had framed their own strategies to implement the programme. The following are the strategies suggested by the NGO network :

1. Conducting a training to the NGO staff/ToT.
2. Training to cultural team.
3. Organising Van Yatra.
4. Printing of wall posters, bit notices, stickers, hand books, charts, and hand bills distribute and paste the same in appropriate places to draw the attention of the public.
5. Group meeting with SHGs/*Dalits* aspiring candidates.
6. Conducting street theatre programme.
7. General awareness and motivational programme to be conducted for public.
8. Block level meeting with the target groups.

The Role of Gandhigram Rural Institute

The Gandhigram Rural Institute had played a key role of a nodal agency and like a bridge between PRIA and NGOs network for the effective implementation of PEVAC activities.

The Coordinator of Rajiv Gandhi Chair for Panchayati Raj Studies Dr. G. Palanithurai, had been in charge of PEVAC activities.

- Rajiv Gandhi Chair for Panchayati Raj Studies, Department of Political Science and Development Administration has taken the assignment of the co-ordinating the whole activities of the PEVAC.
- His informative book and booklets in the Panchayati Raj were distributed to all the NGOs through the networks. The above materials have helped the trainers and the NGO staff to get needed information about New Panchayati Raj System.
- He himself participated in many awareness meetings as resource person and gave a thought provoking speech

which enlightened the women SHG, *Dalits* and aspiring candidates very much.

- Frequent publication of his speech in newspapers on New Panchayati Raj System specifically on awareness among the general voters made the people aware of the democratic system at the grassroots level.
- His two important programmes on New Panchayati Raj System in Sun TV and ten days continuous programme in All Indio Radio on the same subject helped the programme a lot.
- NGO networks had held frequent telephonic conversation as and when they had doubt on electoral process and administration.
- Rules and regulations to be followed in the election process and role of *Dalit* and women and aspiring candidates with regard to local bodies elections were also given in the form of a book.
- Each and every activity of the NGO network proposed and carried out were informed to Dr. G. Palanithurai to update the whole exercise.
- He has also sent the Coordinator PEVAC, Dr. C. Kubendran to different districts to assist the NGO network in carrying out PEVAC activities. Accordingly he has gone to several districts such as Dindigul, Madurai, Villupuram, Kancheepuram and Cuddalore to impart training to the women SHG, *Dalit* and aspiring candidates.

PEVAC Activities carried out by NGOs Network

As soon as the workshop was over, all the networks had started working in their respective districts from 12th September onwards as the days for the local bodies election were nearing very fastly.

District Administration Informed

District Collector and Superintendent of Police were met before the start of the PEVAC activities almost in all the districts where ever they were contacted NGO network and individual NGO have received good response from the government officials for the reasons that PEVAC activities are:

- Supported by the Government.
- Non-party basis commitment of the Election Commission.
- Risk taking activities, sometimes for which opposition may crop up from political parties, elite groups, higher castes and economically affluent candidates.
- It is not anti-government instead it is sharing the burden of Government in generating political awareness among the rural illiterate voters.

Administrative Chart of PEVAC

Government of India
Ministry of Rural Development

PRIA - Tamil Nadu

Gandhigram Rural Institute
[Rajiv Gandhi Chair for Panchayati Raj Studies
Department of Political Science and Development Administration]

Coverage Networks and Districts

TCPR	SAM	ROAD	IFPAAW
1. Trichy	1. Salem	1. Kanyakumari	1. Perambalur
2. Dindigul	2. Kanjeepuram	2. Tuticorin	2. Aryalur
3. Erode	3. Villupuram	3. Tirunelveli	
4. Theni	4. Thiruvarur	4. Ramanathapuram	
5. Karur	5. Tanjore	5. Virudhunagar	
6. Pudukottai	6. Vellur		
7. Namakkal			
8. Nagapattinam			
9. Thiruvarur			
10. Madurai			
11. Coimbatore			
12. Cuddalore			
13. Dharmapuri			
14. Thiruvannamalai			

The District Collector, Superintendent of Police, Project Officer of District Rural Development Agency and Project Officer, Mahalir Thittam (Women Development Corporation in Tamil Nadu) have assured to render help within their capacity to carryout PEVAC activities successfully. In some places it was reported that the Superintendent of Police had ordered the local police station to provide police protection to the NGOs carrying PEVAC message to some sensitive areas. Mahalir Thittam Project Officer had asked the members of SHG in the respective villages to render cooperation to the maximum extent to execute the PEVAC activities. It was really an encouraging trend and a source of strength to the NGO.

1. *Orientation to the NGOs Staff (ToT)*

To begin with, one day orientation was given to all the staff working in the NGOs, no matter whether they had already involved in training on Panchayati Raj or not. In the orientation the staff were briefed about :

- The importance of 73rd Amendment and its basic features.
- Role of villagers in forming a real democratic structure at the grossroots level.
- The role of women in local bodies election as per 73rd Amendment.
- The role of *Dalit* women in general and *Dalit* community in particular in upholding the principle of creation of egalitarian society in India.
- Real meaning of democracy, by participating all voters irrespective of caste, class, religion or any other socio-economic discrimination in the electoral process.
- Role of NGO in bringing about an attitudinal change among rural voters.

2. *Printing of Wall Posters*

As a second step, big size wall posters bearing message fully on local bodies election were printed by each network taking into account the field reality.

- Encouraging *Dalit* and ST in general and women belong to SC and ST in particular not only to vote but to contest in the election.
- Motivating women to contest in the local bodies election as this was the golden opportunity for them to capture the political power to address their long pending problems. Particularly problems faced by women from birth to death like female infanticide, female foeticide, discrimination in school, employment, marriage, dowry system, prevention of widow-remarriage and so on so forth.
- Motivating the women to contest in the local election to ensure their rights.
- Propagating the importance of 33 percentage of reservation of seats allotted for women in Local Bodies.
- Disseminating the information that *Dalits* cannot be prevented from coming to power in the local bodies as there is compulsory reservation according to the 73rd Amendment.
- Informing the rural voters not to be influenced by money or muscle power or any other considerations.
- Appealing the rural voters to select leader who can uphold grassroots democracy social justice, and project natural resources and human rights.
- Emphasizing the importance of voting at high percentage.
- Encouraging the deaf, dumb, handicapped to vote and requesting the healthy person to assist them and take the socially physically handicapped voters to polling station.
- Explained the number of votes to be exercised by the rural voters.
- Giving details about the number of votes to be casted to different posts with respective colours.
- Informing that the electronic machine would not be used, instead, a normal ballot sheet would be used for polling.
- Asking the villagers to help to form a good government with good leadership at the village level to provide good governance.

- Emphasizing that voting is the fundamental rights of every citizen.
- Asking the people not to be a silent spectator in the democratic process and be an active participant in the electoral process, so that grassroots level democracy can be preserved and strengthened.

3. *Bit Notices with Difference by TCPR*

Thousands of bit notices were printed by each NGO working in each district. The information in the notices were according to the local reality. For example, notices printed in the coastal area were related to the problems faced by the fishermen community. Bit notices printed in Madurai, Dindigul, Salem and Namakkal were related to female infanticide and child labour. Bit notices were carrying massages like:

- The major problems faced by the villages in the district.
- Explained the characteristics of a good leader to be elected for the village administration.
- Leader should be familiar with the local people and their problems.
- Leader should be from the local villages of the Panchayat and not outsider.
- Leader should have knowledge, experience and commitment.
- Leader should have earned good name both in his family and village.
- Leader should have thorough knowledge with the basic needs and the burning problems faced by the local people.
- Leader should be able to expose the local problem in the public meeting or in the gram sabha.
- Leader should be more accessible to everyone.
- Leader should respect first people, truth, social criticism and his promises.
- Leader should have a vision towards social reforms and social reconstruction.

- Leader should be able to move with all the people irrespective of caste, class and religion.
- Leader should not be influenced by either money, fame or position.
- Leader should have direct relationship between his speech and action.
- Leader should have ability to tap all the governmental programmes meant for village development to our village Panchayat.
- Leader should have vision towards the future and plan accordingly.
- Leader should have faith in the citizen and democracy.
- Leader should not misuse the power for his self-development.
- Leader should be able to point out the social evils.
- Leader should have intention to protect the natural resources and human rights.
- Leader should have concern for the women, children, and *Dalit* community.
- Leader should have courage to prevent both female infanticide and female foeticide.
- Leader should have love towards our motherland and humanity.
- Leader should preserve the honour and dignity of his position.
- Leader should have a plan to improve the health and hygienic condition of the village.
- Leader should have interest in maintaining and developing common property resources for development.
- Leader should not be a proxy but ability to be independent in decision-making and administration.
- Leader should know the importance of Gram Sabha.
- Leader should be sensitive towards the practice of child labour and bonded labour.

All the above mentioned *details* were printed in the posters and phamplets specifically prepared for PEVAC. After seeing these posters and pamphlets one of the Tamil daily popular newspaper printed all those messages in it for popular consumption by quoting the source.

4. *Distribution of the Bit Notices*

Bit notices were distributed to the rural voters through various means. They are:

(a) Door to Door Delivery

With the help of members of women SHGs and committed staff and youth sangam bit notices were distributed to all individual households.

(b) Distribution through Vehicle

Van, Auto, Cycle, were used for distributing the bit notices with the help of NGO staff to all hamlets.

(c) Important Places

Places like bus stop, street corner, church, temple, mosque and market places, tea shops, educational institutions like, college, school and training institutions were covered by pasting the posters and bills.

5. *Cloth Banners for* **Dalit/*Women***

There were two types of cloth banners printed with multiple colours by each NGO network. The focus given in the banners:

- Encouraging the *Dalits* to make use of the reservation for obtaining political power to move towards mainstream from exclusivism.
- To motivate women to use reservation towards obtaining equality and find permanent solutions to their long pending problems.

6. *Banner Tied*

Places like junction of roads, places earmarked for public meeting and street corners, in front of Panchayat building and Government offices were selected for tieing the cloth banners. Almost, all the women SHGs, youth clubs and volunteers in the villages helped carrying out this activity.

7. *Stickers Pasted*

There were four types of multi-coloured stickers printed in the networks and distributed to the NGO working at districts level. The main themes of the stickers are:

- Appealing the voters to vote for women to protect women rights.
- Encouraging women to contest in the election to protect their rights and solve their problems.
- Motivating *Dalits* to participate in the election as candidate to obtain power to come up in life to the higher level.
- Motivating the voter to support and vote for *Dalit* so that equality and fraternity can be ensured.

Places of Pasting Stickers

Apart from the main places mentioned earlier with regard to the pasting of wall posters and tieing of cloth banners, buses, auto rickshaws were also selected for pasting stickers. It attracted more voters very easily.

8. *Wall Writings*

Some networks have adopted a technique generally the political parties use to adopt like wall writings. They have well in advance reserved the walls outside the houses of the SHG members and common places with the prior permission of the owner of the wall and wrote some messages about.

- Asking the rural voters to vote compulsorily.
- Requesting them to vote for right candidates.
- Emphasizing the rights of *Dalits* and women.

9. *Election Manifestoes Released*

An NGO SAM, prepared and released a model manifesto for the local bodies election. Apart from mentioning all the qualities of a good leader it has also demanded the following :

- 50 per cent of seats are to be reserved for women.
- District Panchayat President should have more powers than the District Collector.
- SC/ST, women should be a part in the decision-making committee at the village level.
- SC/ST, and women should be given importance in the village.

The first copy of this was released by Dr. N. Markandan, Former Vice-Chancellor of Gandhigram Rural Institute in Dindigul on 30 August, 2001. The same was released in all other districts. It has got a very innovative and reformative principles. The SAM network had released the manifesto in all the districts, while carrying out the PEVAC activities.

10. *Rally with Plantain Leaves*

In Tanjore hundreds of volunteers collected by SAM network and it took a procession with banana leaves in which PEVAC messages were written. It attracted the public very quickly.

11. *Training Module for Drama towards Good Governance*

The SAM network has published an innovative training module for generating awareness among the voters on *Dalit* and women representation in the village administration.

12. *Handbook Distributed*

ROAD network has released a handbook on voter awareness particularly the importance and implications of 73rd Amendment.

13. *Pamphlets Distributed*

ROAD has also published a pamphlets consisting of the following details :

- Problems of rural people.
- Instruction to candidates.
- Code of conduct to candidate and political parties.

14. *One-day Training to Cultural Team*

Despite the fact that the cultural team may have rich experience in disseminating messages on various socio-economic problems of the rural mass, it was felt that it is important to provide a one-day orientation to the cultural team about new Panchayati Raj System. It was given at the district head quarters. The training theme was given by the district convener of the NGO.

Cultural Team with PEVAC Messages

A team consists of 10 artists, who have already undergone a training on Panchayat Raj made a round throughout the districts to disseminate the information on

- Rural voting pattern.
- Role of *Dalit*/women in Panchayat,.
- Selecting good leaders for Panchayat.

The theme was very attractive so that villagers were easily attracted. It was done in all the districts under SAM network.

15. *Cycle Yatra*

Some NGOs, almost in all the four networks had adopted this technique as it seemed to be easy to arrange and reach the people quickly and effectively. Display cards were put up at the front of the cycle carrying message of PEVAC. All the printed materials were also distributed during this *yatra*.

16. *Van Yatra*

A van with attached public address system mike was arranged for van *yatra*. This was also followed by many NGOs in major part of Tamil Nadu. The staff of NGO and some professionals were involved in disseminating the PEVAC message to rustic folk. It was quick and easy but costly. Taking into account the time available majority of the NGOs opted for it and justified their role. Political parties also did the same kind of van *yatra*, but the NGO van went to the rural areas with the different messages which attracted the voters. Sometimes the NGOs had to earn the wrath of political parties which is inevitable.

17. *One Day Training to Women SHGs*

As women were one of the major target groups, network NGOs had approached all the members of SHG to carryout the activities under PEVAC. Accordingly, all the SHGs in the adopted union (selected 2-3 in each districts) were contacted. Majority of them attended the one-day training programme organised by the NGO. The participants were motivated to contest in the election and they were given information about:

- The role of SHG in increasing voting percentage.
- The role of SHG in bringing more women leaders.
- The role of SHG in bringing about social change by making use of reservation of seats for women.
- The role of Gram Sabha in social transformation.
- Their participation in the local election.
- How to choose a right candidate?
- Supporting a women candidates from SHG.
- How to file nomination, and take follow up action.

As there were SHGs in every village and they are assisted by the NGOs, majority of the members had participated in the training programme and enriched their knowledge and they made a commitment to this exercise. They were asked to support the PEVAC activities in whatever manner possible. Many members in

SHG were motivated to file nomination in the election. This training was conducted before starting the process of filing nomination.

18. *One-day Training for* Dalits

This programme was organised exclusively for *Dalits* in some parts of Tamil Nadu particularly in Chidambaram and Nagapattinam and they were motivated to file nomination both in the reserved and general constituencies.

Training for the Aspiring Candidates

A one-day training was organized by the every NGO under the network for aspiring candidates during and after the nomination date was over. Intimation through formal letter and wall posters were sent to every candidates filed nomination for various posts asking them to attend the meeting. A marriage hall for either in the taluk or district headquarters was selected for holding the meeting and candidates particularly women and SC/ST were requested to attend the meeting. The following *details* were shared with them:

- How to file correct nomination so that it will not be rejected?
- How to take follow-up activities successfully?
- How to make canvassing to attract the voters?
- How to compete with other political party candidates?
- Code of conduct and official norms for various activities.

Resource persons were invited from different fields. The service of Dr. G. Palanithurai, Coordinator, Rajiv Gandhi Chair for Panchayati Raj Studies, Dr. V. Ragupathy, Assistant Coordinator, and PEVAC Coordinator Dr. C. Kubendran and research scholars Mr. M. A.Thirunavukkarasu were also sought. In the training programme our concentration was only for women and *Dalit*, yet all the candidates, *i.e.* non-SC women had also participated and benefited.

Issues Focused

Some important issues/messages disseminated by the NGO:

- No one should get money for voting.
- Select good, committed and knowledgeable leaders.
- Support women/*Dalit* as president.
- Method to find out a suitable leader.
- Different colours and respective posts the rural voter should know.
- Importance of *Dalit*/women in Local Administration.
- How to be an independent administrator and take decision on their own?

Problems Witnessed

- Conflicts among *Dalits* and sub-castes of *Dalits* in many places.
- *Dalits* were prevented from contesting in the election at the village Panchayat level in Madurai and Virudhunagar districts continuously.
- SC women were prevented from filing nomination in the general seat itself.
- Poor SC women candidates purchased by elite women after the nomination.
- SC women/*Dalits* expected financial support from NGOs.
- Wife of government employees and political leaders particular and rich candidate in general had spent more money for campaigning, the poor SHG women lost hope and interest.
- Auctioning and rotation methods were also adopted in Madurai, Ramnad, Salem districts.
- NGOs were prevented to conduct campaign on PEVAC activities in the village where *Dalits* were prevented in Madurai district.
- No campaigning in the villages where lottery and auctioning methods were practiced for electing village presidents in Madurai district.

Implications

Despite there were some hurdles in caryingout PEVAC activities. The NGO partners could achieve some positive changes in the election. The important development observed during PEVAC activities in the rural areas are :

- Women were motivated to contest in the election in the general seats apart from reserved seats.
- *Dalits* were enlightened towards not only voting but to contest in the election as well.
- The level of political awareness among the rural people in general and *Dalit* and women in particular has been increased considerably.
- District Collector has encouraged, Superintendent of Police has appreciated and Mahalir Thittam Project Officer has supported our work in many districts. It is a good beginning for the local NGOs to get support from the government officials to carryout PEVAC activities in the future towards strengthening democracy.
- Women developed confidence in managing power.
- *Dalits* were encouraged and come out to fight against elite group.
- *Dalits*, no doubt if we constantly support would definitely fight against the so called upper caste people who have prevented them from filing nomination in four village panchayats in Madurai, Virudhunagar districts.
- Women were motivated to attend Gram Sabha meeting four times in a year without fail and make use of it for the wholistic development of the rural society and particularly to solve the problems faced by the women for centuries together.
- Wall posters with different messages in multi-colour were appreciated by social activist, government officials, and other NGOs as the information given in the posters were educative, motivative and timely needed.
- More independent candidates were contested in the election by the direct support of NGOs and women SHGs.
- It created an opportunity for many NGOs to join together to fight against the upper caste and male

domination in the rural areas. Thereby the NGOs have covered a platform to sustain their activities in the future.

- SHGs in some villages were the deciding factors for the selection of village president.
- There was no complaint against women SHG candidate in the villages.
- Separate bit notices were printed in the name of SHG forum.
- *Dalits* were very happy that NGOs had taken up their cause and responded to the their feelings.
- Deputy speaker of Tamil Nadu Legislative Assembly appreciated the PEVAC activities.
- Women candidates were made assertive to act independently.
- Percentage of voting in the rural areas has gone up.
- Prevented the free distribution of *Dhoties, Sarees,* tumblers to poor voters to attract them in Perambalur areas.
- The concept of 'proxy' has gone. Women and *Dalits* have contested on their own not behalf of some one. Now they are independent.

Number of Nominations from SHG and *Dalits* was high

Due to constant support, motivation and appropriate guidance, given by the NGO network, the number of candidates contested for different posts from village Panchayat, ward member, village Panchayat president, Panchayat union counsellor and district counsellor, was high compared to the previous election. NGO network concentrated only in the third-tier of Panchayat, namely Gram Panchayat. The number of candidates for Gram Panchayat ward members and president posts were so high that even the NGO could not expected this number especially in some districts, Salem, Kanjeepuram.

Follow-up Activities

Even after the campaign process was over some NGO had taken follow-up activities like.

- A village visit was done on the day of polling in Madurai district where auctioning was done and against there was a formal election as some one field nomination against the victor.
- Tensed village in Usilampatti, Thathanpatti was visited by TCPR NGO, and helped the police and the public for smooth polling.

Table 2.1 : Targets and Achievements

Sl. No.	NGO/ Position	Village Ward Member		Village President		Panchayat Union Ward Member		District Panchayat Counsellor		Total	
		P*	E**	P	E	P	E	P	E	P	E
1.	TCPR	998	467	243	104	145	54	23	9	1409	634
2.	SAM	1075	414	211	43	73	11	21	2	1380	470
3.	ROAD	460	350	75	30	40	15	4	2	579	397
4.	IFPAAW	344	131	30	13	29	7	7	3	410	154

Source : Computed.
* Promoted
** Elected

From Table 2.1, we can understand that NGOs working in the rural area have played a significant role in motivating rural people participated and won in the local bodies election and educated rural voters to elect a right person to a representative.

These representatives are mostly from women SHG and SC/ST.

Reasons for the Success

Some of the major reasons for success of the programme are:

- Constant follow-up and motivation of NGOs to the *Dalit* and women candidates.
- Committed staff and fullest cooperation of the SHG members.
- Timely intervention of the PRIA-GRI and network NGO.
- SHGs were already motivated in the rural self-government.
- They had already known the village administrative structure and its function and the role of the village president in rural development activities hence they immediately plunged into the tray.
- They were expecting some external help and guidance to contest in the election and that was given by NGOs.
- *Dalit* had already known the reservation but hesitated to come out to contest in the election. They were badly in need of guidance and encouragement and support either from Government or NGO. As PEVAC went at right time they made use of it.
- Informative meeting conducted frequently specifically for women and *Dalit* and PEVAC motivated them to contest in the election against the dominant caste people within the village.
- SHGs were already waiting for such support to protest against to existing power holder as they were exploiting women and *Dalits*.
- They were fed up with the government officials.
- NGO had given thorough knowledge about 73rd Amendment, provision of reservation of seats for women/*Dalit*.
- A combined campaign by PRIA-Network-GRI had effectively focused only on the suppressed people.
- Solid support by women *sangam* in rural areas.
- Door-to-door canvassing by NGO SHGs.
- Implementation of PEVAC activity at the right time.
- The election for the village ward member and presidents was not on party basis. So women/*Dalit* who don't even have membership card from any political party could contest in the election.

Reasons for the Failure

Though NGO network could achieve a lot, yet there were some shortcomings in the programme. They were as follows :

- The duration of the PEVAC activities was very short.
- Immediate implementation without much preparation for the PEVAC activities.
- In the Local Bodies elections majority of the candidates were from the same village. Same caste and among the relatives, it was more sensitive for the SHGs and even to NGO to work in this environment.

1. *Male Opposition in the Family*

However motivation, the NGO network has given unless there is support from either husband or father of the women SHG member whom the SHG or NGO motivates, it ends in failure in many villages. Male members in the family prevented the women candidates from contesting.

2. *Male Domination in the Villages*

The women candidates, who contested in the general seat, were opposed and threatened by the male nominee in some villages in many districts.

3. *Sensitive Campaigning by other Candidates*

In many places the opposite candidates had conducted the campaign with caste and religious sentiments. Which attracted with literate voters very easily. Under such circumstances promotion of our general candidate was found difficult.

4. *Higher Caste Opposition*

- Higher caste people could not tolerate the emergence of SC and ST in their own village.

- Moneylenders and business people who can spend money lavishly get more support from the villages.
- Votes were purchased by the government officials whose wife had contested in the village.
- Money, liquor, muscle power were the deciding factor for winning the seats in many villages.
- NGO/SHG candidates were struggled for want of money, for canvassing at the last moment.
- Villages do not support the candidate with social concern but they were after money and material.
- Violence prevented considerable women voters to exercise their voters in the rural areas.
- *Dalits* divided among themselves, in the reserved area.
- Non-*Dalits* prevented *Dalits* from filing nomination.
- People gave importance to political party candidate rather than the qualified independent.

Suggestions

Some NGO have come out with suggestion for effective follow up of the PEVAC activities in future.

Three days training programme for elected representatives at all level may be arranged and imparted training on :

- Administration
- Account keeping
- Conducting Gram Sabha
- Knowledge about PRA
- Government programmes
- Planning with people
- Resource mobilization

- Printed materials are to be supplied on duties and the responsibilities of the leaders in the respective tiers of panchayati system.
- Exposure visit to successful area within Tamil Nadu and other states like Kerala.
- Setting-up of resource centres on Panchayat system.

- A monthly newsletter may be circulated to all the Panchayat in Tamil Nadu where success/failures stories can be shared.
- Group discussion with bureaucrats academicians and politician may be arranged.
- Training programme should be conducted at least once in a year for five years.

NGOs and Area of Operation under each NGO Network

Name of the Network : **Tamil Nadu Campaign on Panchayati Raj (TCPR)**

Area Covered

Sl. No.	District	Name of NGO	Name of the Block(s) Covered	No. of Panchayats Covered
1.	Pudukottai	ISSI	Karamadai 15	
			Thiruvankulam	10
			Annavasal 2	
			Kannandarkovil	2
2.	Namakkal	KKEO	Sendamangalam	10
			Kabilaramalai	10
3.	Karur	GRAMIUM	Kulithalai Krishnarayapuram	20
4.	Dindigul	CHERU	Vadamadurai	15
		PEACE Trust	Dindigul	40
5.	Erode	PEACE Trust	Bhavani	10
			Bhavanisagar	10
			Uthukuli	10
6.	Nagapat-tinam	SEVALAYA	Nagapattinam	4
			Keeliyur	7
			Kilvelur	7
			Thalanayar 2	
7.	Cuddalore		Centre for Parankipettai	10
			Peace Action Keelapalayam	10
8.	Madurai	REFORM Trust	Usilampatti	11
			Chellampatti	10
			Sedapatti	10
9.	Theni	CHANDRD	Uthampalayam	10
			Periyakulam	10

(Contd.)

Sl. No.	District	Name of NGO	Name of the Block(s) Covered	No. of Panchayats Covered
10.	Trichy	SEVAI	Arthanallur Lalgudi	20
11.	Dharmapuri	REDC	Dharmapuri	14
			Nallampalli	10
12.	Thiruvan-namalai	Rural Development SEVA Centre	Perambalur	15
			Thellar	10
			Vandavasi	5
			Vempakkam	5
			Pudupalayam	5
			Thiruvannamalai	5
13.	Thiruvarur	Bharati Women Development Centre	Thiruthuraipoondi	10
			Koradachery	10
14.	Coimbatore	CSSR	Madukkarai	9
			Thondamuthur	10

Name of the Network: **Social Action Movement**

Area Covered

Sl. No.	District	Name of NGO	Name of the Block(s) Covered	No. of Panchayats Covered
1.	Salem	Karunya Gender Development Trust	Kadayampatti Mettur, Vellor	
		WEED Trust	Yercaurd	
		PHDT Trust	Ayothipattinam	
		PSDI	Bethanayakanpalayam	
		CROSS	Thalaivasal	
		Human Resource Development Centre	Gengavalli	
		VEEDU	Namagiripettai	
		POETS	Rasipuram	
		MALAR	Senthamangalam	
			Thiruchengode	
			Sangagiri	
			Veerapandi	30
2.	Kanchee-puram	PERT	Thiruppatur	
		WEDS	Kottnkulathur	
		SEAT	Thirukalukundram	
		DET	Maduranthakan	
		RWT	Acharapakkam	
		WEETT	Uthirmerur	65

(Contd.)

Sl. No.	District	Name of NGO	Name of the Block(s) Covered	No. of Panchayats Covered
3.	Villupuram	GAWD	Thiruvunnialannur	
		ATSSS	Thirukovilur	
		REAL	Vikkiravandi	
		POWER	Kanai	
		STS	Kolianoor	
		CHF	Olakkoor	16
4.	Thiruvallur	URDS	Solavaram	
		SERAPHS	Gummidipoondi	
		GNNS	Ambathur	
		SPAD	Uthukottai	
		SEED	WDWA	
		SAFE INDIA	ARDS	
		SERVING HANDS	SEVAI	10
5.	Tanjore	SAM	Kumbakonam	
		Network	Thiruvarur	
			Thirthuraipoondi	
			Tanjore	
			Papanasam	
			Mannarkudi	
			Orathanadu	
			Peravoorani	
			Pattukottai	
			Mayiladuthurai	
			Sivakali	
			Thirupananthal	15
6.	Vellore	CRSHS	Vaniambadi	
		SAM	Kudiatham	
		Network	Sevoor	
			Aryur	
			Jolarpettai	
			Tripathur	
			Vellore	11

Name of the Network : **IFFPAW Network**

Name of the Partner NGOs

1. Akila Bharathi Social Development Centre
2. Community Rehabilitation Organisation for Progress
3. Gandhigram Odhaya Society
4. Indo Trust
5. League for Education and Development

6. Organisation for Action and Social Integration
7. Organisation for Social Action and Improvement
8. Perambalur Social Service Society
9. Peoples Action for Transformation
10. Rural Education and Action Development
11. Rural Welfare Organisation
12. Rural Welfare Society
13. Subiksha
14. Society for Daughters of Mary Immulcate
15. Star

Area Covered

Sl. No.	District	Name of NGO	Name of the Block(s) Covered	No. of Panchayat Covered
1.	Perambalur	IFPAAW Network	Perambalur Alathur Veppur Veppanthapattai	87
2.	Aryalur	IFPAAW Network	Jayakondam Andimadam Sendurai T. Palur Thirumanur Ariyalur	122

Name of the Network: **ROAD**

Area Covered

Sl. No.	District	Name of NGO	Name of the Block(s) Covered	No. of Panchayats Covered
1.	Kanyakumari		Kuruthankodu	15
			Vilavangadu	5
2.	Tuticorin		Srivaigundam	15
3.	Tirunelveli		Nanguneri	9
4.	Ramanathapuram		Ramanathapuram	12
5.	Virudhunagar Sathur			3

III. PEVAC BY NGOS NETWORK

Pre-Election, On the Day of Election and Post-Election

Generation of awareness among the voters prior to the local bodies election was the prime aim of the Pre-Election Voter Awareness Campaign (PEVAC) activities. The activities were expected to be completed on the day before polling, as the title of the activities suggested. But all the NGOs network and district level NGOs have extended their activities to the day of polling and even after the results of the election were declared, as the nature of the problems and the work requires more than the stipulated period in the form of follow up activities. A significant observation made in this regard is that:

- All the networks and district level NGOs were hectically involved in carrying out PEVAC activities prior to the election.
- Very limited NGOs imparted training to the elected members after the election was over.

The activities carried out in the three phase pre-election, on the day of election and post-election, are presented hereunder one by one. As soon as the workshop was over, all the networks started working in their respective districts from 12th September, 2001 onwards as the days for the local bodies election were approaching.

District Administration Informed

District Collector and Superintendent of Police were met before the start of the PEVAC activities in almost all the districts. The NGO networks and individual NGOs received good response from the Government officials for the reason that PEVAC activities are :

- Supported by the Government.
- In non-party basis, as recommended by the Election Commission.

- Risky activities sensitive in nature, to which opposition may come from political parties, elite groups, higher caste and economically affluent candidates.
- Not anti-Government but a sharing of the burden of Government in generating political awareness among the rural illiterate voters.

The District Collector, Superintendent of Police, Project Officer of District Rural Development Agency and Project Officer, Mahalir Thittam (Women Development Corporation in Tamil Nadu) offered to render help to carry out PEVAC activities successfully. In some places, it was reported that the Superintendent of Police ordered the local police station to provide police protection to the NGOs carrying PEVAC message to some sensitive areas. Mahalir Thittam Project Officer asked the members of SHGs in the respective villages to render cooperation to the maximum extent to execute the PEVAC activities. It was really encouraging and a source of strength to the NGOs.

1. ***Orientation to the NGOs Staff (ToT)***

To begin with, an one-day orientation programme was organised for all the staff working in NGOs, no matter whether they were trained in Panchayati Raj or not. The staff were briefed about the following aspects:

- The importance of 73rd Amendment and its basic features relating to village development.
- Role of villagers in creating a real democratic structure at the grossroots level.
- The role of women in local bodies under 73rd Amendment.
- The role of *Dalit* community in general and *Dalit* women in particular in upholding the principle of creation of egalitarian society in India.
- Real meaning of democracy, in terms of participation on by all the voters irrespective of caste, class, religion or

any other socio-economic discrimination in the electoral process.

- Role of NGOs in increasing the voting rate among rural voters.

2. *Printing of Wall Posters*

As a second step, big size wall posters bearing messages fully on local bodies election were printed by each network taking into account the field reality.

- Encouraging *Dalits* and STs in general and women belonging to SC and ST in particular not only to vote but to contest the election.
- The theme was motivating women to contest the local bodies election as this was a golden opportunity for them to capture political power to address their long pending problems. Particularly problems faced by women from birth to death like female infanticide, female foeticide, discrimination in school, employment, marriage, dowry system, prevention of widow-remarriage and so on so forth.
- Motivating the women to contest the local bodies election to ensure their rights.
- Propagating the importance of 33 per cent reservation of seats allotted for women in local bodies.
- Disseminating the information that *Dalits* cannot be prevented from coming to power in the local bodies as there is compulsory reservation according to the 73rd Amendment.
- Informing the rural voters not to be influenced by money or muscle power or any other considerations.
- Appealing to the rural voters to select a leader who can uphold grassroots democracy, social justice, and protect natural resources and human rights.
- Emphasizing the importance of voting in large numbers.
- Encouraging the deaf, dumb, handicapped to vote and requesting the healthy persons to assist them and take

the socially and physically handicapped voters to the polling station.

- Explaining the number of votes to be exercised by the rural voters.
- Giving details about the number of votes to be caste for different posts with respective colours.
- Informing that the electronic machine would not be used—instead, a normal ballot sheet would be used for polling.
- Asking the villagers to help to form a good government under a good leadership at the village level to provide good governance.
- Emphasizing that voting is the fundamental right of every citizen.
- Asking the people not to be silent spectators in the democratic process and be active participants in the local bodies election, so that grassroots level democracy can be preserved and strengthened.

3. *Bit Notices with a Difference by TCPR*

Thousands of bit notices were printed in each district. The information and issues in the notices were according to the local reality. For example, notices printed in the coastal areas covered the problems faced by the fishermen community. Bit notices printed in Madurai, Dindigul, Salem and Namakkal included female infanticide and child labour. The major information the bit notices carried were: The major problems faced by the villages in the district. The characteristics of a good leader for the village administration was given as below:

- Leader should be familiar with the local people and their problems.
- Leader should be from the local villages of the Panchayat and not an outsider.
- Leader should have knowledge, experience and commitment.
- Leader should have earned good name both in his family and in his village.

- Leader should have thorough knowledge of the basic needs and the burning problems faced by the local people.
- Leader should be able to expose the local problem in the public meeting or in the Gram Sabha.
- Leader should be accessible to everyone.
- Leader should first respect people, truth, social criticism and his promises.
- Leader should have a vision inclining towards social reforms and social reconstruction.
- Leader should be able to move with all the people irrespective of caste, class and religion.
- Leader should not be influenced by either money, fame or position.
- Leader should maintain direct relationship between his speech and action.
- Leader should have ability to tap all the governmental programmes meant for village development.
- Leader should have vision inclining towards the future and plan accordingly.
- Leader should have faith in the citizen and democracy.
- Leader should not misuse the power for his self-development.
- Leader should be able to point out the social evils.
- Leader should have intention to protect the natural resources and human rights.
- Leader should have concern for women, children, and *Dalit* community.
- Leader should have courage to prevent both female infanticide and female foeticide.
- Leader should have love towards motherland and humanity.
- Leader should preserve the honour and dignity of his position.
- Leader should have a plan to improve the health and hygienic condition of the village.
- Leader should have interest in maintaining and developing common property resources for development.

- Leader should not be a proxy but to be independent in decision-making and administration.
- Leader should know the importance of Gram Sabha.
- Leader should be sensitive towards the practice of child labour and bonded labour.

All the above mentioned *details* were printed in the posters and pamphlets specifically prepared for PEVAC. After seeing the posters and pamphlets one of the Tamil daily newspapers printed all those messages for popular consumption.

4. *Distribution of Bit Notices*

Bit notices were distributed to the rural voters through various means. With the help of members of women SHGs and committed staff and Youth Sangam bit notices were distributed to all individual households. Van, Auto and Cycle, were used for distributing the bit notices with the help of NGO staff to all hamlets. Places like bus stop, street corner, church, temple, mosque, market place, tea shops, educational institutions like, college, school and training institutions were covered by pasting the posters and bills.

5. *Cloth Banners for* Dalit *Women*

There were two types of cloth banners printed with multiple colours by each NGO network.

The focus given in the banners:

- Encouraging the *Dalits* to make use of the reservation for obtaining political power to move towards mainstream from exclusivism.
- To motivate women to use reservation towards obtaining equality and finding permanent solutions to their long pending problems.

6. *Banner Tied*

Places like junction of roads, places earmarked for public meeting and street corners, infront of Panchayat building and government offices were selected for displaying the cloth banners. Almost all the women SHGs, Youth Clubs and volunteers in the villages helped in carryingout this activity.

7. *Stickers Pasted*

There were four types of multi-coloured stickers printed by the networks and distributed to the NGO working in districts. The main themes of the stickers were:

- Appealing to the voters to vote for women to protect women's rights.
- Encouraging women to contest the election to protect their rights and solve their problems.
- Motivating *Dalits* to participate in the election as candidates to obtain power to come up in life.
- Motivating the voters to support and vote for *Dalits* so that equality and fraternity can be ensured.

Places for Pasting Stickers

Apart from the main places mentioned earlier with regard to the pasting of wall posters and tying of cloth banners, buses, auto rickshaws were also selected for pasting stickers. It attracted the voters very easily.

8. *Wall Writings*

Some networks adopted a technique which generally the political parties use, namely wall writings. Well in advance they reserved the walls outside the houses of the SHG members and common places with the prior permission of the owner of the wall and wrote some messages about:

- Asking the rural voters to vote compulsorily.
- Requesting them to vote for right candidates.
- Emphasizing the rights of *Dalits* and women.

9. *Election Manifestoes Released*

An NGO, SAM, prepared and released a model manifesto for the local bodies election. Apart from mentioning all the qualities of a good leader it also demanded the following:

- 50 per cent of seats are to be reserved for women.
- District Panchayat President should have more powers than the District Collector.
- SC/ST women should be a part of the decision-making committee at the village level.
- SC/ST, and women should be given importance in the village.

The first copy of this was released by Dr. N. Markandan, Former Vice-Chancellor of Gandhigram Rural Institute, Dindigul on 30 August, 2001. The same was released in all other districts. It pronounced very innovative and reformative principles. The SAM network released the manifesto in all the districts while carrying out the PEVAC activities.

10. *Rally with Plantain Leaves*

In Tanjore hundreds of volunteers collected by SAM network took out a procession with banana leaves on which PEVAC messages were written. It attracted the public very quickly.

11. *Training Module for Good Governance*

The SAM network published an innovative training module for generating awareness among the voters on *Dalit* and women representation in the village administration.

12. *Handbook Distributed*

ROAD network released a handbook on voter awareness, particularly the importance and implications of 73rd Amendment.

13. *Pamphlets Distributed*

ROAD also published a pamphlet consisting of the following details:

- Problems of rural people.
- Instruction to candidates.
- Code of conduct for candidates and political parties.

14. *One Day Training to Cultural Team*

Despite the fact that the cultural team may have rich experience in disseminating messages on various socio-economic problems of the rural masses, it was felt that it is important to provide a one-day orientation to the cultural team about the new Panchayati Raj System. It was given at the district headquarters. The training theme was given by the district convener of the NGO.

Cultural Team with PEVAC Messages

A team consistsing of 10 artists, who have already undergone a training in Panchayat Raj, made rounds throughout the districts to disseminate information on

- Rural voting pattern.
- Role of *Dalits*/women in Panchayat.
- Selecting good leaders for Panchayat.

The theme was so attractive that villagers were easily attracted. It was done in all the districts under SAM network.

15. *Cycle Yatra*

Some NGOs, almost in all the four networks, adopted this technique as it seemed to be easy to arrange and reach the people quickly and effectively. Display cards were put up at the front of the cycles carrying message of PEVAC. All the printed materials were also distributed during this *yatra*.

16. *Van Yatra*

A van with attached public address system was arranged for a van *yatra*. This was also followed by many NGOs in most parts of Tamil Nadu. The staff of NGOs and some professionals were involved in disseminating the PEVAC message to rural folk. It was quick and easy but costly. Political parties also did the same kind of van *yatra*, but the NGO van went to the rural areas with different messages which attracted the voters. Sometimes the NGOs had to earn the wrath of political parties which was inevitable.

17. *One-Day Training to Women SHGs*

As women were one of the major target groups, network NGOs approached all the members of SHG to carry out the activities under PEVAC. Accordingly, all the SHGs in the adopted unions (2-3 in each district) were contacted. The majority of them attended the one day training programme organised by the NGO. The participants were motivated to contest the election and they were given information about:

- The role of SHGs in increasing voting percentage.
- The role of SHGs in bringing more women leaders.
- The role of SHGs in bringing about social change by making use of reservation of seats for women.
- The role of Gram Sabha in social transformation.
- Their participation in the local election.
- How to choose a right candidate.
- Supporting women candidates from SHGs.
- How to file nomination, and take follow up action.

As there were SHGs in every village and they were assisted by the NGOs, the majority of the members participated in the training programme and enriched their knowledge and they made a commitment to this exercise. They were asked to support the

PEVAC activities in whatever manner possible. Many members in SHGs were motivated to file nomination in the election. This training was conducted before starting the process of filing nomination.

18. *One-Day Training for* Dalits

This programme was organised exclusively for *Dalits* in some parts of Tamil Nadu, particularly in Chidambaram and Nagapattinam and they were motivated to file nomination both in the reserved and general constituencies.

Training for the Aspiring Candidates

A one-day training programme was organized by the every NGO under the network for aspiring candidates before and after the nomination date was over. Intimation through formal letter and wall posters was sent to every candidate who filed nomination for various posts asking them to attend the meeting. A marriage hall in either the taluk or the district headquarters was selected for holding the meeting and candidates, particularly women and SC/ST, were requested to attend the meeting. The following details were shared with them:

* How to file correct nomination so that it will not be rejected?
* How to take follow up activities successfully?
* How to make canvassing attractive to the voters?
* How to compete with other political party candidates?
* Code of conduct and official norms for various activities.

Resource persons were invited from different fields. The service of Dr. G. Palanithurai, Coordinator, Rajiv Gandhi Chair for Panchayati Raj Studies, Dr. V. Ragupathy, Assistant Coordinator, and PEVAC Coordinator Dr. C. Kubendran and research scholars Mr. M. A.Thirunavukkarasu were also sought. In the training programme the concentration was only on women and *Dalits*. Yet all the candidates, *i.e.* non-SC and women also participated and benefited.

Issues Focused

Some important issues/messages disseminated by the NGO:

- Select good, committed and knowledgeable leaders.
- Support women/*Dalits* as president.
- Method to find out a suitable leader.
- Different colours and respective posts, the rural voter should know.
- Importance of *Dalits*/women in Local Administration.
- How to be an independent administrator and take decisions on one's own?

Problems Witnessed

- Conflicts among *Dalits* and sub-castes of *Dalits* in many places.
- *Dalits* were prevented from contesting in the election at the village Panchayat level in Madurai and Virudhunagar districts continuously.
- SC women were prevented from filing nomination for the general seats.
- Poor SC women candidates were purchased by elite women after the nomination.
- SC women/*Dalits* expected financial support from NGOs.
- Wife of government employees and political leaders, particularly rich candidates, spent more money for campaigning so that the poor SHG women lost hope and interest.
- Auctioning and rotation methods were also adopted in Madurai, Ramnad, Salem districts.
- NGOs were prevented from conducting campaign on PEVAC activities in the village where *Dalits* were prevented in Madurai district.

- No campaigning in the villages where lottery and auctioning methods were practised for electing village presidents in Madurai district.

Implications

Though there were some hurdles in carrying out PEVAC activities, the NGO partners could achieve some positive changes in the election. The important development observed during PEVAC activities in the rural areas were:

- Women were motivated to contest the election in the general seats apart from reserved seats.
- *Dalits* were enlightened towards not only voting but to contest the election as well.
- The level of political awareness among the rural people in general and *Dalits* and women in particular has been increased considerably.
- District Collector has encouraged, Superintendent of Police has appreciated and Mahalir Thittam Project Officer has supported our work in many districts. It is a good beginning for the local NGOs to get support from the Government officials to carry out PEVAC activities in the future towards strengthening democracy.
- Women developed confidence in managing power.
- *Dalits* were encouraged and came out to fight against elite groups.
- *Dalits*, no doubt if we constantly support, would definitely fight against the so-called upper caste people who have prevented them from filing nomination in four village Panchayats in Madurai and Virudhunagar districts.
- Women were motivated to attend Gram Sabha meeting four times in a year without fail and make use of it for the holistic development of the rural society and particularly to solve the problems faced by the women for centuries together.
- Wall posters with different messages in multi-colour were appreciated by social activists, Government

officials, and other NGOs as the information given in the posters was educative, motivating and timely.

- More independent candidates contested in the election because of the direct support of NGOs and women SHGs.
- It created an opportunity for many NGOs to join together to fight against upper caste and male domination in the rural areas. Thereby the NGOs have covered a platform to sustain their activities in the future.
- SHGs in some villages were the deciding factors for the selection of village president.
- There was no complaint against women SHG candidates in the villages.
- Separate bit notices were printed in the name of the SHG forum.
- *Dalits* were very happy that NGOs had taken up their cause and responded to their feelings.
- The Deputy Speaker of Tamil Nadu Legislative Assembly appreciated the PEVAC activities.
- Women candidates were made assertive and to act independently.
- Percentage of voting in the rural areas has gone up.
- Prevented the free distribution of *dhoties, sarees,* tumblers to poor voters to attract them in Perambalur area.
- The concept of 'proxy' has gone. Women and *Dalits* have contested on their own, not on behalf of someone. Now they are independent.

Number of Nominations from SHGs and *Dalits* was High

Due to constant support, motivation and appropriate guidance given by the NGO network, the number of candidates who contested for different posts from village Panchayat, ward member, village Panchayat president, Panchayat union councillor and district councillor, was high compared to that in the previous election. NGO network concentrated only on the third-tier of Panchayat, namely Gram Panchayat. The number of candidates for Gram Panchayat ward members and president posts was so high that even the NGO could not have expected this number especially in some districts, like Salem, Kanjeepuram.

On the Day of Election

In addition to generating awareness among the voters on the local bodies election and New Panchayati Raj before election, NGOs also carried out certain important activities in support of the candidates to be promoted on the day of polling as described hereunder.

1. *Nomination of Booth Agent*

As part of the polling process, some NGOs nominated their local volunteers as booth agents for the candidates, the NGOs and women SHGs intended to promote.

2. *Personal Visit to SC Colony*

SC voters were personally and individually met at their residence, mostly in the colonies, and they were once again reminded to vote for a particular candidate, namely the NGO promoter.

3. *Organised Informal meet with SHGs*

On the day of election, all the members of SHGs in the early morning gathered in a particular house and discussed how to motivate the voters to support the candidates being promoted.

4. *Written Vote Slips*

A group of volunteers and the staff of NGOs and office bearers of SHGs were actively involved in writing the voter slip throughout the night in support of a particular candidate.

5. *Handicapped and Aged were Assisted*

Both NGOs and members of SHGs very actively took part in taking the aged and physically handicapped to the polling station to exercise their vote. They were also taken back home safely, which created a good impression in favour of the candidates they promoted.

Ensured High Percentage of Votes

A group of NGO staff along with local volunteers and members of SHGs went round the village, going street by street and door by door, to ensure that all the voters exercised their vote. They also convinced some voters who were not interested to vote. They did this exercise till the last minute of the polling.

Prevented Bogus Votes

With keen watch and verification by the volunteers nominated as booth agents a large number of bogus votes were prevented from the elite groups of the local people.

Tried to Avoid Violence and Untoward Incidents

The personnel deployed by the NGOs and SHGs played the role of mediator to prevent any clash between two groups about to clash. In some places disputes were settled within the village limit avoiding police cases.

Protected the Ballot Boxes after Polling

Once the voting process was over, after completing all the formalities to be followed, the voted ballot sheets were preserved safely as it was the time when rival groups may lift or damage them. So a group of volunteers and NGO staff were physically present in front of the hall where the ballot boxes were kept.

Minimum Expenditure Met

Some NGOs met the expenditure incurred on refreshment to the booth agents and volunteers in support of their candidates.

Rushed to the Riot Village

Apart from promoting candidates in different ways NGOs also made visits to some villages identified as sensitive in their area on the day of polling where there was clash between two groups which stopped the polling process for hours. NGO personnel were also involved in pacifying the rival groups with the support of the local police and the Deputy Superintendent of Police (DSP) leading to resumption of polling.

Visited the Village which Auctioned the President's Post

In order to understand the attitude of the people and the local reality in the village where president was elected through auctioning, a team of members from an NGO working in Madurai district visited the village (Ayyanarkulam) and had a discussion with the people about the auctioning and the polling performance.

Visited the Village where Lottery System was Adopted

It was a surprise that a candidate who was elected through lottery method was forced to contest the election as there was a competitor who filed nomination against him. A team of members from the local NGO visited the village, V. Agurani, to observe and understand the opinion of the voters towards rival candidates.

Interviewed the Person Elected through Lottery System

The one who was elected through lottery method and was contesting the election was met and interviewed about the probability of his winning in one of the hamlets where the polling was going on. It was documented photographically.

Post-Election

Before and on the days of election were not the end of the activities carried out by the NGO network under PEVAC in Tamil Nadu. It extended even after the election in different forms as follows:

1. *Felicitation to the Elected Representatives*

As a mark of encouragement, NGOs started organising a public meeting at the block level and district level, where newly elected representatives at different levels—ward members, Panchayat presidents, Panchayat union councillors and district Panchayat councillors—were honoured in two batches. The first batch was organised for the two lower levels, *i.e.* ward members and panchayat presidents. The second batch was specially organised for the top two levels, Panchayat union councillors and district Panchayat councillors. Every individual representative was honoured.

Politicians, academicians and research staff from Gandhigram Rural University, particularly from the Department of Political Science and Development Administration, were invited as resource persons. The elected representatives were briefed about the importance and relevance of three-tier system in the contemporary socio-economic development.

2. *Training to the Elected Representatives*

After the felicitation was over, a few NGOs had made arrangement for imparting formal training to the representatives and that too only for the village presidents, as they are the ones who possess the supreme power and more responsibilities rest with village presidents.

The important themes on which the training was given were:

- Salient features of 73rd Amendment.
- The role of women and *Dalits* in village development.
- Powers and responsibilities of village president.
- Village administration.
- Maintenance of 31 records and accounts.
- 29 powers given to village presidents according to 73rd Amendment.

They were also supplied with printed materials on these aspects.

3. *Awareness Programme*

A few selected and interested presidents were imparted awareness programme on various aspects, particularly the strengths and weakness of the previous presidents and their achievements and failures.

Promoted Gram Sabha

Unlike in previous years when the attendance of villagers in Gram Sabha meeting was very poor after the local bodies election was over, NGOs were particular in strengthening the Gram Sabha meeting. So, the NGOs, through women self-help groups (SHGs) and with the help of the staff and volunteers, took all the steps necessary to make the Gram Sabha meeting much better than in the past years.

Suggestions

- The majority of the NGOs have proposed to conduct a formal training to the elected representatives.
- It was suggested that a resource centre may be established at the district level to cater to the needs of all the elected representatives for getting guidance and assistance.

Follow-up Activities

- A village visit was made on the day of polling in Madurai district where auctioning was done but there was a formal election as some one filed nomination against the selectee.
- A tense village in Usilampatti, Thathanpatti, was visited by TCPR NGO, who helped the police and the public to ensure smooth polling.

IV. ROLE OF STATE ELECTION COMMISSION

An autonomous body set-up by Government of Tamil Nadu specifically for conducting of local bodies election played its role very clearly from the time of announcement of the dates for the poll to the declaration of election results. In order to conduct a smooth, fair and free election, the State Election Commission released reports, statements and information periodically through both print and electronic media.

- It appointed election officers at various levels to take follow-up activities from state level to Panchayat union level.
- It announced two phases of polls for easy administration and security purposes.
- It nominated high level officials for constituting monitoring committees which periodically monitored every activity of the officials below their level.
- State Election Commission had clearly earmarked assignments to Government officials at different levels and supervised their functioning to speed up the process.
- District Collectors were encouraged and involved very effectively in the conduct of election in their respective district.
- In order to speed up the polling and make the counting accurate without confusion, the State Election Commission had dropped the idea of using electronic machines for voting. Instead ballot sheet was used.
- As local poll election was a little different from general assembly election, with regard to number of votes a voter has to vote for general election only 2 votes (MP and MLA), but in local poll, they have to exercise 4 votes, *i.e.* district councillor, panchayat union councillor, panchayat president and ward member, it gave different colours to the ballot sheets to distinguish them from one another. It published the information to the voters through all the daily papers, which was really a good work and which helped rural voters to get a clear idea as for whom to vote and on which colour.
- In order to prevent any untoward incidents and any other anti-social activities during the election it laid down some restrictions for the candidates, such as :

— The duration of campaign was fixed in rural and urban areas differently. The loudspeaker was allowed from 6.00 am to 10.00 pm in urban areas and up to 11.00 pm in rural areas.

— The District Collectors were asked to hold all party meeting to discuss the poll arrangements. Accordingly each District Collector, submitted reports to the State Election Commission periodically.

— So as to prevent bogus votes the District Collector warned that: Those who indulged in casting fake votes would be booked under Goondas Act.

— A phone number which can be used by the people to inform the collectorate of any untoward incident during polling and during counting was given to the public. Frequent meetings were also held on security arrangements.

— With the past record, as witnessed in the general assembly elections, the State Election Commission identified sensitive polling booths in the two phases and made necessary security arrangements for smooth conduct of election.

— In order to ensure 100 per cent voting, the State Election Commission declared that the voters who do not have photo identity card could use anyone of the 19 proofs already suggested by State Election Commission.

— This flexibility, in allowing eligible voters to vote, really paved the way for a high rate of polling. The booth officers were also given proper instructions in this regard.

— State Election Commission fixed the maximum amount to be spent for election according to the post in the local poll. It also warned that the candidates who violate the limits would be punished and that their candidature, even if they won the election, would be cancelled.

— It also fixed a deadline for the submission of expenditure account— within 30 days of the election.

— State Election Commission asked the District Collectors to give orientation and training to the poll officers.

— State Election Commission through newspapers periodically informed the public about the steps being taken towards free and fair conduct of poll which was encouraging to the innocent and exploited people.

— Voters list was released much earlier to the public so that the voters could verify their names and those whose names were not included could enroll their name in the voters list. It gave an opportunity to the new voters to enroll their name.

— A lot of precautionary measures were taken, *i.e.* the district authority issued orders to surrender licensed guns throughout Tamil Nadu till the election was over.

— It also ordered the owners of the wineshops to close down the wine shops for three days, *i.e.* two polling days and the counting day.

— The district authority issued orders to the polling officers wherein it gave clear instruction as to how to conduct a fair and free election. The officials also performed their role to the maximum possible.

Gaps Identified

- Though the State Election Commission conducted the local poll election in a successful manner with violence only here and there it would have still been more effective and a higher percentage of voting would have been observed if it had gone some steps further. There were some gaps identified in the role played by the State Election Commission. They were :

  — State Election Commission had not taken any steps to generate awareness among the people in the remote areas on the number of votes they had to vote, and the different colours for each position.

— People were not aware of the difference between general election and local bodies election.
— State Election Commission had not taken steps to hold election in the areas where election had not been held successively three times, *i.e.* Keeripatti, Pappapatti and Nattarmangalam of Madurai district and Kattachienthal in Virudhunagar district.
— No serious steps were taken against the candidates or the village people who had adopted lottery method and auctioning of village president posts.
— There were a number of problems during polling as the majority of the voters, even those who had photo identity card, were prevented from voting as their names did not appear in the voters list. Such problem, could have been averted, had the State Election Commission taken proper steps a little earlier.

Symbols allotted to independent candidates were not easily identifiable and understandable by the rural voters, particularly symbols like grinding machine, banana, lorry etc., which confused the voters. Many candidates found it very difficult to popularise their symbols among the rural voters. There were some symbols which had sentimentally wrong notions like broom, flying vessels. Candidates who were allotted these types of symbols lost interest in campaigning. Though there was prior information about the selection of Panchayat presidents through lottery method and auctioning (the media persons were able to cover the news with photographs), no steps were taken against them. Even after the first incidence of such selection of candidates for village president posts either police or other functionaries concerned could have taken precautionary steps to prevent such happenings so that auctioning could have been averted in other places. Basic rights of citizens were denied by this practice.

Dalits were prevented from filing nomination in the reserved areas. It was well known to all the officials, both district administration and State Election Commission. It was the third time that they refrained from the election. No appropriate step was taken so that SC could file nomination. Hence the fundamental right under democracy was demanded. Of the total booths where repolling was demanded in one-fourth cases re-polling was ordered. There was no mention of the number of votes one should cast at ward level in the ballot sheet.

— Colours, differentiating various positions, like ward members, councillor, president, chairman was not intimated to the voters properly.

— No steps were taken to conduct re-polling in the places where none cast their vote in the re-polling, particularly in Ramanathapuram district, Mala Kannucheri Panchayat, with 500 voters.

— The performance of election observers was not so serious as in the general election or in the previous Panchayat election held in 1996.

No guarantee and security was given to *Dalits* in the villages reserved for *Dalits*, who were prevented from filing nomination. It was also observed that some people of *Dalit* community had left their village due to the attack of the dominant community on them and their houses protesting against the *Dalits* proposing to file nomination in Natarmangalam, one of the villages where election not held in Madurai district.

Symbols and Dissatisfaction of Candidates

There was utter confusion, unhappiness and dissatisfaction and dejection, on the part of candidates for the posts of village president and ward members. It was due to the symbols allotted to them.

1. *Symbol of Violence*

Some symbols like sickle, axe, saw, spear, allotted for village level were symbols of violence. The candidates who were allotted these symbols found it embarrassing to use the symbol for canvassing. There was already tension, and enmity even among the relatives and the opponents of the same village and ward. Canvassing with symbol of violence further developed tension between candidates and among the public.

2. *Bad Omen*

Some symbols like broomstick, well, candle, cap were considered bad omens in the villages. The candidates to whom these symbols were allotted felt sentimentally that they could not campaign for votes with these symbols as these were symbols of failure, destruction, and cheating (the negative aspects).

3. *Confused/Unknown Symbols*

There were some symbols like grinder, tomtom, large horse, which were not known to rural people and the candidates. It was difficult for both the voters and the candidates to understand the symbols and publish the same within a short period of time.

4. *Very Small Symbols*

Key, comb, ball, hammer, kettle were some of the symbols allotted to candidates at the village level which were very difficult for the candidates to draw on the wall and popularise among the village people.

5. *Difficult for Drawing*

It was difficult to draw pictures of scooter, tractor during campaign. The State Election Commission could have taken some steps in this regard so that all the candidates, voters and supporters would not have found it difficult to popularise the symbols and thereby facilitated the campaign more effectively. In general the role of State Election Commission really deserves appreciation though some changes are needed with regard to the selection of symbols.

V. EXTENSION OF RESERVATION FOR WOMEN AND *DALIT*

Women Panchayat presidents in Tamil Nadu had been pressing the Government to extend the tenure of reservation for another period. The representatives from the State Association of Women Presidents met the leaders of all the political parties and sought their support in influencing the Government in this regard. They explained that they demanded the extension of reservation period for another term because it had taken five years for the women representatives to break even after the initial struggle to establish themselves in their constituencies.

Sudden announcement of local poll election in Tamil Nadu and reservation for women and *Dalits* in position at every level was really a surprise. Women and *Dalits* were neither trained nor prepared for contesting the election. Untrained, unprepared, inefficient persons were made to contest the local election on behalf of the elite group of the village. With regard to women candidates the wives/daughters/sisters of the ex-presidents, and for SC candidates (both men and women) the candidates who were working in the agricultural field of the so called upper caste group were fielded.

The proxy candidates were:

- Mostly illiterates.
- Unaware of even their own village and hamlets and the people there.
- They did not know the problems of their own people.
- They did not have knowledge about the power and responsibilities of a village representative for which they were contesting.
- They did not even know the formalities to be followed for contesting the election.

Many candidates did not know how to file nomination. Many of the nominations of such candidates were rejected in the previous election. It was very difficult for the candidates to campaign for votes. Women were reluctant to go out for campaign in a village where a male has always been the ruler.

The situation was worse in the case of SC women candidates who had to seek support from all the males of the upper caste, including the ex-president. Women candidates found it difficult to go round with women group in their own village, street by street and door to door, for campaigning for votes, which was uncommon in rural life. Though voters were not satisfied with the quality and qualifications of the candidates, they selected the proxy candidates knowing fully well that it was not the elected candidate who was going to function but the elite who would function in the name of the elected one. (That was what exactly happened after the election.) There were some incidents where the husbands of elected women representatives not only accompanied them wherever they went, even to attend meetings held in the collectorate and to attend training in far off places.

- Males, either husband, brother or father of elected women acted as presidents for a full term in many Panchayats.
- They were always sitting in the Panchayat office and attending to complaints and receiving the official communications.
- They collected taxes of all kinds in all the hamlets.
- They even gave interview to the press on behalf of the real president.
- It is not out of place to mention that a husband of a woman president went to the extent of conducting Gram Sabha meeting and affixing his signature in the place of his wife in the records. It so happened not deliberately but due to lack of knowledge about the power/ responsibility and the role of the president.
- There were some debates in this regard. Some women complained that the males played the role of women presidents just to show their supremacy and establish their dominant role, as in the case of their role in the family administration preventing women from functioning independently in the key aspects.

Another section of women activist argued that men did so because they did not want women to enjoy power in any form more than what men enjoyed at every level in any field. It was easy for men to dominate over women as they have already exercised their superior power in all their domestic activities. It is to be noted here that both men and women don't understand the reasons for reservation for women in the election. The perception of those people on democracy is far from the perception of the political analysts, social thinkers and women activists. The main reason why the allocation of 33 per cent reservation for women has not served its purpose in many places is the lack of awareness on the part of women. As it has been mentioned already it was the Government which announced elections all of a sudden and imposed local poll election on the people, for its own survival as there was pressure from Central Government. People found with no option but to accept the Government decision of participating in the election according to the 73rd Amendment with reservation. Just for the sake of fulfilling the required number of seats on reservation the people fielded candidates of their choice.

Compulsory reservation of 33 per cent for women made the people give preference to women. Males could not tolerate the emergence of the leadership of females in their own villages. Males considered the women presidents only equivalent to the heads SHGs in the village and treated them so. But the extension of reservation for women has created good impact in the overall personality of women leaders.

Impact Created

In the first period women were forced to contest the election, whereas, the second time they themselves came forward and contested. It shows that women, given a chance, would take up any responsibility. Women in the previous election were proxy candidates, depending totally on men for all activities. Women leaders were reluctant to speak in public, whereas with 5 years of experience, almost all the women leaders started speaking informatively in the midst of people and in public meetings. Due to lack of knowledge on their role and responsibilities, the women leader had developed an inferiority complex to move with Government officials, but now, due to attending meetings and training programmes constantly, women candidates have developed confidence and courage to express their thoughts and opinions freely and interact with officials confidently.

- The same candidates are able to contest once again. More or less it is an evolution of their performance. Only those who very actively administered the Panchayat during the previous tenure have been selected in the subsequent election also.
- As the extension of reservation was given the general candidates felt disappointment and complained as if their right was denied.
- In some villages, where the *Dalit* and women Panchayat leaders failed to improve their skill and talent, the public lost faith in reservation. As there is no other way to elect a suitable leader, they are forced to elect from among the available women and *Dalit* candidates during the second time also.

In the previous term women leaders were only executors of the programmes evolved and implemented by Government. But now women leaders, along with other women representatives and self-help group members, started raising voice against social evils in general and women related issues in particular prevalent in the village like alcoholism, rape, wife beating, easy divorce and so on and so forth. During the last 5 years of their leadership the males of their family were accompanying the leaders wherever they went, even to attend training programmes and meetings conducted exclusively for women. Some males went to the extent of attending intensive training programmes arranged specifically for women. But now one could witness women candidates attending a residential training programme alone even for a week. Once women presidents found it very difficult to bring rural people to Gram Sabha. But due to constant meeting and transparency, the women leader made the women self-help group in each hamlet attend the Gram Sabha.

The attendance at Gram Sabha was encouraging because of the effort taken by women leaders and it was made possible only through extension of reservation for women. Previously the mobility of women presidents was restricted by the family members and even the village people looked down upon them due to social and caste customs and norms whenever the leaders went out of the village. But now the mobility of a woman leader is considered very important and none looks at it differently as she has carried out a lot of development activities with the support of local people.

Innate Ability Comes Out

As long as women were engaged in only kitchen activities they were looked at only as servants but after assuming power, they have started showing their innate qualities.

Team Spirit Developed

Among women representatives and women leaders a sense of cooperation has developed towards village development. Five long years of their experience has improved their leadership quality. They are now capable of taking decisions on their own. In the previous term, women Panchayat leaders were treated as servants by the government officials at every level. In the present term due to extended reservation every woman leader has started enquiring about the schemes and other provisions from the government officials. The time has come when the women would treat the Government official as their servant. In short, extension of reservation for women has brought about positive changes in the administration, implementation, gender sensitization, and overall individual personality of women. Political awareness has increased, the number of candidates proposing to contest the election has also increased. Quality of service, perception towards village and social issues have also changed. Extension of reservation for women has really been a milestone in the process of women empowerment.

VI. NEW SYSTEM OF SELECTION OF CANDIDATES

Ever since the first election was held, every election has been witnessing changes both positively and negatively in terms of the characteristics of candidates, campaigning techniques, electoral procedures, ceiling on election expenditure, involvement of religion, caste and alliance with political parties with contradicting ideologies and so on so forth. But the local bodies election held in the year 2001 in Tamil Nadu witnessed some unexpected and disheartening changes, threatening the fundamentals of democracy and human rights. They were:

1. Selection of representatives through lottery system.
2. Selection of leaders through auctioning of posts.
3. Selection of leaders by rotation.
4. Preventing *Dalits* from filing nomination in the reserved areas also.

Auctioning

This is the first time that people elected their representatives through auctioning of the local body positions. This is mainly because they could mobilize sufficient money to take care of their welfare activities in their villages. Even though the people in Ayyanarkulam Village Panchayat had two higher level functionaries, *i.e.* Union Chairman and MLA, they could not get any meaningful delivery from them for their socio-economic improvement. On occasions of urgency and necessity the village people had to depend upon their own resources. Even to meet the basic needs which are supposed to be taken care of by the village administration, such as laying of link roads, maintenance of schools and other common utility buildings, providing of street lights etc. So they thought that the alternative left to them was only to have people of their choice elected through auctioning which would prevent both violence, unnecessary conflict among the villagers and add a definite amount to the village common fund. The emerging trend among the villagers only showed their disbelief in the representatives elected through democratic system who could not do anything for the development of the village. On the contrary, people could have their own fund for their development work on the day of auctioning itself.

Villagers have developed the practice of attending to infrastructure work like laying link road leading to village temple and installing street light with the money earned through public property like village tank based for fish or collecting contribution from every household. Villagers said that even very recently they laid a road to the temple of a village God, Nalla Gurumban. They estimated that nearly Rs. 20 lakhs from common fund has been spent to carry out all such activities and that they needed still more money for worshipping the God every year grandly. More contestants in the election for the same post only developed violence, enmity, disintegration of the village unity and misunderstanding among relatives leading to clashes, damaging individual and common properties. Formal election also paved the way for unnecessary expenditures like printing wall posters in various colour.

- Drawing symbols and writing names of candidates on walls.
- Erecting board.
- Expenditure on campaigning.
- Everyday expenditure for the supporters of the candidates till the end of the election process. They usually demand 3 meals and adequate quantity of liquor for the men.
- For women supporters the candidate used to give a minimum of Rs. 50 per head and the maximum depends upon the economic condition of the candidate or political party.
- It was estimated that on an average a person decides to contest in the election only if he has the capacity to spend from Rs. 2 lakhs to Rs. 8 lakhs. There was a case wherein a candidate contested the election by selling all his properties and borrowing money from relatives/ moneylenders at high rates of interest and then lost, that his family was ruined. So his children prevented him from contesting the present election.
- If every candidate spends money lavishly for campaigning and purchasing every single vote by cash, the total amount would be much higher than the estimated amount. All the amount so spent was a sheer gone waste as the amount was given to the men for unproductive purposes.

There was a belief that if a voter receives money from the candidate in person, his vote is ensured. But contrary to this earlier belief voters of the present election started collecting money from all the candidates and the decision to whom to vote was finalised according to the amount of money received. Many candidates were cheated by this. The person who was defeated in the election formed group with his own supporters and started working against the existing president and this created a tense situation in the village everyday after the result was announced. SC people were beaten up by the defeated candidate on the charge that they had not voted for him. This has been a common behaviour of the defeated candidates in almost all the villages in this area.

- Auctioning of posts is a sign of healthy development in a village where people feel that peace and integration among the people are essential.
- The money earned through auctioning would be used for the common activity suggested by the majority of the villagers in all the hamlets.
- Auctioning was done only after informing all the voters irrespective of village, caste or socio-economic status. Anybody could participate and help to increase the common fund which would be used for solving common problems.

Table 2.2 : Comparative Statement on the Seats won by AIADMK and DMK, the Major Political Parties

Double the Time	Total Seats	Seats Won by		Inde-pen-dent	%
		AIADMK	DMK		
Panchayat Union ward member	6489	2582	1411	1,171	18.04
District panchayat ward member	654	369	134	7	1.00
Municipal Councillor	3346	945	952	746	22.29
Equal Municipal Chairman	102	34	34	9	8.82
Corporation Councillor	473	169	172	51	10.78
Corporation Mayor	6	3	2	—	—
With considerable differences					
Town Panchayat ward members	9023	2178	1902	3.355	37.18
Chairman	601	198	143	130	21.60

Notes : The above table shows that it is AIADMK which has won majority of the seats followed by DMK.
Independent candidates are more in numbers.

Auctioning can't be Considered a Legal Election

The State Election Commissioner Mr. P.S. Pandiyan said that auctioning of some posts in village Panchayats does not have legal sanctity and anyone can contest regardless of any prior deal. He also said that only after the electoral officer's declaration a particular a contestant becomes winner and in no other way can a winner be declared.

Table 2.3 : Details of Selection of Candidates

Adress	Post	Rs.	Purpose	Remark/No. Participants
Ayyanarkulam Chellampatti Union Madurai	Village Panchayat	5.43 lakhs	Road, Koil	1. Koil Promise 2. Village Committee
Eanthi Village Thirupuvanam Union Sivagangai	Village President	260 lakhs	Union Committee Former President and a competitor	1. Two instalments 2. Won the ex-president 3. No deposit (2 persons)
Eanthi Village Thirupuvanam Union Sivagangai (Lottery)	Panchayat Union Councillor	25,000 fixed		5,000 deposit, 13 persons
Muthuvan Thidal Thirupuvanam	V. Pt. (Women)	4000		2 persons, temple construction
Padamathur Sivagangai	Village Panchayat	1.5 lakhs		
Chenai Union Ananthapuram Pannankuppam Thantipatti	Village Panchayat Councillor Ward Members	5.6 lakhs		SC are not satisfied
Madanthai Pt Paramakudi Union Ramanathapuram	Village Panchayat	31,000 Village fund	Avoid caste clash, local dispute	Families

(Contd.)

Adress	Post	Rs.	Purpose	Remark/No. Participants
Nedunkulam	Village Panchayat	41,000 fund two-equal+ 27,000 caste organisa-tion = 68000	Went day full amount (1001 advance) caste organisation	One member from each tank (300) – same caste – caste organisation fund – $7\frac{1}{3}$ of the total voters participated
Anthiyer Town Pt Erode	Town Panchayat 4th Ward Members	15,000 fixed, 45,000 fisher men (35,000)	No faith is in government programme to development ward facility	
S. Keelapatti T. Kallupatti Union Madurai District	(Reserved) SC (Customs) Village Panchayat	35,000 (caste) 1,10,000 fixed 1,10,000		Chellanji Ammal construction pledged on soil will not misuse, illicit seller be booked – work for village develop-ment
Earaikeni T. Kallupatti, Madurai District	Village Panchayat (women)	12,000 fixed		Ammankoil construction
Muthulunga-puram T. Kallupatti Madurai District	Village Panchayat	1 lakh	Not less politics	
Tirunelveli Kadayanathur Ward	(Ward Councillor) 4		Rotation thevar muthaliar	
	Anaiseri Village Panchayat	Caste 1.00/2.00 lakhs		– young sanmugapandi
Kadaladi Union Kidathikai	Village Panchayat	5 lakhs	No talk in political parties	– shared to 2 hamlets

(Contd.)

Adress	Post	Rs.	Purpose	Remark/No. Participants
Kilan Kadu Tenkasi	Village Panchayat (women)	20,000		– koil renovation
	Ward 13,6	13,500 20,000		
Thiruvannamalai Cheyyar Ankavar Pt	Village Panchayat	5.71 lakhs		– koil renovation – independent in the koil promises
Muthukapatti Senthamayalam Namakkal	Village Panchayat	4 lakhs		– Village development – After 9 nomination – Village committee decided – Mariamman kovil promises – Remaining 8 agreed in writings

Source : Computed.

- The highest rate for village president was Rs.5.75 lakhs in Thiruvannamalai district and the lowest rate was Rs.0.20 lakhs in Thenkasi.
- Almost all the auctioning was done in the premises of a temple or in front a temple.
- Village committee is a powerful tool in operating the village life.
- Caste interaction and integration are considered more important than political affinity.
- Amount earned through auctioning is mostly to be used for either renovation or construction of temple, or any other religious activities.
- Mostly the aim of the winner was to defeat the former president.

- The rate of auctioning for village Panchayat post increased many times in the current election.
- Even the reserved seats for women/SC were also auctioned.
- Even poor fishermen got the post of VP through auction.
- An independent candidate won the auction.
- Money can be given on instalment basis also, if the winner does not have money ready.
- The remaining candidates accepted their defeat in the lottery method gave the same in writing.
- The candidates and the people unanimously accepted the decision taken/judgment rendered by the village committee with regard to lottery/auctioning.
- The aspiring candidates/previous representatives agreeded to the decision taken by the village committee, *i.e.* not to contest in a particular ward where the candidate was unanimously elected.

It is assumed that all the representatives elected through either lottery or auctioning would have good/positive relationship with the Village Committee. In many villages some basic needs like the laying of road, construction of compound wall for the school etc. were done by the Village Committee with the village common fund. The candidates who won the auctioning promised that they won't indulge in any anti-social activities or misuse funds for personal development. As every one accepted the verdict all would support him to ensure good performance. They would keep an eye or his money transactions that he can not engage in any corrupt activities. As people did not believe in governmental programmes and the promises of representatives, they opted for this technique. In a way it seems to be a healthy, new dimension in recent democracy. It is the government and representatives who taught this auctioning method to the villagers.

Moreover, the villagers picked up this practice from their traditional method, wherein they increased the village common fund through auctioning of tamarind trees found on either side of the Panchayat road, tank with fish and other common properties. The money was utilised for common purposes. The villagers felt that the village president's post was also one of the common village properties which could be auctioned for the common fund.

Negative Aspects of Auctioning

- It has created a negative opinion and enmity towards the previous president and his supporters.
- Only the rich can enjoy the political power at the grassroots level. The main purpose of 73rd Amendment, namely equal choice to all citizens failed.
- The fundamental rights/bottom level democracy is damaged.
- The leader elected through auctioning may not be accepted by all the villagers as only a handful of elite people in the village committee has finalised the decision.
- The leader would be very particular in only earning money by any means even affecting the welfare and development programmes.
- People would lose their right to control over the village president.
- Village president will perform according to his wish.
- If the majority ward members are against the village president, no programme could be implemented successfully.
- Anybody who is rich by any means will become the president. Persons with social concern, commitment, involvement and good character may not be respected. The whole value system in the village will collapse.
- It will really become a business rather than a service.

Suggestions

- Representatives should be not based on caste but on economic status.
- Every president elected through these methods should declare his income and current assets before he assumes office.

- They should be asked the reasons behind the purchase of the post at high rate which is not a salaried one. How would they regain the amount? Though it is totally against democracy both the Election Commission and the Government of Tamil Nadu have not taken any stern steps against this immediately.

Auctioning was Opposed by Political Parties

Members from a political party (Marxist Communist) prevented the auctioning of village Panchayat post in Kumanan Thozhu of Maiyladumparai, threatening that the party would field a candidate against the person elected through auctioning. Followed this the villagers, who had assembled in a common place for auctioning, dispersed. Intervention of political parties at appropriate time prevented auctioning. But in many places political parties did not react to it for reasons unknown yet.

Entry of Political Party can Prevent Auctioning of Posts

There was a news column in *The Hindu* about the workshop on Panchayati Raj held in Madurai to hold local bodies elections wherein Dr. G. Palanithurai, Professor, Gandhigram Rural Institute, who heads the Pre-Election Voters Awareness Campaign (PEVAC) in Tamil Nadu stated that the entry of political parties at the grossroots level would prevent the auctioning of posts in the villages. He also quoted the Melavalavu incidents wherein 6 persons including the village president were murdered and condemned the political parties for not taking the issue up in a big way.

He also pointed out that it was because of the political affiliation that the murder of Leelavathi, an active member of CPI(M) and corporation councillor was strongly taken up at several levels. The group of academicians argued that if Panchayats are left to political parties, they would ensure the election at correct time by fielding their respective party candidates at the panchayat level as in the case of elections to the higher structure.

Media Must Help Stop Auctioning of Panchayat Seats

Dr. B. S. Bhargava, a Panchayati Raj expert from Bangalore, at a one day media workshop held in Madurai, expressed his view that, though auctioning was practiced in Madhya Pradesh, Karnataka, Kerala. and Andhra Pradesh, the spreading of the disease, should be stopped, for which the print and electronic media should voice their concern and enable the Government to curb it legally. He also suggested that instead of simply exposing such auctioning the media should also highlight the better performance of Panchayat institutions. Dr. Regina Pappa from Alagappa University said that auctioning of some posts in Tamil Nadu was no doubt disturbing. The trend should be discouraged on a warfooting. Dr. G. Palanithurai, Coordinator, recalled that in olden days the elders practised nominating/ electing a person for Panchayat post by consensus. But the trend adopted (auctioning of posts) in villages today was a threat to the very fundamentals of democracy. Various women and *Dalit* fora in Tamil Nadu strongly condemned auctioning of the village Panchayat posts. A unit of Peoples Union for Civil Liberties (PUCL) urged and demanded the Election Commission to initiate necessary action immediately and make those elections null and void and also to conduct fresh elections in those places in a democratic way as it may lead to heavy corruption in villages and become a big menace in future. The State General Secretary, John Moses in his statement, expressed his surprise that both the Sate Government and the SEC did not take any step against auctioning and he also demanded fresh elections in such villages.

Auctioning was Termed as a Mafia-type Takeover

Prof. G. Palanithurai looked at the auctioning of posts as an attempt by the traditional Panchayat system trying to re-establish itself. He condemned the practice very strongly and also insisted that the State Election Commission should take immediate action. The practice was tantamount to allowing a mafia-type takeover of the local bodies. He also informed that this practice was in vogue only in some places in the previous election, but due to conducive climate, this practice has spread to many places. He also questioned how this type of presidents would get their money back. Dr. G. Palanithurai also criticized that the bureaucracy was in no mood to share power with the people and hence turned a blind eye to the auctions. The Government should send officials to the panchayats where auctioning was held and take necessary action. He also suggested that Panchayats should be told in clear terms that the development works cannot be carried out unless the due process of local body elections is followed. The action is seen as a direct threat to the 73rd Constitutional Amendment. All the political parties do not act against auctioning. All the voters in the village are members of anyone of the political parties which were also responsible for auctioning. The parties themselves had not come forward to condemn the auctioning. There was a series of news items in the local Tamil papers about the proposal for auctioning of Panchayat posts in many parts of South Tamil Nadu. The Mettupatti Village Panchayat in Chellampatti Union and Pappinayakanpatti Village Panchayat in Sedapatti Union along with the Sathur Panchayat were some of the examples where auctioning was done.

In the last week of September Chennai High Court advocate and President of the legal wing of the Tamil Nadu Congress Party A.P. Suriyaprakasam filed a case in the High Court demanding the arrest of the people responsible for auctioning. Referring to the report of auctioning of posts, the State CPI(M) Secretary Mr.N. Sankaraiah urged the State Election Commission to ensure the conduct of local bodies poll in a democratic manner and also said persons were being prevented from contesting after the auctioning. He also commented that such auctioning went against the basic democratic principle of power to the people.

Mr. E.V.K.S. Elangovan, the Tamil Nadu Congress President, said that auctioning should be checked throughout India. There was a tense situation: if some one files nomination against the one elected through auctioning, what would happen, and what would be the role of political parties, and if anything goes wrong with the competitors leading to violence, what would be the role of the police and the Election Commission and the

State Government. But as expected there was some opposition to the elected ones and many withdrew their nomination on the last day for withdrawal. In the village where lottery system was adopted for selecting a candidate for the post of village Panchayat some persons contested against the elected candidate.

Law and Auctioning

1. According to Section 120 of the Tamil Nadu Panchayat Act the ceiling on expenses for the village president in local body polls was put at Rs.10000 only.
2. According to IPC 171 C(1) auctioning a post is a crime.
3. According to the Constitution, all the people must be involved in electing a leader. But just contrary to the law,
   - Posts have been auctioned even for up to 5.7 lakhs.
   - *Dalits*, women and other minority people did not participate in the process of auctioning and there was no compulsory attendance of the majority of the voters.
   - In some places one-third of the total voters did not attend the gathering to protest against auctioning.
   - When all the voters did not attend the gathering it meant that there was an opposition to the process.
   - It is not necessary that all the people including voters in the various hamlets accept or respect the elected candidate.
   - The decision for auctioning of post was taken by a handful of elderly people in the village belonging to the older generation. They imposed their ideas on the younger generation who might have a different vision. The young generation and women were forced to accept the decision of elderly men.

The poor innocent people simply kept mum though they had some difference of opinion regarding the decision, because anybody opposed the decision it might create tension in the village.

- Those who are really committed, honest, broad-minded, selfless, educated but poor miss the chance of contesting for or becoming president.
- There was confusion as to whether the amount given to the village committee for auction be included in the election expenditure or not.
- Mostly caste committee (Uravin Murai) decided and fixed the amount. It means that in the local poll caste organisation played a crucial role, particularly in auctioning.
- The money is used mostly neither for welfare nor for productive purposes but for unproductive purpose. But villagers are satisfied and content because something is better than nothing.

Collector Warned of Action Against Auctioning

Mr. K. Dhaneedra Reddy, Collector of Perambalur district, talking to the press, said that action would be taken against any one who tried to kill the spirit of democracy by auctioning. Authorities would keep a vigil on other Panchayats where such attempts were reported.

The Hindu Condemned the Auctioning

In the last week of September there was a column in *The Hindu*, wherein the columnist vigorously condemned the act of auctioning of posts and asked the SEC to check such moves and deal with those behind the auctions under provisions of law and the political parties to challenge it in earnest.

Court Notice to State Government to Answer

In response to the plea filed by the Chennai High Court advocate, the First Bench sent a notice to the Government of Tamil Nadu. The hearing was put off to the fourth of October.

Lottery Method

The ancient system of lottery (Kudavolai, *i.e.* pot system) has come back to Vagurani Village Panchayat in Usilampatti Taluk. When there several contestants of the same qualities (one is equivalent to the other) people in the ancient period preferred the pot system to elect their representatives. But now, in Vagurani Village, people adopted this method not because all the contestants were equally qualified, but to get money for common fund and restrict the number of candidates contesting the election.

The villagers were badly in need of money for the construction of additional building for the school recently upgraded to high school from middle school. So, the village committee decided to collect Rs. 2 lakhs from the selected candidate. If several persons aspired to contest, the candidates might be elected by following the lottery method. Accordingly the village committee informed all the people in all the hamlets under the village Panchayat that each espirant was to deposit Rs. 1 lakh and that the one who was elected through lottery must pay another Rs. 1 lakh. One fine morning the people assembled in the premises of the village temple of Kamatchiamman. There were 13 competitors. The villagers found no option but to adopt the lottery method.

So the names of the competitors were written on a small pieces of paper and they were rolled and put into a pot kept at the centre of the crowd. It was informed clearly that a child would be asked to pick up any one of the pieces of rolled paper. The person whose name was picked would be declared elected and the remaining competitors could get their deposit money back on the spot. Everyone accepted the condition. The child was ready. All the competitors and family members, relatives, friends and supporters were eagerly watching the event. The name of the candidate whose name was picked was Nallathambi *alias* Parthipan. He was declared elected. The others got their deposit money back. Everyone greeted him including the competitors. The event was over just a month before the election date.

The main reasons for adopting the lottery method were:

- To get village common fund for school building.
- People have no faith in the fund to be allotted by the Government for rural development.

This is the only village in Tamil Nadu where election for Panchayat president post was done under the kudavolai method.

Rotation Method for Electing the President

Reservation for women and SC in the local bodies is a new concept. Under this reservation, new entrants have occupied the various positions. The first period of five years is a new experience to them. But it is incomplete as the Panchayati Raj governance itself is new and has been introduced for the first time under the 73rd Constitutional Amendment. The purpose of reservation is to give opportunity to the so called marginalised sectors, women and *Dalits*, to participate in the activities of local bodies as well as administration of the local bodies directly.

Being a ward member or president in a village Panchayat, the women and *Dalit* representatives are legally entitled to sit and share their opinions and take part in decision-making. Only by this opportunity their social justice in ensured. But, in several villages, the traditional committee has its own concept of reservation for various posts. In a multi-caste village, the committee listed the names unanimously as their representatives without contest to avoid conflict among the various castes.

1. *Unanimous Selection in a Multi-Religious Village – Case Studies*

Rajakambeeram is a village near Manamadurai, where people of the three major religions, *i.e.*, Hindus, Christians and Muslims live almost in equal number. In order to avoid religious clash over power, the villagers had decided to allot the positions of local bodies to all three religions on rotation basis.

Accordingly, in the previous election the village president post was allotted to a Muslim and the post of vice-president was given to a Christian. This time, a Hindu was given village president's post, the vice-president's post was given to a Christian and the post of Union Councillor was given to a Muslim. After allotting the three posts to three religions, according to the village committee's direction each religious group constituted a committee with 10 members (six elders and four youths). The three committees jointly decided the individuals from the different religions for ward members.

2. *Unopposed from Caste Ridden Village*

Of all the unopposed selection of the president, the most unexpected and surprising are was the selection of candidate from the Yadava community in Karuvanoor Village of Madurai West Union. It was the village where the Joint Secretary of DPI Sri. Modakatthanpandi was murdered by caste Hindus followed by continuous caste clashes and damaging of properties of each other and burning buses and huts of poor people.

Tension was prevailing as the day for local election was nearing. Foreseeing the caste clashes among the various caste groups, the village elders (village committee) convened a meeting to decide on a candidate for village president. Accordingly one Mr. Manivannan, a caste Hindu, was elected village president. Vice-President's post was given to SC community and nine ward members were also selected unanimously. It is a good sign for putting an end to the caste conflict in the village where SC, Yadava, Mukkulathore and Muslims live together in tension.

3. *Villagers Convinced the Only Opponent*

A women was elected president in Nattum Union. Lingawadi is the name of the village Panchayat where Mrs. Palaniammal was elected unopposed by the intervention of the village committee which convinced the only other person who filed nomination. Though there are three hamlets under this Panchayat having 4312 voters, yet none opposed it. Vice president and ward members were also unanimously elected by the village committee. The voters given full freedom to choose their union councillor and district Panchayat member. In Dindigul district according to the official report 248 candidates were elected unopposed, of whom five were for village presidents, 240 for members of village Panchayat and 2 for members of town Panchayats and 1 for union council.

4. *Ward Members and Chairman were Elected Unanimously*

A distinction was observed in town Panchayat which is a model to be followed. People of several castes and religions live together in this area. For the 15 wards in the town Panchayat more than 50 candidates filed nominations from different castes and religious groups. Each caste group was very particular in capturing the chairman's post, not letting in any political parties. For this the different caste groups collectively formed an alliance. The same alliance was also used for selecting the ward members. Accordingly, ward members were elected giving due representation to all the caste groups. The main reason they gave for rejecting the political parties was to create communal harmony and friendly relationship among various caste groups.

5. *Town Panchayat Chairman was Elected Unopposed*

In Abiramam town Panchayat, the chairman was elected without competition as the only competitor (his own sister) was made to withdraw her nomination and 8 ward members were also elected unopposed. In Muthukulathoor also 6 ward members were elected unopposed.

6. *A President was Elected Thrice Successively*

The same president has been elected thrice successively in a multi-caste village. Kandilan is a Panchayat in Kaddaladi Union of Ramnad district where Thevars, Devendrakula Vellalars and Yadavas live together. Though the villages around this panchayat are noted for caste clashes and the prevalence of tension frequently created by the two caste groups, Thevars and

Devendrakula Vellalars (SC), they elected a member from the Thevar community Mr. Malaikannan, a B.A. Graduate, as village president. He has been elected successively three times just because of his personal character and selflessness and accessibility to the villagers of all hamlets.

Better Performance Paved the way for Second time President

A gram seva awardee, Ms. Lakshmi Pongaroo Adikalar has been unanimously elected a second time as village president of Melmaruvathur Village Panchayat. She was elected president unopposed this time. The voters said that she has been elected by the people because of her unbiased selection of beneficiaries and for implementing well the Government programmes (both state and central), for which she was awarded 'Gram Rathna Award'. She was also appreciated by the district administration for her achievement in reaching the target fixed for savings in a year.

New System of Elections and the Kind of Leadership it has Developed

- The leader elected through auctioning will always be keen on minting money —double and triple the amount he had spent on the purchase of the post through auctioning.
- He will act according to his wish. The villagers cannot have control over his behaviour.
- Identification of beneficiaries in any programme would be based on his choice. He will give priority only to his relatives and supporters.
- The leader will perceive the role of village president as a duty of recovering the money spent with high interest.
- All his intention and activities will only be towards getting more benefit and profit in all the activities.
- The perception of Government officials towards this type of leader would be negative. There will be a suspicion on the part of bureaucrats about the leader that he would be profit oriented rather than programme oriented or problem oriented in relation to the implementation of any Government programme.

- The leader will not respect even the local sentiments of the people and village traditional committee.
- The powerful body in the 73rd Amendment, *i.e.* Gram Sabha would lose its importance. Neither would people attend the Gram Sabha nor would the leader respond properly. Even ward members would not have any say in Gram Sabha and in executing any activities.
- There will not be good relationship between people and the president and between ward members and the president.
- Auctioning of posts is nothing but letting the house on lease for five years where in the house owner cannot control the tenants till the tenure is over. Similarly villagers will also be helpless.
- The pattern of leadership has been changing. People will not have any respect for the village president. The dignity of the post will be damaged.
- It will be a negative role model for the villagers.
- The next generation will not respect, the values and the sentiments of people with social concern and selfless commitment. Instead, villagers feel that any body who is capable of purchasing the president's post could become president. This trend is not good for any social development.
- Only rich people can participate in either auctioning or lottery system.
- The fundamental rights of a citizen, namely any individual can contest the election, is denied by the elite group.
- Persons belonging to a particular village and living outside, probably in the cities, may become president of the village, just because he has vote in the village and has enough money to win the lottery or auction.
- Such persons might not have understood the real problems faced by the local people as they have not gone street by street and door to door for canvassing.
- The president will not consider the local people either as his villagers or relatives or voters, because the leader was elected through auctioning or lottery or rotation, as

decided upon by a handful of members of traditional village committee.

- The leader will not have dream or vision towards the development of the village. Instead he would have only an urge to develop himself and his economic status.

Implications of Auctioning

- Aspiring candidates could not contest the election.
- People are not able to use their right to select their own candidate.
- Right and suitable candidatures have not come forward.
- The decisions are taken at the higher level and not at the grassroots level. Hence people lose interest in the Panchayat system.
- Problems and felt needs of the people are not addressed. But priority is given to getting money from the selected candidate as the seats are auctioned.
- Very openly the power of money is acknowledged which is against the law and democracy.
- Participation of the people after the election also is not up to the mark. It is learnt that the villagers are not able to question the activities of the president who assumed office through auction.

Implications of SHG Putting up Candidates

- NGOs make use of this opportunity to involve directly or indirectly in local politics.
- Trained women leaders get opportunity in the election process and taste both sides sweetness and bitterness.
- The election created an opportunity to test the solidarity of SHGs. Even within SHGs there were rivalries.
- Cutting across caste, religion and close relationships the SHGs. Stood united and showed their unity in selecting their own candidates.
- The local leaders of political parties met the SHG members and sought their support for their party candidates.

- In several villages the political parties threatened the candidates of SHGs.
- When the SHG women opposed the men candidates they faced enmity from the community on several social issues like community toilet, alcoholism, public distribution system, health and sanitation, schools and *balwadies* during the campaign.

VII. ROLE OF PRINT MEDIA

The fourth pillar of democracy, the media, plays a key role in upholding the principles of democracy in any country. The status of democracy can be assessed by the degree of freedom a state has given to the press. Through public opinion press people can do wonders in various fields, particularly in politics and notably in the election. In recently held local bodies election also the media contributed a lot in different aspects.

- Regional coverage in all the dailies helped people to understand the micro level problems and perspectives and to assess the performance of the parties contesting the election.
- Inter-state comparison on policies of the State as well as the Centre focused by the press made people understand the manifesto of the parties clearly.
- The press also acted as a forum to all political parties to publish their ideology and manifesto and also to elicit opinion from opinion makers.

Dinamalar sought opinion on the current issues everyday over telephone.

- Articles on election awareness were published periodically.
- Periodical publication of SEC's report and information.
- Gave coverage to the voters' opinion letters to the editor.
- Analysis of past performance of the different political parties was presented for comparison.

- Ideological deviation of the political parties emerging out of alliances.
- Focused on local issues like auctioning of posts.
- Exposing leaders chosen by lottery method and auctioning through photographs. Subsequently, it also criticised academicians, parties and social workers.

Role of Media in Generating Awareness

Even before the declaration of election dates for the local bodies election, the print media started publishing news items indicating the expiry dates of the local bodies' tenure. It also reminded the Government to conduct elections. News items related to dismissal of village presidents was appearing very frequently towards the end of the tenure.

- Tamil dailies had been expressing concern over the conduct of election as the State Government was keeping mum in this regard. There was a sequence of problems from Ms. Jeyalalitha assuming power to the arrest of former Chief Minister M. Karunanidhi and central ministers.
- There were news items on the delay in sanctioning of money to village Panchayats for the execution of works proposed in the Gram Sabha. Bureaucrats unduly delayed the passing of bills which caused many problems for the smooth functioning of local bodies. The print media highlighted these.
- By the end of July the Tamil daily *'Dinamani'* published a news column wherein it urged the State Government to conduct local bodies election. It also criticized the Government stating that the Chief Minister of Tamil Nadu J. Jeyalalitha was not interested in conducting elections for local bodies, that she had taken all possible steps, so as to prevent the conduct of elections, but, immediately after her assumption of power, she pretended as if she was very particular about conducting local bodies elections.

- The daily also criticized that cooperative organisations in Tamil Nadu were functioning without popular representation and that, similarly, J. Jeyalalitha wanted the local bodies to function elected representatives and thereby being them under the Government's administration. It created awareness among the people about the attitude of the Chief Minister towards holding elections.

Removal of District Collector's Power to Dismiss Village President

There was a news column in *'The Hindu'* demanding the repeal of Section 205 of the Tamil Nadu Panchayat Act, dealing with the removal of Panchayat presidents by District Collectors. The main reason for the demand was that these provisions were being misused by bureaucrats to keep the presidents under their control and on most occasions victimize the elected representatives.

Separate List IV for Local Bodies to be Incorporated

It also urged that the Government should devolve the powers under XI Schedule of the Constitution to the three-tiers of the Panchayat and recommended that a separate list IV for local government should be incorporated in the Constitution.

Convert State Officials as Public Servant

The Hindu published a news item even before the election dates were announced that all the departments to be engaged in overseeing the activities must be decentralised and the state officials should be made to work as public servants of the Panchayat Government.

The present reserved constituency for women should be extended to the next election also. It was really a disappointment for the men in the village, who had an intention to become presidents and worked towards it that they could not contest the election since the constituencies were again allotted for women. Men were not in a position to digest a local woman becoming president, very particularly a woman belonging to SC becoming president. Under such sensational environment news was published in the dailies demanding extension of reservation for women.

The newspaper had explained the justification for the demand: in many village Panchayats only after the 73rd Amendment had woman gained an opportunity for entering public life and trying to manage the Panchayat administration. The 5 year experience of the first term had helped them to understand the administration and functions of Panchayat bodies. Just when the representatives were gaining confidence in themselves the term was over. All they had gained would go waste and the newly elected representatives will have to undergo the same process for five years. This will continue for ever and no woman can be trained as president in the near future. This news has very effectively created an impact on the minds of women SHGs to contest in the election. The office bearers of the self-help groups started preparing their mind towards contesting the election if the reservation was extended.

More Funds Sought

A news in an English paper stated that the allocation of eight per cent of the State's revenue tax to local government bodies was not adequate. The Government should devolve 50 per cent of its total revenue to local bodies.

Tax Exemption for Panchayats

It was before the filing of nomination that some news items appeared regarding reforming the functions and structures of the three-tier system. The media urged that the Government should come forward to give exemption from payment of electricity bills for better Panchayat administration. This is an important suggestion because a discussion with a village president in one of the training programmes revealed that the electricity charges for village panchayats was high and it was a heavy burden for many panchayats particularly panchayats with poor revenue resources. It was also observed that, in many panchayats, the payment of electricity bills was made from other heads of expenditure. This created a good deal of awareness among the rural voters on the difficulties faced by the president in running the village Panchayat. The presidents and aspiring candidates also perceived the scarcity of funds to meet the basic expenditure of the village.

DRDA to be Merged with District Panchayat Council

In the same month a Tamil daily published a press report released by the chief of the Village Presidents' Association of Tamil Nadu which recommended that the DRDA should be merged with the District Panchayat Council and the district and taluk administration must function as subordinate agencies to the District Panchayat and any information on the implementation of works under DRDA schemes must be made public through district or union panchayats.

For the distribution of patta the district administration should receive the list of persons from the village Panchayat presidents. Such suggestion-packed news items have not been in the past 15 years before the election. Print media, particularly the Tamil dailies, have played a crucial role in publishing the power and responsibilities of presidents as and when situations arose. On reading news items of this kind both the presidents and villagers gain knowledge about the role of village Panchayats.

Periodical Publication of News on Election

Almost all the dailies in Tamil Nadu have been publishing news about the development taking place in the process of conducting election. Even before the declaration of local poll elections the media published a news item that the Government of Tamil Nadu had passed order to nominate an election officer to conduct the election.

With regard to enrolment of voters for the current election, the print media clearly informed the schedule for enrolling the names of eligible voters in the list. It also published the basic eligibility conditions for a citizen to enroll his/her name.

Stimulated the Government to Conduct Election

At the end of July the Tamil daily *Dinamani* published a news item criticising the State Government for delaying the conduct of local polls without any genuine reason.

- It clearly mentioned that it was the State Government which deliberately delayed the steps to be taken to conduct election by issuing an order not to take any steps towards conducting election.
- This news items evoked good response from the people. People everywhere started talking about the local election. The press gave further statistical information in a simple form for the rural people which were hitherto not made available.
- It motivated people to elect representatives in an unbiased way by publishing slogans everyday.
- It offered platform for leading opinion makers and field level workers to air their views on the importance of local self-government through democratic means.
- It clearly projected the structure, function and power of local self-government, which helped people to understand their need for participating in the governance.
- It pointed out the responsibility of the people in exercising their voting right.
- Steps to increase the voter turn out in the election were also published.
- Continuous pre-election articles highlighting the importance of local self-governance led the people to know more about it.
- People's views on electoral reforms were mobilised for the consideration of the State Election Commission.
- A good coverage of the candidates' bio-data helped the common people understand about the candidates and people could make comparison for their best choice.
- The exposure by the press on the process of alignment of different parties for electoral gains made the parties more vigilant regarding public opinion.

- A separate supplement was issued by the *'Dinamalar'* which specially covered the election issues and drew the attention of the people.
- It sensitized the people to the issue of the auctioning and lottery method for the election of their representatives through proper election process.
- From the date of declaration of dates for election till the election was over newspaper had been publishing news items periodically on the steps taken by the government to conduct free and fair elections. This created confidence, overcoming the fear and tension prevailing in the minds of voters in all the areas.
- It also published clear statistics on total voters in a district.
- The number of voters at district, block, Panchayat and ward level was made known to the voters.
- The number of booths established in at each level was given in the news.

Suggestions to Media

- It published only matters which are rather sensitive. Sometimes the incidents were magnified and the news was released just to draw the attention of the masses.
- It gave more importance to the violent and anti-social activities, and also the violation of rules and regulations of the Election Commission by the candidates.
- It only highlighted the events but it hardly gave reasons and suggestions. For example, it described very elaborately how the candidates spent money very lavishly to attract the voters.

Media Task Force that Visited Tamil Nadu

Reporters from two leading Delhi based dailies, namely *Pioneer* and *Navbharat Times* arrived in Madurai on 9 October, 2001 for covering news on PEVAC. Generally, a special reporter or senior reporter would be very much involved in collecting only sensitive information on burning issues. Pre-Election Voters

Awareness Campaign (PEVAC) carried out by PRIA, New Delhi for local bodies election held in the second term in Tamil Nadu in October 2001 received such attention from these two leading dailies.

It seemed that the press people felt that at was uncommon for a private agency to be involved in generating political awareness among the general public for the creation of good governance at the bottom level (in the rural local government).

The PEVAC emphasised the followings:

- emphasizing increasing the voting percentage.
- Generating awareness on 73rd Amendment among the public.
- Motivating the women and *Dalits* to contest the election.
- Encouraging the voters to support and elect women/*Dalit* representatives to the rural local bodies.
- Creating a suitable environment for free and fair elections by sensitizing the voters.
- Reducing the number of proxy candidate from women and SC/ST.

The State Election Commission had openly made a plea that the NGOs can involve themselves in generating awareness among the voters about the role of voters in strengthening the rural local bodies. Accordingly PRIA (Society for Participatory Research in Asia) which had experience of the same type of activities in other states, *i.e.* Madhya Pradesh, Uttar Pradesh, Himachal Pradesh, Haryana, Bihar and Kerala in the previous election extended its activities to Tamil Nadu for generating awareness among the voters in general, and women and *Dalits* in particular. Accordingly, PRIA carried out the PEVAC activities in the entire state —29 districts—with GRI as a coordinating agency.

Press People and PEVAC

On 9th October 2001, two senior reporters, one from *Navbharat Times*, and the other from *Pioneer*, arrived at Gandhigram. They were briefed about the activities carried out by PRIA in Tamil Nadu. Mr. Shagun, in-charge of the Hyderabad Office of PRIA explained the programmes of the media people in Tamil Nadu and their purposes. Dr. G. Palanithurai Coordinator Rajiv Gandhi Chair for Panchayati Raj Studies had given proper guidelines to Dr. C. Kubendran, Coordinator, PRIA to make all the arrangements for field visits. Dr. G. Palanithurai, also described, the structure of the institutions/NGOs involved in the activities and the method of selection of 4 NGO networks and district level coordinating NGOs under this programme. He further explained the role of Gandhigram Rural Institute and the Rajiv Gandhi Chair for Panchayati Raj Studies, Department of Political Science and Development Administration in Gandhigram Rural Institute in coordinating, monitoring, guiding the NGOs in the successful implementation of all the activities under PEVAC.

Mr. Shagun was given details of the names of NGO networks and NGOs involved and their previous experience in generating awareness in general and political awareness in particular and their area of operation with approximate people proposed to be covered and the target group aimed at. The media held a formal discussion with Dr. G. Palanithurai, Mr. Shagun and Dr. Kubendran and finalised the issues to be covered.

Media Visit

Accordingly the media team first visited Pappapatti village where *Dalit* people were prevented from filing nomination for the village president's position. The team first had an informal discussion with SC people whose residences were located a little away from the main settlement of the so called upper and dominant caste people, the Piramalai Kallars. It was so decided because the settlement of the Kallar community was on the way to the SC colony. It was assumed that the Kallar community people might also accompany the team to the SC colony as soon as the discussion was over. Then the SC people might not be in a position to express their opinion/feelings very openly in the presence of Kallar community people.

It was understood from the discussion with the SC people that though the SC people feel that it is really a God's gift—for obtaining power without taking any effort. But considering the local situation where the Kallar community is wehemently opposing the reservation, the SCs could not take any step against their wish. They admitted that none from the Kallar community came and prevented directly or made any warning to anybody from the SC community. People belong to SC themselves decided not to think of filing nomination against the wish of the Kallar community. SC people also realised that the Kallar community trusted that the SC people would not file nomination when Kallars are boycotting the election successively for the second term. Moreover, the SC people were not in need of power at this stage. But what is needed is food, cloth, shelter and employment for guaranteed survival.

They also refused to contest because they were not trained or prepared mentally and financially. They also ciriticised the Government that it had all of a sudden announced Pappapatti as a constituency for SC and just because there was no nomination from here the Government officials and NGOs, media people have started coming and enquiring about it but they were not really interested in the welfare of SC people in this area. They stated that power is not a priority compared to basic needs. The existing reality in that area is:

- SC people do not have land of their own.
- No alternative employment to agricultural bodies.
- Most of the people have migrated to different parts of Tamil Nadu and India in search of livelihood.
- There is no security for education and quality of life locally.
- The majority of the families do not have houses of their own.
- There is no irrigation facilities and the fertility of the soil is so poor that no profit is received from rainfed agriculture and the quality and quality of yields are deteriorating every year.

Such being the case how can we think of ruling the Panchayat and the people of the Piramalai Kallar community on whom we depend totally for every activity in the village from morning to evening, the SCs asked. The media team interviewed persons belonging to SC community, of both the sexes and of different age groups and engaged in different occupations with different educational levels. Though the older generation admitted that the agitation/opposition of the Kallar community against reservation is right from their point of view as they were numerically dominant and Pappapatti was one of the important, religious centres for the Kallars community, the younger generation, due to their education, exposure and contact with some political parties, expressed their inability to enjoy the power which is knocking at their door through reservation.

Some active persons from the Kallar community come casually to the spot and enquired about the reaction of the SC people about contesting the election. It was really embarrassing for the team as well as the coordinators. But they were satisfied to learn that SC people had also reflected the feelings of the Kallar community regarding reservation. The second part of the discussion in the same village was held exclusively with the Pirmalai Kallar community in their place. Some selected members of the traditional village committee, youths and some women were interviewed on the issue of boycotting the election continuously.

The response of all the sections was almost similar that they were not against the *Dalit* people in their village who are not interested in contesting the election but they were angry with the Government which has allotted Keeripatti and Pappapatti villages to SC candidates without any logic and justification as the number of Kallar voters are more than the SC voters. They also felt that the Government was deliberately insulting these people by reserving the 'Kallar fort' of Pappapatti and Keeripatti for SC community who are the minority, landless, dependent and serving community. They also stated that they may go to any extent to prevent the election. Having finished the interview with the two sections in Pappapatti, the team moved on to Sangarapatti, one of the hamlets of Pappapatti Panchayat, where the SC community are numerically equal to the Kallars and where one person tried and failed to file nomination.

It was the topic of the day which created a lot of tension among the villagers. As the person concerned, Mr. Narasimman, was not available in the village, the team had an interaction with some key persons from the SC community of the village. Their response was somewhat encouraging and they felt that they were ready to file nomination but because of the unpreparedness of the people and lack of cooperation even among the sub-castes of the *Dalit* community, they dropped the idea of contesting the election.

But Mr. Narasimman from their village tried to file nomination at the last minute of the last day. But he failed in his attempt. They also informed that Mr. Narasimman was threatened by the Kallar community very frequently. He also confined himself to his house fearing that the Kallar community may murder him at any time if he moves outside the house or village.

Next, the media team went to Chellampatti Panchayat Union, to cross-check the information given by the Pappapatti people that they do not have any difficulty in the absence of village president and the clerk and special officer take care of all the needs of the villages. The clerk said that the work and activities allotted to these two villages, *i.e.* Pappapatti and Keeripatti, were carried out properly under the instruction of the higher officials. When the interview was on, persons from different villages, who came to the union office, said that election should not be conducted till it was declared a general seat. Otherwise, every member of the Kallar community will become Osama-bin-Laden of Afghanistan.

From Chellampatti the team shifted to Ayyanarkulam village where the village president was selected by auctioneering. As soon as the team reached the village a crowd surrounded them and refused to accept that auctioning took place. Everyone concealed the event very cleverly. Some admitted the auctioning and tried to convince the team that the system was banned, and formal election was to be held openly with heavy competition. This was said by the group of the selected president's rivals. The supporters of the ex-president approached the team and revealed the fact with authentic evidences. Dr. C. Kubendran displayed the press clippings which had appeared in the local dailies on auctioning which took place in the same village, which motivated the team to go further. The detailed information on auctioning like the genesis of the auctioning method, persons responsible, rules and regulations framed, reaction of the people from other hamlets and the response of the government were collected.

They then unanimously justified that auctioning was preferred for some specific reasons such as

- For fulfilling the basic facilities needed for the village which is otherwise not possible. They criticized the local MLA and the Union Chairman who are from the same village for not doing anything for the improvement of the village.
- For preventing unnecessary tension and clash between two groups which were witnessed in the previous Panchayat election.
- For increasing the village common fund. The villages have the habit of creating and increasing the 'village common welfare fund' through auctioning of village common properties like tamarind trees growing on either side of the link road or main road, *poramboke* land, pools, tanks, Panchayat common buildings, shopping complexes situated within the boundary of village Panchayat etc.

When the Government and the elected representatives fail to meet the demands/needs of the people village committee fulfils them with their own money. For the villagers, the village president's position is also one of the common properties which also can be auctioned for increasing the common fund. So they did so. It was observed that village Panchayat is the third government but it is the village committee of the traditional Panchayat which decides the system of selection of president. It increased the common fund through auctioning and carried out all the activities needed for the villagers with participation of the beneficiaries. They justified that when a body, no matter whether it is elected or selected, is able to select a leader, able to mobilize funds and plan with the people and execute it with the people's participation without depending on any external support it is really self-government.

But it was observed from the interview with the people that they feared the Government since there was an announcement made by Sri P.S. Pandian, Tamil Nadu Election Commissioner or that selection through auctioning is not legally acceptable. Vagurani of Usilampatti Union in Madurai district was the next destination for the media team to cover the incidence of lottery system adopted for the selection of village Panchayat president. Vagurani village was situated some 8 km from Usilampatti towards the south on the way to Sedapatti.

The reasons given by the village committee for preferring lottery method were quite reasonable:

- The villagers wanted to purchase a land for the construction of additional building for the high school. The Government was ready to construct an additional building if the villagers contributed land. There were eight hamlets including Vagurani, namely Muthiampatti, Navarpatti, Mettupatti, Aithupatti, Santhaipettai, Vagurani and SC colony.
- The people, particularly the members of traditional village committee from Vagurani village, decided to collect money from the candidates interested in contesting for the post of village Panchayat president. The idea was informed to all the hamlets through local medium of communication a week before the date of filing nomination.

The message was that the committee intended to collect Rs. 2 lakh as deposit from the aspiring candidates with the condition that the selected candidate should pay another Rs. 1 lakh for which it invited the representatives of village committee from all the hamlets on 25th September to express their opinion. Accordingly, representatives of all the hamlets assembled and endorsed the proposal as there was no high school in many hamlets and no school at all in two hamlets Navarpatti,

Santhaipettai and SC colony. They also fixed a date for the aspiring candidates to deposit the money. There were 12 candidates ready to give Rs. 2 lakh for the same post. So the village committee decided to elect a candidate through lottery method. The 12 aspirants deposited the amount of Rs.1 lakh. Their names were written on separate pieces of paper which were rolled and put into a pot and mixed properly in the midst of villagers from all the hamlets who assembled in front of the village God in the temple premises. The village temple was selected deliberately so that the selection of president will not be questioned by anybody as it was done in the presence of God. It is conceived that the president's selection was done by God indirectly.

It was a thrilling experience, not only for the depositors but the villagers also. With the consent of all the people a child was asked to pick up any one of the paper pieces from the pot. It was P. Nallathambi *alias* Parthipan whose name was picked up and he was declared elected president of Vagurani Village Panchayat. All the participants including voters and aspiring candidates greeted him. All eleven remaining aspirants were given their deposit money back, Mr. Nallathambi paid the remaining Rs. one lakh. It was well before the formal election that the president for Vagurani was elected. But one Mr. Palani from one of the hamlets, Kanavaipatti, in the midst of opposition from different hamlets, filed nomination against the selected president which was not only against Mr. Nallathambi but against the village committee and the village norms and regulations which paved the way for the conduct of formal election. The team after collecting the information met both the elected village president and the rival candidate in person and had interview with them individually.

The rival said that he was not satisfied with the system of selection and he had confidence that he can win the election as his party is very strong in his village and he has served 30 years for village welfare. Mr. Nallathambi was dissatisfied with the strength of village committee which could not prevent the rival from filing nomination. He also demanded his money back as he had to spend money for election campaign and other activities.

The interview was over by 9.30 p.m. on the day. Kulithalai of Trichy district was visited by the media team on the second day, where it had a discussion with the staff of the NGO Gramium, on the role of NGOs in promoting women SHGs and *Dalits* in the local bodies election.

Mr. Narayanan, Head of the NGO gave some printed materials on how SHGs were formed and promoted and the different types of small trades women members engaged in and the extent of socio-economic development through awareness programme and skill development training and financial assistance from the bank where they had been operating accounts for more than one year. The team finalised two villages to be visited. Accordingly, it went to a village situated some 20 km away from Trichy and organised the women SHG members to file nominations for the reserved seats for various posts in local bodies election. In another village it was observed that women filed nominations in the general constituencies. In both the villages, women members expressed the hope that they would definitely win the election at various levels with the constant support of NGOs working there. It was also observed that the majority of the women were very particular in contesting for Panchayat president post rather than for other posts. All the members from SHGs assured that they will extend their support to the common candidates till the results are declared.

NGOs Network and the Media

In addition to the conventional method of disseminating information towards generating awareness among the general voters about the salient features of 73rd Amendment and reservation for women and *Dalits* and importance of three-tier system in the overall development of the rural area, the NGOs have made use of the print media and electronic media.

Electronic Media: Television

An exclusive interview with Dr. G. Palanithurai, Head of the Department of Political Science and Development Administration and Coordinator, Rajiv Gandhi Chair for Panchayati Raj Studies on Panchayati Raj was telecast.

This interview was telecast about for 40 minutes, in the morning in the Vanakkam Tamilzhagam programme of SUN TV. Vanakkam Tamilzhagam has been one of the informative programmes of SUN TV, which is one of the well reached satellite TV networks in Tamil Nadu.

In his interview Dr. Palanithurai covered:

- The political climate prevailing when 73rd Amendment was made.
- Achievements of Central and State Governments in providing basic facilities to the rural people.

Publication in the Print Media — Newspaper

News items of NGO activities relating to PEVAC were being published as and when the NGOs conducted their programmes like:

- Public meeting with different target groups such as women SHGs, aspiring candidates, *Dalit* people and general voters.
- Cycle rally, van rally and human procession on generating awareness.

Letter to the Editor

The network called ROAD, in a letter to the Editor of the *New Indian Express* stressed the need for three-tier system for the upliftment of rural poor in Tamil Nadu. The letter opposed the views of some political parties in Tamil Nadu which were demanding the Central Government to retain only two-tiers in place of three-tiers. The letter was published during the election process.

News on the Qualification of a Good President

Bit notices printed and distributed by the NGOs under TCPR on the qualifications of a good president were published in the local Tamil daily *'Dinamalar'* one of the leading dailies with a wide circulation in Tamil Nadu.

- Strengths and weakness of the existing Government system, power centralisation, top to bottom planning.
- Relevance of New Panchayati Raj in the contemporary social and political conditions.
- The important components of 73rd Amendment towards equal distribution of wealth and resources, empowering women and *Dalits* through compulsory reservation.
- Planning with people at micro level.
- Implementing the programme with people's participation.
- Combining human life with environment.
- Towards a holistic development of the people.

He also emphasised the role of voters in strengthening village Panchayat principle of democracy at the grassroot level. This interview evoked a good response from all the sections of the people. Academicians, politicians, NGOs, scholars, bureaucrats, students and general voters received a lot of inputs and information on Panchayati Raj System. It was well received by all the sections of the society as there were not many publications on the current issues and there is no institute or academic expert in Tamil Nadu to promote New Panchayati Raj System except Dr. G. Palanithurai and Gandhigram Rural University in Tamil Nadu.

Regional News Telecast on PEVAC Campaign

Almost all the satellite-based Tamil channels covered and telecast the PEVAC activities carried out by the NGOs, particularly the public meetings with various target groups like SHGs, aspiring candidates, and *Dalit* candidates. The news on public meetings organised by some district level NGOs under

TCPR were telecast in the regional news items wherein the speeches of resource persons like Dr. G. Palanithurai, Dr. V. Ragupathy and Dr. C. Kubendran were covered. Of all the information provided the speeches on

- The role of women SHGs in improving the standard of life of rural poor, particularly women, through exercising their duties by obtaining some position at the panchayat bodies.
- Encouraging *Dalit* people to contest the election at various levels not only for the reserved seats but also for the general seats.
- Motivating SHGs and general voters to support both women and *Dalits*.
- Were well received and attracted the attention of all the sections of the people.

Radio Talk by Dr. G. Palanithurai

Dr. G. Palanithurai gave an informative and thought-provoking talk on New Panchayat System and its possible anticipated impact in rural areas. His radio talk was broadcast during local bodies election process. The major contents of the talk were:

Video Show

A video show depicting the story of a president in a village Panchayat was distributed to all the NGO networks and the respective district level coordinating NGOs. In turn they screened the cassette titled Namma Ooru, Nalla Ooru (our village is a good village) in their respecctive villages. The story was about a talented woman president in the village who performed well and fought against upper caste people, elite groups and male chauvinism and also other anti-social activities and the elements involved in it. The response of the rural women on seeing the stories was good in every village and hamlet. The theme story was the topic of the talk of the women working the agriculture field the next day morning. All the NGO networks have used both print media and electronic media to some extent to disseminate the messages of PEVAC. But they have not done to fully/effectively throughout Tamil Nadu. It may be due to lack of time and financial constraints.

VIII. PEVAC IN NILGIRI AND SIVAGANGAI BY THE HUNGER PROJECT

Introduction

PEVAC activities were carried out throughout Tamil Nadu by PRIA in association with Gandhigram Rural Institute. Out of 29 districts in Tamil Nadu in 2 districts the PEVAC activities were undertaken by 2 NGOs, Rural Development Organisation (RDO) and Rural Welfare Trust (RWT) respectively under the Hunger Project. The main activities undertaken by these NGOs are narrated hereunder.

The main objectives of PEVAC are:

1. To create good leadership in the local bodies election.
2. To train independent leadership, particularly from women and *Dalit* candidates.
3. To promote leadership from SHGs for various levels of positions under local bodies.
4. To increase voting percentage among rural voters.
5. To create a conducive political environment towards fair and free elections.

Target Area and the People

In both the districts, the two NGOs concentrated only on the village panchayat level, *i.e.*, Panchayat president and Ward members. As already mentioned the target group of the PEVAC activities are rural women members in SHGs and *Dalit* people.

Blocks Covered by the NGOs

BDO Nilgiri	Villages	Blocks covered under RWT in Sivagangai
Erumadu	Kattacombai	Kallal
Devar Shola	Anna Nagar	Singampunari
Uppatti	Aravenu	S. Pudur
Nilakottai	Thutturmattam	Thirupathur
Pandalur	Kothagiri	
Manjolai	Konavarari	
Athikuna	Kookal	
Mel Gudalore	Masakkal	
P. Soundi	Kattapettu	
Cherumulli	Thumanatti	
O'Velley	Ithalar	
Devala	Emarald	
Nadugunai	Arukuchi	
Masinagunchi	Kolakomabi	
Mavanalla	Selas	
Nelliyalayam	Adhikavatti	
Cherambadi	Kutti and Sugathala	

With regard to RDO

- A cultural team conducted 35 street theatre camps in 35 village Panchayats.
- RDO mini bus with a big banner reading "Panchayati Raj-Election Voters Awareness Campaign", and with a public address system, plied in difficult hilly terrain in all the 35 village panchayat areas.

Major Activities Carried Out

Special Programme for Aspiring Candidates

Apart from normal awareness programme a special programme/ training was organised mainly for the aspiring candidates in order to prepare their mind towards winning the election and accepting the decision to be given by the voters in the election.

Printed Wall Posters

1. 4,000 copies of wall posters were printed by RWT, Sivagangai. The themes were:

- Vote for good candidates irrespective of caste, class, party, identity, relationship and so on so forth.
- Select the candidates who are accessible, uncorrupt, socially concerned.
- Prefer youth, specifically women and *Dalits*.
- Emphasison the three-tiers, particularly the village Panchayat as the base for the creation of Gram Swaraj which was dreamt of by Mahatma Gandhiji throughout his lifetime.

2. 50,000 notices were printed on various themes like:

   - Salient features of New Panchayati Raj Act.
   - Structure and functions of three-tier system.
   - Do's and don'ts during election.
   - Role of booth agent and returning officer.

   The same posters were printed in A4 size also.

An Appeal Letter

An appeal letter explaining the objectives of the programme was distributed to the public.

Handouts

Handouts describing details of the constitutional amendments relating to Gram Panchayati Raj duties and responsibilities were printed.

An Appeal Letter to the Voters for Unanimity

An appeal letter was distributed to the voters in order to generate awareness among the rural voters to select the representative unanimously so that election expenditure and tension between two groups would be reduced.

Steel Frames

The 29 subjects provided to village presidents were written in bold letters as bill boards and inserted into steel frames designed for the purpose.

Dissemination of Information

- These posters and printed materials were exhibited in tea shops, petty shops etc.
- Women SHGs were fully used for distribution of letters to the voters.
- Debates and discussions were also conducted with the help of SHG members.
- The steel frames/boards were kept outside the programme venue in order of priority.
- Musical programme/street play/theatre were also conducted to generate awareness.

Response to Messages

There was a good response to each technique adopted for PEVAC activities. Particularly seeing the wall posters there were a number of telephone calls and letters and personnel comments by the public. Even some political party members were asking for the posters to exhibit in their respective villages.

- People started discussions with others in the tea shops and saloons.
- Aspiring candidates very eagerly participated in the training programme voluntarily.
- The printed materials relating to rules and regulations of village Panchayat were very useful to the representatives. They attended the meeting after reading the materials which helped them to acquire more knowledge.

Response to Awareness Programme

Contrary to expectations there was a good response from different sections of the society like all political parties and Government officials and high school and college students who extended whole-hearted support to the movement. The cultural team obtained signatures from important persons including police officers in the respective areas. Police gave protection to the team.

Orientation Programme

An orientation programme was held in 5 places aiming at orienting the women self-help groups towards taking part in the electoral process. Each participant was given printed materials covering information on the 29 subjects the presidents are empowered with and the ralationship among president, vice-president and ward members,

- A debate was also conducted on the information.
- Doubts were clarified.
- The participants were divided into three groups for group discussion.

Village Meeting

Eleven meetings were conducted at the village and hamlet level. The village voters were given proper information on the 29 subjects of the village panchayats and the role and responsibilities of local bodies representatives at various levels, particularly at village Panchayat level, ward members, village Panchayat president. All their doubts were clarified and suggestions and recommendations were also sought from the people to take follow-up action.

Potential Candidate Training

Following invitations distributed to the potential candidates personally by self-help group members and the staff of RWT, a formal meeting was organised at the village level to impart training on electoral ethic and code of conduct to these aspiring to contest.

Candidates Promoted-Rural Development Organisation (Nilgiris)

Village Panchayat Presidents	35, of when
	Women – 45.7%
	Men – 54.3%
	Dalits – 17.0%
	SHGs – 30%

Rural Welfare Trust

	Male	Female
Village Presidents	34	26
Vice-presidents	5	–
Ward members	124	74

Post-Election

The RWT and RDO did not stop their activities with the election for local bodies. They extended their work even after the election was over. It was felt essential that all the elected representatives, particularly women who won various positions in the local bodies like ward members, vice-president, village presidents, had to be felicitated and encouraged in a public meeting, so that the women will gain confidence and be motivated to function with social recognition. Accordingly a meeting was organised where resource persons from Gandhigram Rural University, were invited. Dr. G. Pankajam, the Vice-Chancellor of Gandhigram Rural Institute, in her felicitation address expressed her hope that women presidents can show better performance than the men presidents. Dr. Palanithurai, Head of the Department of Political Science and Development Administration, in his address, analyzed the development taking place in successfully, functioning of village Panchayats in the midst of various hurdles social cultural and economical. Appealing to the newly elected women presidents to perform well, he also assured that he and his department would always be in support of effective functioning of village Panchayats. Mr. S. Balasubramanian, Director of the IFPAAW also spoke. The important topics which the resource persons dealt with in the post-election training were as follows:

- Functioning of three-tier system.
- Salient features of Panchayati Raj System.
- Role and responsibilities of elected representatives.
- Panchayat Administration.
- Linkage with role of Government officials and NGOs.
- Importance of Gram Sabha meetings.

- Conduct of Panchayat and Gram Sabha.
- Panchayat Fund, Budget.
- Administrative report and audit.
- Planning and complementation of schemes.
- Anticipated problems and solutions.

RDO in Nilgiris had invited resource persons, who were prominent in panchayati raj like Mr. G.A. Rajkumar IAS, Prof. Dr. G. Palanithurai, Mr. N. Balachandran, Mr. M. A. Thirunavukkarasu and Mr. N.K. Perumal, V. Raman through his meaningful song enlightened the women representatives on the role and responsibilities in good performance of village panchayats. It was proposed to create a model panchayat with distinction in many respects through personal discussions, interaction and appeals to all the voters by printed letter. Discussing and analysing various aspects P. Karunkulam, in Thiruppathur Block, was selected unanimously to be the model panchayat followed by, P. Verpugaptti in Kallal Block, Vadavanpatti in Singampunari Block and Uthirapatti in S. Pudur Block.

Observations

It was observed that the PEVAC activities carried out by RWT created good impact in the minds of rural voters. The misunderstanding was prevalent that women have right to contest only in the 33 per cent reserved seats and not the remaining seats which was alloted only for men. In fact, the allocation of 33 per cent seats for women is meant for women where men can't contest. At the same time there is no restriction on women contesting in the seats not reserved, which are general seats. This was cleared up. In many places women who wanted to contest for the general seats were denied due to this misunderstanding. But the intervention of RWT helped the women to contest.

Problem Faced

Though there was careful planning and execution of the plan there were two important problems RWT, RDO faced.

1. Males, particularly the aspiring candidates and their relatives, were dissatisfied with the NGO's act of encouraging only women members.
2. There was opposition from the upper caste people as the NGOs were always in support of *Dalit* people.

Expectations

The two NGOs, RWT and RDO carry out PEVAC activities under the Hunger Project put forth some suggestions:

1. Instead of focusing on awareness programme only for women it should include men also.
2. Necessary training should be given to Panchayat presidents and vice-presidents and ward members, union and district councillors immediately after the election is over.
3. Exposure visits for representatives must be arranged.
4. The programme should be started much earlier.

I. SIVAGANGAI DISTRICT – THE HUNGER PROJECT

Introduction

The Pre-Election Voters Awareness Campaign organized by RWT in collaboration with Gandigram Rural Institute funded by the Hunger Project had yielded positive results. In this connection a training programme was conducted in Thirupathur at the Algappa Bagyam Marriage Hall on 3 November, 2001, for newly elected women Panchayat presidents and ward members. The elected women are members of SHGs who actively participated in the campaign. The programme started with a prayer and oath taking. The Vice-Chancellor of Gandhigram Rural Institute lighted the lamp to begin the sharing session. While welcoming all the participants Mr. V. Subbiah of RWT said that RWT had covered few blocks in the district in rural welfare activities of the villages. Some of the works have been completed by RWT by struggle. All the problems of the local villages are addressed by RWT and efforts are made to find solutions to all these problems. RWT had helped in forming a building workers association in 1995. This association now has 1,000 members. In 1996 women SHGs were organized by RWT. The current number of SHGs are 200 comprising about 10,000 women. The local saving of these SHGs now stands at Rs. 1 crore. He appreciated Prof. G. Palanithurai's help in funding and sponsoring the campaign through the Hunger Project.

The newly elected women representatives were felicitated with a shawl.

Speaking on this occasion, Kalaiarasi, Panchayat president of Papankulam said that for the past five years she had done a lot of work as Panchayat president. The people have re-elected her for the second term by evaluating her performance. Of all the representative institutions in Indian Democracy Local Bodies are the one which are evaluated by the people closely and on the basis of their evaluation, people cast their votes.

Ms. Chinnammal of Varathupatti who is the Panchayat president, said that she had been re-elected because she had been engaged in service to the people at all times. She considers this as a certificate given to her by the people. Ms. K. Rakku Vadavanpatti who is the Panchayat president said that Gramiya Iyakkam has to be thanked for such a service, and this function will encourage us more to do service to the people and that they are duty bound to Gramiya Iyakkam. Now we realize the power of women. Ms. K. Selvi, Panchayat president of Vadamavalli said that she is thankful to all who voted for her and to this Iyakkam for its support to me to contest in the election. Ms. Leelavathi of Esmapatti who is the Panchayat president said that she is thankful for such a meeting and to all who voted for her and she hopes to get cooperation from all to discharge her duties effectively and efficiently.

Ms. Kanniayye of Kattukuripati who is the Panchayat president said that she and others who have shared our views and vision are privileged to be here. She said three people contested against her and she won the election. It means that more number of people reposed confidence in me. She said that she will keep up this sentiments and continue to work for the people. S. Subbulakshmi of Kunnakudi a ward member said that she never imagined that she could became a ward member. She said

Gramiya Iyakkam encouraged me to contest in the election. She said this training is very much useful to them. T. Chitra, a ward member of Vairavanpatti said that training is very essential for efficient discharge of functions and to get role clarity for effective functioning in Panchayat as member or leader.

It is a meeting to make the elected Panchayat presidents to realize their worth. They have been drawn from SHG and oriented by RWT. Now they have come to occupy the political space and through which they have determined to take up the real issues of the people on development. After this, Vice-Chancellor of Gandhigram Rural Institute delivered the presidential address. The following is the summary of the address.

There are about 117 ward members and 25 village presidents from the four blocks in which Gramiya Iyakkam is active. The reason for the women to be here is for felicitation. But this felicitation should be repeated at the end of fifth year for successful accomplishment of duties. In this same place the function was held to strengthen the SHGs three years before. Five years ago no one thought that training is an imperative one. But now training becomes inevitable. Only now power has been given to those who really need it. 33.3 per cent reservation of seats in local governance for woman have been useful here and many have been newly elected and re-elected. But this opportunity should not be to occupy the seat of power but to discharge the duties and responsibilities and so that the position of the elected member is not by the title but by the amount of work she has done by being in position. Responsibility vested with women is like a narrow road with a lot of obstructions. But all elected members should face these obstacles and come out victorious. This position is not for self-service but should be considered as an opportunity to serve the people. Panchayat president is like a neighbour. It is not like MP or MLA. People will ask for every thing from the president, as they are nearer to them and familiar to them. By doing your work and fulfil the demands of the people you will be recognized and re-elected. Your works in panchayat would strengthen the women movement. This women power should grow and this movement should grow. Here you have to notice an important point that you have no role models in front of you and you should become role models for the coming generations.

After this Mr. Raman sang some women movement songs to encourage all the participants.

Mr. Balasubramaniam of IFPAAW said that PEVAC is a good beginning. Appreciable work has been done by the Panchayats. Now the hope is in Panchayats to address the basic issues and problems of the people. Quoting Barathiar (a poet) he said Education and Nutrition are the two legs of a human being. The following is the summary of the lecture given by Prof. G. Palanithurai in RWT during the interactive session with elected women leaders.

Elected women representatives are to be appreciated and complimented because of one important reason that the existing myth of proxy has been broken. They are in position now not on the basis of the support extended by any male member of her family. Self-help group members are just like army men to support the activities of the Panchayat. They would help the panchayats in tackling the social and economic issues. They are an array of problems unattended so far have to be addressed and attacked and for which self-help group members would be helpful. Going back to the people to get solution is the best way of providing good leadership. In this effort Gandhigram Rural Institute will provide all the necessary help, in association with RWT. It is not possible for the newly elected women representatives to know all they have to do as leaders. The aim of all this effort is that people should recognize the leaders and leaders should recognize the people.

Regarding the role perception of a good leader, the women should be convinced that being a leader is not being an ordinary person. She must know that what are the requirements and status of the people who have elected her. One example is how many of the elected leaders know how many of the people in their respective villages have enough food to eat? How many people do not have basic amenities? Only if leaders know all these things, efforts could be taken to improve the quality of life. Thus to improve the situation, knowledge is necessary. In the same way the health of the children in the rural areas to be taken note of and leaders should ensure that every child in the village is hunger free and infection free. By knowing things irrelevant works done commonly by elected leaders can be stopped. Women leaders should set an example for others in this regard. To do this, women should convince themselves that they are not subordinate to men. They can be on par with men if they do not copy what men do. They should believe in themselves and be independent. If women start speaking independently and boldly then it is the first step towards self-realization.

A woman should not feel shy. They should discuss problems like sanitation, woman and child health and other women related problems openly among themselves as well as with Government authorities. In all this effort the leader is the guiding force. One thing must be kept in mind. It is a well known fact that women candidates faced a lot of obstacles to win the elections. In the same way they should face all the obstacles in implementing welfare measures. Effective leadership is recognized only when in spite of all opposition, respect for the common people is maintained. This can be achieved only through discipline. Finally, what is important to remember is social ills are not the fault of the common people. If one says less and does more then much can be achieved.

Mr. Raam, the Director of Gramiya Iyakkam said that of the 200 candidates of various SHG who contested in elections, 109 were elected. Before election candidate evinced keen interest in the process. The RWT workers are living with a mission to succeed. This result was achieved because of the different kind of assistance given by many. Hard work, self-confidence, and honesty are the three characteristics required for Panchayat leaders for their success. After 5 years the same felicitation should be arranged for the women leaders for successful completion of works. There should be cordiality among winners and losers. This will ensure full participation of all the people in the village.

Healthy Practice

One could notice a major development in Sivagangai district in the Local Bodies Election that all candidates contested in the election barring a few are from the SHG. A healthy competition was in the election and after the declaration of results the candidate who lost in the election shook hands with the victorious candidates and pledged their support to the elected representatives. A healthy democracy has been evolved at the grassroots and for which SHG members are responsible.

This was well received by all the participants. The following is the list of participants:

List of Leaders elected for Village Panchayat from RWT SHGs (Female)

Sl. No.	Name	Panchayat	District
1.	Ms. S. Pushpalatha, President	S.R. Pattanam	Sivagangai
2.	Ms. Malarkodi, President	Keelappattamangalam	Sivagangai
3.	Ms. R. Yasodai, President	Veliyathur	Sivagangai
4.	Ms. A. Santha, President	Koothaloor	Sivagangai
5.	Ms. A. Vennila, President	Kurunthampattu	Sivagangai
6.	Ms. K.R. Shiyamala, President	Ulagampatti	Sivagangai
7.	Ms. S. Gomathi, President	Manalur	Sivagangai
8.	Ms. V.R. Kalaiarasi, President	Veppangulam	Sivagangai
9.	Ms. M. Tamilchelvi, President	Malaikandan	Sivagangai
10.	Ms. R. Vimaladevi, President	Vetriyur	Sivagangai
11.	Ms. K. Rakku, President	Vadavanpatti	Sivagangai
12.	Ms. S. Gandhimathi, President	Kalippuli	Sivagangai
13.	Ms. A. Rani Aron, President	Aalangudi	Sivagangai
14.	Ms. S. Amutha, President	Piramanapatti	Sivagangai
15.	Ms. K. Muthulakshmi, President	D. Mampatti	Sivagangai
16.	Ms. S. Ratha, President	N. Melaiyur	Sivagangai

(Contd.)

Sl. No.	Name	Panchayat	District
17.	Ms. A. Pushpam, President	P. Nerpugapatti	Sivagangai
18.	Ms. N. Valli, President	Aalampattu	Sivagangai
19.	Ms. P.L. Vasuki, President	Eriyur	Sivagangai
20.	Ms. Y. Nallammal, President	A. Kalappur	Sivagangai
21.	Ms. P. Thangam, President	Kannamangalapatti	Sivagangai
22.	Ms. Y. Nagajothi, President	Kozhikudipatti	Sivagangai
23.	Ms. V. Chandra, President	A. Melaiyur	Sivagangai
24.	Ms. T. Vallimayil, President	S. Mathur	Sivagangai
25.	Ms. T. Vasanthal, President	Melapatti	Sivagangai
26.	Ms. V. Poongothai, President	S. Sevalpatti	Sivagangai
28.	Ms. J. Jeyasumathi, President	Melapattamangalam	Sivagangai
29.	Ms. S. Kamila Beevi, President	Karisalpatti	Sivagangai
30.	Ms. G. Sumathia, President	Kilavayal	Sivagangai
31.	Ms. C. Chinnammal, President	Urathupatti	Sivagangai
32.	Ms. G. Thanasundari, President	Valasipatti	Sivagangai
33.	Ms. G. Pushpa, President	Varappur	Sivagangai
34.	Ms. M. Selvi, President	Vadamavasi	Sivagangai
	Vice-President		
1.	Ms. R. Meenakumari, Vice-president	Kattampur	Sivagangai
2.	Ms. S.P. Rajalakshmi, Vice-president	Veppangulam	Sivagangai
3.	Ms. S. Kaliammai, Vice-president	Kuruthampattu	Sivagangai
4.	Ms. A. Mary, Vice-president	Sembanur	Sivagangai
5.	Ms. M. Vasanthal, Vice-president	Vadavanpatti	Sivagangai
Ward Member			
1.	Ms. M. Pandidevi, Ward member	Malaikandan	Sivagangai
2.	Ms. S. Malar, Ward member	Vadavanpatti	Sivagangai

(Contd.)

Sl. No.	Name	Panchayat	District
3.	Ms. M. Preama, Ward member	Koothalur	Sivagangai
4.	Ms. M.Chandra, Ward member	Koothaloor	Sivagangai
5.	Ms. M. Nangamuthu, Ward member	Patharakudi	Sivagangai
6.	Ms. M. Annalakshmi, Ward member	Koothaloor	Sivagangai
7.	Ms. Sp. Parvathi, Ward member	Nariyangudi	Sivagangai
8.	Ms. Sp. Rakkayee, Ward member	Melapattamangalam	Sivagangai
9.	Ms. M. Rajakumari, Ward member	Keelapattamangalam	Sivagangai
10.	Ms. S. Kala, Ward member	Veliyahur	Sivagangai
11.	Ms. M. Umayatchi, Ward member	SR Pattanam	Sivagangai
12.	Ms. KR Sarasu, Ward member	Aalampattu	Sivagangai
13.	Ms. S. Annapoorani, Ward member	Nerpugapatti	Sivagangai
14.	S. Rajeshwari, Ward member	Kattampur	Sivagangai
15.	Ms. V. Muthulakshmi, Ward member	P. Nerpugapatti	Sivagangai
16.	Ms. V. Panchavarnam, Ward member	N. Keelayur	Sivagangai
17.	Ms. V. Valliammal, Ward member	D. Mampatti	Sivagangai
18.	Ms. K. Nagarathinam, Ward member	Kundrakudi	Sivagangai
19.	Ms. S. Subbalakshmi, Ward member	Kundrakudi	Sivagangai
20.	Ms. K. Nachammai, Ward member	Kattampur	Sivagangai
21.	Ms. A. Devi Abragham Ward member	Aalangudi	Sivagangai
22.	Ms. C. Chitra, Ward member	Thirukkostiyur	Sivagangai
23.	Ms. D. Neelavathi, Ward member	S. Mampatti	Sivagangai
24.	Ms. C. Sigappee, Ward member	Eriyur	Sivagangai
25.	Ms. S. Muthulakshmi, Ward member	Patharakudi	Sivagangai

(Contd.)

Sl. No.	Name	Panchayat	District
26.	Ms. A. Panchali, Ward member	S. Pudur	Sivagangai
27.	Ms. K.R. Gandhi, Ward member	Vadavanpatti	Sivagangai
28.	Ms. T. Arumugam, Ward member	Vetriyur	Sivagangai
29.	Ms. SP. Sundaram, Ward member	Veppangulam	Sivagangai
30.	Ms. S. Amaravathi, Ward member	Kuruthampattu	Sivagangai
31.	Ms. V. Palaniyayee, Ward member	Manalur	Sivagangai
32.	Ms. P. Kalyani, Ward member	Ulagampatti	Sivagangai
33.	Ms. C. Parvathi, Ward member	Minnamalaipatti	Sivagangai
34.	Ms. M. Chinnammal, Ward member	Melavannariruppa	Sivagangai
35.	Ms. K. Vasanthal, Ward member	Malaikandan	Sivagangai
36.	Ms. V. Thamilarasi, Ward member	Parmanampatti	Sivagangai
37.	Ms. S. Palaniammal, Ward member	Karisalpatti	Sivagangai
38.	Ms. P. Palaniammal, Ward member	Karisalpatti	Sivagangai
39.	Ms. A. Fatima Beevi, Ward member	Karisalpatti	Sivagangai
40.	Ms. P. Kavitha, Ward member	Kilavayal	Sivagangai
41.	Ms. A. Nachammal, Ward member	Kilavayal	Sivagangai
42.	Ms. A. Pappathy, Ward member	Kulathuppatti	Sivagangai
43.	Ms. V. Dhanapackiam, Ward member	K. Kulathupatti	Sivagangai
44.	Ms. V. Palaniyayee, Ward member	Manalur	Sivagangai
45.	Ms. C. Chellammal, Ward member	Manalur	Sivagangai
46.	Ms. M. Amuthavalli, Ward member	Manthakudipatti	Sivagangai
47.	Ms. P. Poomani, Ward member	Manthakudipatti	Sivagangai
48.	Ms. M. Chinnammal, Ward member	Melavannariruppu	Sivagangai

(Contd.)

Sl. No.	Name	Panchayat	District
49.	Ms. P. Muthupalani, Ward member	Melavannariruppu	Sivagangai
50.	Ms. C. Packiyam, Ward member	Minnamalaipatti	Sivagangai
51.	Ms. K. Muthulakshmi, Ward member	Musundupatti	Sivagangai
52.	Ms. C. Gangalakshmi, Ward member	Musundupatti	Sivagangai
53.	Ms. S. Buvaneshwari, Ward member	S. Pudur	Sivagangai
54.	Ms. C. Nachammal, Ward member	S. Pudur	Sivagangai
55.	Ms. K. Rajamani, ward member	K. Pudupatti	Sivagangai
56.	Ms. D. Saroja, Ward member	Puluthipatti	Sivagangai
57.	Ms. P. Lalli, Ward member	Puluthipatti	Sivagangai
58.	Ms. A. Yamuna, Ward member	Ulagampatti	Sivagangai
59.	Ms. M. Nallammal, Ward member	Ulagampatti	Sivagangai
60.	Ms. T. Krishnaveni, Ward member	Valasaipatti	Sivagangai
61.	Ms. G. Indirani, Ward member	Valasaipatti	Sivagangai
62.	Ms. V. Ponnalagu, Ward member	Varappur	Sivagangai
63.	Ms. A. Vasantha, Ward member	Varappur	Sivagangai
64.	Ms. V. Jeya, Ward member	Pramanampatti	Sivagangai
65.	Ms. V. Thamilarasi, Ward member	Pramanampatti	Sivagangai
66.	Ms. A. Rajeshwari, Ward member	Kattampur	Sivagangai
67.	Ms. N. Kala, Ward member	P. Karungulam	Sivagangai
68.	Ms. G. Ulagi, Ward member	P. Karungulam	Sivagangai
69.	Ms. A. Thavasumani, Ward member	P. Karungulam	Sivagangai
70.	Ms. A. Mallika, Ward member	Vannariruppu	Sivagangai
71.	Ms. R. Kavitha, Ward member	Vannariruppu	Sivagangai

(Contd.)

Sl. No.	Name	Panchayat	District
72.	Ms. A. Sittu, Ward member	Vannariruppu	Sivagangai
73.	Ms. P. Karuppayee, Ward member	Thirukkostiyur	Sivagangai
74.	Ms. S. Jamuna, Ward member	Thirukkostiyur	Sivagangai
75.	Ms. C. Chitra, Ward member	Thirukkostiyur	Sivagangai
76.	Ms. K. Pandiammal, Ward member	Vadamavali	Sivagangai
77.	Ms. S. Jeyamani, Ward member	Vadamavali	Sivagangai
78.	Ms. K.R. Valli, Ward member	Aalampattu	Sivagangai
79.	Ms. K. Sarasu, Ward member	Aalampattu	Sivagangai
80.	Ms. V. Shanthi, Ward member	Alangudi	Sivagangai
81.	Ms. P.L. Vairamuthu, Ward member	Kallal	Sivagangai
82.	Ms. V. Deivanai, Ward member	Kallal	Sivagangai
83.	Ms. G. Meiyammai, Ward member	Kallipattu	Sivagangai
84.	Ms. P. Kavitha, Ward member	Kallipattu	Sivagangai
85.	Ms. C. Thamilarasi, Ward member	Kallipattu	Sivagangai
86.	Ms. K.R. Valliammai, Ward member	Kallippuli	Sivagangai
87.	Ms. M. Saroja, Ward member	Kalllippuli	Sivagangai
88.	Ms. K. Soundavalli, Ward member	Kambanur	Sivagangai
89.	Ms. K. Chandra, Ward member	Kambanur	Sivagangai
90.	Ms. N. Pushpam, Ward member	Kandramanickam	Sivagangai
91.	Ms. M. Rajeshwari, Ward member	Kandramanickam	Sivagangai
92.	Ms. K. Meenal, Ward member	Kandramanickam	Sivagangai
93.	Ms. N. Mutharasi, Ward member	Keelapoongudi	Sivagangai
94.	Ms. K. Kannammal, Ward member	Keelapoongudi	Sivagangai

(Contd.)

Sl. No. Name	Panchayat	District
95. Ms. A. Lakshmi, Ward member	Kovilur	Sivagangai
96. Ms.T. Sunthanthiramani Ward member	Kovilur	Sivagangai
97. Ms. P. Annamayil, Ward member	Nariyangudi	Sivagangai
98. Ms. V. Kamalam, Ward member	Nachiyapuram	Sivagangai
99. Ms. M. Devayani, Ward member	N. Melaiyur	Sivagangai
100. Ms. S. Amutha, Ward member	N. Keelaiyur	Sivagangai
101. Ms. V. Panchavarnam, Ward member	N. Keelaiyur	Sivagangai
102. Ms. S. Muthulakshmi, Ward member	Patharakudi	Sivagangai
103. Ms. G. Chitra, Ward member	Sevarakkottai	Sivagangai
104. Ms. M. Manimekalai, Ward member	Sevarakkottai	Sivagangai
105. Ms. S. Pillammal, Ward member	Sevarakkottai	Sivagangai
106. Ms. M. Thilagavathy, Ward member	SR. Pattanam	Sivagangai
107. Ms. P. Amali, Ward member	SR. Pattanam	Sivagangai
108. Ms. S. Anthoniammal, Ward member	Sembanur	Sivagangai
109. Ms. K. Santhamani, Ward member	Thattatti	Sivagangai
110. Ms. K. Vasanthal, Ward member	Thalakkavur	Sivagangai
111. Ms. K. Devaki, Ward member	Thalakkavur	Sivagangai
112. Ms. G. Poomayil, Ward member	Visalayankottai	Sivagangai
113. Ms. K. Jothi, Ward member	Visalayankottai	Sivagangai
114. Ms. M. Vasanthal, Ward member	Veliyathur	Sivagangai
115. Ms. G. Kaveri, Ward member	Veppangulam	Sivagangai
116. Ms. S. Rama, Ward member	Eriyur	Sivagangai
117. Ms. P. Shanthi, Ward member	Mallakottai	Sivagangai

(Contd.)

Sl. No.	Name	Panchayat	District
118.	Ms. M. Indiragandhi, Ward member	Mallakottai	Sivagangai
119.	Ms. S. Banumathi, Ward member	Mallakottai	Sivagangai
120.	Ms. R.M. Meenal, Ward member	D. Mampatti	Sivagangai
121.	Ms. K. Boomayil, Ward member	D. Mampatti	Sivagangai
122.	Ms. M. Chitra, Ward member	S. Mampatti	Sivagangai
123.	Ms. S. Sasikala, Ward member	S. Mampatti	Sivagangai
124.	Ms. T. Neelavathi, Ward member	S. Mampatti	Sivagangai

List of Leaders Elected for Village Panchayat from RWT SHGs (Males)

Sl. No.	Name	Panchayat	District
President			
1.	Mr. K.R. Bose, President	Devapattu	Sivagangai
2.	Mr. S. P. Vadivelu, President	Kallal	Sivagangai
3.	Mr. Ambalatharasu, President	Kandramanickam	Sivagangai
4.	Mr. N. Murugesan, President	Keelapoongudi	Sivagangai
5.	Mr. M. Thirunavukkarasu, President	Kovilur	Sivagangai
6.	Mr. R. Veeraiah, President	Nariyangudi	Sivagangai
7.	Mr. C. Ramasamy, President	N. Keelayur	Sivagangai
8.	Mr. G. Ponnaiah, President	Patharakudi	Sivagangai
9.	Mr. N. Subramanian, President	Sevarakkottai	Sivagangai
10.	Mr. R.M. Chokkalingam, President	Sembanur	Sivagangai
11.	Mr. S.P. Rajendran, President	Thattati	Sivagangai
12.	Mr. P.R. Murugappan, President	Thalakkavur	Sivagangai

(Contd.)

Sl. No.	Name	Panchayat	District
13.	Mr. V. Ramachandran, President	Kattampur	Sivagangai
14.	Mr. C.T. Manivannan, President	P. Karungulam	Sivagangai
15.	Mr. M. Manickam, President	Thirukkostiyur	Sivagangai
16.	Mr. S.Pillappan, President	Aralikkottai	Sivagangai
17.	Mr. V. Ramachandran, President	Mallakottai	Sivagangai
18.	Mr. M. Manickam, President	S. Mampatti	Sivagangai
19.	Mr. S. Seevili Alagan, President	Kulathuppatti	Sivagangai
20.	Mr. K. Mani, President	Manthakudipatti	Sivagangai
21.	Mr. M. Ponnuschamy, President	Melavannayiruppur	Sivagangai
22.	Mr. A. Sundarama, President	Minnamalaipatti	Sivagangai
23.	Mr. A. Alagan, President	N. Neduvayal	Sivagangai
24.	Mr. A. Rajmohan, President	S. Pudur	Sivagangai
25.	Mr. A. Sathan, President	K. Pudupatti	Sivagangai
26.	Mr. C. Chinnameiyan President	Puluthipatti	Sivagangai
Ward Member			
1.	Mr. K. Karuppiah, Ward member	Kilavayal	Sivagangai
2.	Mr. A.R. Ponnusamy, Ward member	Kilavayal	Sivagangai
3.	Mr. N. Vellaichamy, Ward member	Kilavayal	Sivagangai
4.	Mr. P.A Palaniyandi, Ward member	Kulathupatti	Sivagangai
5.	Mr. S. Alagan, Ward member	Kulathupatti	Sivagangai
6.	Mr. A. Vellaichamy, Ward member	Kulathupatti	Sivagangai
7.	Mr. P. Rengaraj, Ward member	Manalur	Sivagangai
8.	Mr. C. Venkatachala-pathy, Ward member	Manalur	Sivagangai
9.	Mr. C. Ayyasamy, Ward member	Manthakudipatti	Sivagangai
10.	Mr. A. Malaichamy, Ward member	Manthakudipatti	Sivagangai

(Contd.)

Sl. No.	Name	Panchayat	District
11.	Mr. K. Periyasamy, Ward member	Manthakudipatti	Sivagangai
12.	Mr. A Vellapoosari, Ward member	Melavanniyiruppu	Sivagangai
13.	Mr. C. Kariyan, Ward member	Melavanniyiruppu	Sivagangai
14.	Mr. M. Ayyavu, Ward member	Minnamalaipatti	Sivagangai
15.	Mr. V. Veeriah, Ward member	Minnamalaipatti	Sivagangai
16.	Mr. A. Palani, Ward member	Minnamalaipatti	Sivagangai
17.	Mr. A. Selvaraj, Ward member	Urathupatti	Sivagangai
18.	Mr. C. Kasilingam, Ward member	Urathupatti	Sivagangai
19.	Mr. A. Kumar, Ward member	S. Pudur	Sivagangai
20.	Mr. N. Nagarajan, Ward member	K. Pudupatti	Sivagangai
21.	Mr. S. Sathan, Ward member	K. Pudupatti	Sivagangai
22.	Mr. A. Periyasamy, Ward member	Ulagampatti	Sivagangai
23.	Mr. A. Vallinathan, Ward member	Varapur	Sivagangai
24.	Mr. A. Palanisamy, Ward member	Varapur	Sivagangai
25.	Mr. A. Asirvatham, Ward member	Varapur	Sivagangai
26.	Mr. S. Subbiah, Ward member	Aalampattu	Sivagangai
27.	Mr. V. Tharmalingam, Ward member	Kallal	Sivagangai
28.	Mr. C. Sundaravadivelu, Ward member	Kallal	Sivagangai
29.	Mr. S. Palanikumar, Ward member	Kallal	Sivagangai
30.	Mr. U. Karuppiah, Ward member	Kallipattu	Sivagangai
31.	Mr. K. Soman, Ward member	Kandramanickam	Sivagangai
32.	Mr. V. Murugan, Ward member	Keelapoongudi	Sivagangai
33.	Mr. M. Subramanian, Ward member	Keelapoongudi	Sivagangai

(Contd.)

34.	Mr. T. Mathiyalagan, Ward member	Keelapattamangalam	Sivagangai
35.	Mr. S. Banikkan, Ward member	Kurunthampattu	Sivagangai
36.	Mr. K. Kalimuthu, Ward member	Kurunthampattu	Sivagangai
37.	Mr. A. Karuppiah, Ward member	Kurunthampattu	Sivagangai
38.	Mr. N. Kannan, Ward member	Kovilur	Sivagangai
39.	Mr. R. Mariappan, Ward member	Kovilur	Sivagangai
40.	Mr. S. Rakkappan, Ward member	Kovilur	Sivagangai
41.	Mr. R. Arumugam, Ward member	Melapattamangalam	Sivagangai
42.	Mr. A. Shanmugam, Ward member	Melapattamangalam	Sivagangai
43.	Mr. Manickam, Ward member	Melapattamangalam	Sivagangai
44.	Mr. S. Karuppiah, Ward member	Nariyangudi	Sivagangai
45.	Mr. P. Mohammed Ali, Ward member	Nariyangudi	Sivagangai
46.	Mr. Ramaiah, Ward member	Nariyangudi	Sivagangai
47.	Mr. M. Karuppaiah Ward member	Nariyangudi	Sivagangai
48.	Mr. P.R. Subramanian, Ward member	N. Melaiyur	Sivagangai
49.	Mr. A. Chandran, Ward member	N. Melaiyur	Sivagangai
50.	Mr. K. R. Palanichamt, Ward member	N. Keelaiyur	Sivagangai
51.	Mr. V. Elangeshwaran, Ward member	N. Keelaiyur	Sivagangai
52.	Mr. A.L. Seenivasan, Ward member	P. Nerupugapatti	Sivagangai
53.	Mr. R.M. Subramanian, Ward member	P. Nerpugapatti	Sivagangai
54.	Mr. M. Sekar, Ward member	P. Nerpugapatti	Sivagangai
55.	Mr. P. Ramanathan, Ward member	P. Nerpugapatti	Sivagangai
56.	Mr. R. Muthu, Ward member	Patharakudi	Sivagangai
57.	Mr. A. Arumugam, Ward member	Patharakudi	Sivagangai

(Contd.)

Sl. No.	Name	Panchayat	District
58.	Mr. R. Chinnaiah, Ward member	Sevarakkottai	Sivagangai
59.	Mr. A. Raman, Ward member	Sevarakkottai	Sivagangai
60.	Mr. S. Palanimurugan, Ward member	Sembanur	Sivagangai
61.	Mr. C. Ashok Kumar, Ward member	Sembanur	Sivagangai
62.	Mr. S. Erutthayaraj, Ward member	Sembanur	Sivagangai
63.	Mr. M. Muthukumar, Ward member	Sembanur	Sivagangai
64.	Mr. M. Karuppiah, Ward member	Sembanur	Sivagangai
65.	Mr. V.S. Rajendran, Ward member	Sembanur	Sivagangai
66.	Mr. S. Sathiah, Ward member	Thattatti	Sivagangai
67.	Mr. N. Vellakannu, Ward member	Thallkkavur	Sivagangai
68.	Mr. A.L. Nedunche-zhilyan, Ward member	Veliyathur	Sivagangai
69.	Mr. A. Lakshmanan, Ward member	Veliyathur	Sivagangai
70.	Mr. C. Ayyakannu, Ward member	Veliyathur	Sivagangai
71.	Mr. A. R. Meiyappan, Ward member	Veppangulam	Sivagangai
72.	Mr. N. Soundararaj, Ward member	Veppangulam	Sivagangai
73.	Mr. V. Nagarajan, Ward member	Veppangulam	Sivagangai
74.	Mr. S.P. Sundaram, Ward member	Veppangulam	Sivagangai

IX. OVERALL IMPACT OF THE CAMPAIGN

Citizens' Point of View

The communication techniques adopted by different NGOs depend upon the level of awareness of the people in the district and the techniques and tools available with the NGOs. Though techniques and people were dissimilar, the messages that all the NGOs disseminated were similar. All the messages were mostly related to generating awareness among the voters about their voting rights and selecting suitable candidates to create good governance. The following are the themes of the campaign.

- Voting rights of the people in general and women and *Dalits* in particular.
- Number of votes to be cast by villagers and urbanites.
- Selecting women and *Dalit* candidates for social justice.
- Role of 73rd Amendment in upholding the principles of democracy.
- 33 per cent reservation for women towards women empowerment and equality.
- *Dalit* reservation aiming at fraternity and social equality.
- Powers, duties and responsibilities of village president according to 73rd Amendment.
- Quality of a good leader at village level administration.

Communication Techniques

1. *Materials Produced*

Sl. No.	Material	Type	Information focused on
1.	Charts	Cartoon style	Women & *Dalit* support
2.	Phamplets	7 pages	73rd Amendment salient features
3.	Display cards	Multi-colour	No. of votes right to vote
4.	Bit notices	Multi-colour	Qualities of good leader and role of Women/*Dalits*
5.	Wall posters	Medium and big size	Supporting *Dalit*/women candidates
6.	Booklets	26 pages, multi-colour	Leadership training
7.	Cloth banners	Multi-colour quality cloth	Canvassing vote for women and *Dalits*
8.	Training module	Folded type	Promoting women leadership
9.	Stickers	Multi-colour	Awakening women/*Dalit* candidates
10.	Model manifesto	Book form	All voters, candidates and NGOs

2. *Dissemination Methods*

The respective NGOs at the district level along with the personnel from PRIA and GRI used the following methods to disseminate the information.

- Informal meeting with target group women and *Dalits*.
- Formal meeting with target group.
- Public meeting with villagers in general.
- Focus group discussion with SHGs/*Dalit* groups and aspiring candidates.
- Distribution of printed materials to all the workers.
- Wall writings with prior permission.
- Cycle really with volunteers, NGO staff, SHG members and aspiring candidates.
- Van rally and *yatra* conducted by NGO staff for general voters.
- Procession for general voters promoting voting rights.
- Procession with banana leaves for general voter awareness and reservation.

3. *Personnel Involved*

In order to disseminate the messages of PEVAC, personnel from various levels werc involved. They were NGO heads, staff of NGO, women SHG office bearers, youth club members, school children and volunteers from different fields and school and college students.

Resource Persons

Personnel from Gandhigram and other academic institutions, NGOs, Government departments were involved in the campaign activities and for imparting leadership training to the nominees.

1. NGO staff who had already undergone training on Panchayati Raj conducted either in State Institute for Rural Development (SIRD) in Maraimalai Nagar or Rajiv Gandhi Chair for Panchayati Raj Studies, Department of Political

Science and Development Administration, Gandhigram Rural Institute, Gandhigram were used.

2. The heads of the NGOs were involved in PEVAC at the district level.
3. Resource persons from Gandhigram Rural University are

   (a) Dr. G. Palanithurai, Head, Department of Political Science, Coordinator, Rajiv Gandhi Chair for Panchayati Raj Studies;
   (b) Dr. V. Ragupathy, Reader, Department of Political Science, Associate Coordinator;
   (c) Dr. C. Kubendran, Coordinator PEVAC, PRIA; and
   (d) M.A. Thirunavukkarasu, Research Associate;

were also engaged in imparting training to the target groups.

Duration of Dissemination of Message

The time schedule was fixed according to the convenience of the local people and at the time they were free from the campaigning of political parties. Public meetings and canvassing were conducted both early in the morning and in the evenings.

Efficiency of Communication Techniques

Impact of Campaign

Since the majority of the NGOs were already experienced in conducting similar campaigns, to some extent much more sensitive than PEVAC activities, it was easy for the majority of the NGOs to communicate the message very effectively through different media. It benefited the voters, particularly women and *Dalits*.

Impact of Campaign from Citizens' Point of View

It was observed from the several responses of the people to the PEVAC activities that:

- All the members in SHGs have become aware of the rights of women in contesting the election by using 33 per cent reservation and the campaigners, particularly the office bearers, motivated many members to contest the election even in the general seats against male candidates and upper caste candidate.

- It was only through PEVAC wall posters that the voters came to know that they had to cast 4 votes at the village level, thus preventing the confusion of voters. The four votes and the respective positions were clearly depicted in the colour wall poster very clearly which made the villagers understand it all easily.
- Colours, and respective positions like ward members, Panchayat president, Panchayat union councillor, district panchayat president were understood only through the wall posters.
- Small bit notices which were distributed by the NGOs to described the characteristics of a good leader. This was very useful for every voter to vote for a good candidate.
- Though it was not possible to understand the extent of its impact in voting for a good candidate, it was observed that there was a good response to the notice from the people.
- We were stimulated and motivated either to contest the election or to support SC candidates on reading the stickers carrying messages supporting women/*Dalit* candidates pasted in public places, said voters belonging to SC.
- Women in rural area said that they are encouraged to organise women's group to support women candidates due to the presence of the big sized multi-coloured cloth banner carrying messages which encouraged women to contest the election.
- The women self-help group members felt that the training module released by SAM developed confidence in their mind that only women presidents can carry out all development programmes unbiased and promote social justice at the local level.

3

LOCAL BODY ELECTION

I. ELECTION COMMISSION AND THE GOVERNMENT IN THE ELECTION

As the tenure of the local bodies was nearing completion there was suspicion and uncertainty among the people over the conduct of election to the same. To put an end to the uncertainty, the Tamil Nadu State Election Commission, on 3rd September, 2001, announced the dates for polls to both rural and urban local bodies in two phases, one on 16th and the other on 18th October, 2001. It was just three months after the Legislative Assembly elections. When the election was announced, the political climate of Tamil Nadu was so hot and nobody knew what would be the course of action of the Government.

The decision was announced in a tense climate prevailing in Tamil Nadu, particularly in Chennai, as the Municipal Administration Department of the Government of Tamil Nadu had issued a show-cause notice to the Chennai Corporation Council as to why it should not be dismissed. (Chennai Corporation Mayer M.K. Stalin was the son of M. Karunanidhi the arch enemy of J. Jayalalitha).

The State Election Commission had also given the dates for different stages of the election process. Accordingly, the last date for filing nomination was 27th September, 2001; scrutiny of applications was scheduled for 28th September; the date for withdrawal was 1st October; polling was to be held on 16th and 18th October, 2001; and the date of counting of votes was to be 21st October, 2001. The whole process of the election was over by 23rd October, 2001. The newly elected representatives were to assume office on 25th October, 2001.

Election had to be conducted for the following bodies:

Corporations	-	6
Municipalities	-	102
Town Panchayats	-	611
District Panchayats	-	29
Panchayat Unions	-	385
Village Panchayats	-	12618

Ethnic Parties Two-Tier System

The Government of Tamil Nadu sought a constitutional amendment to restore the old two-tier system of Panchayat in the state. It was an irony that both the DMK and the AIADMK which never agree upon any issue in Tamil Nadu polity, hold the same opinion on one issue, namely creation of two-tier system of Panchayat in Tamil Nadu. When the late M.G. Ramachandran was a member of the Ashoka Mehta Committee, he recorded a dissent note against the three-tier system suggested by the committee. The AIADMK as the ruling party, passed a resolution in the Legislative Assembly of Tamil Nadu requesting the Government of India to bring in an amendment to the 73rd Amendment by which two-tier system of local bodies could be created. Mr. M. Karunanidhi, the President of the DMK and former Chief Minister of Tamil Nadu, in a statement in one of the leading Tamil dailies, *Dinamani* on September 9th expressed his full support to the Government seeking a constitutional amendment to restore the two tier system in Tamil Nadu. Only on this issue both M. Karunanidhi and J. Jayalalitha concurred with each other.

State Election Commission

The Tamil Nadu State Legislature enacted the Tamil Nadu Panchayat Act, 1994 for the conduct of election to panchayats. The District Municipalities Act, 1920 and the City Municipal Corporation Acts relating to Chennai, Madurai, Coimbatore, Trichy,

Salem and Tirunelveli were also amended for conducting elections to municipalities and city corporations. The Tamil Nadu Election Commission was established as an autonomous body mainly for the purpose of conducting Local Bodies elections and looking after all the matters related to elections like the preparation of electoral roll and conduct of elections periodically. Accordingly, the first election for local bodies after the enactment of the State Conformity Act, 1994 was held in October 1996 successfully at one stroke.

Problem in Electoral Rolls

Though it was the responsibility and duty of the State Election Commission (SEC) to prepare the electoral rolls (the names of the eligible voters, *i.e.*, every citizen of India, aged above 18 with sound mind) by revising and updating the electoral rolls by proper door-to-door enumeration and verification, the State Election Commission failed to do so. The SEC was very particular about conducting the election rather than about the revision of electoral rolls. It failed to fulfil its duty. Updating and revising the electoral rolls by door-to-door enumeration and verification are very much essential for fair conduct of elections.

The Need for Revising Electoral Rolls

- After a long gap of five years of general and local body elections the eligible voters who have crossed the age of 18 have to be included. This can be done even on the last day for filing of nominations.
- Those who are dead or have changed their place of residence and permanent migrants have to be excluded from the electoral rolls to avoid duplication of voters.
- Deletion of names can also be done in the case of those who have indulged in corruption, illegal practices and other offences related to elections.
- Names left out in the electoral rolls have to be included if the voters produce valid certificate of residence.

The electoral rolls so prepared, revised and updated should also be published. Electoral rolls which are not published should not be used in elections. Even during the Parliamentary elections in 1999 there were complaints that eligible voters on a large scale were not included in the list. It was not an updated electoral roll. During the revision in 1999, voters on a large scale were deleted from the list which was used in May 2001 in Tamil Nadu Assembly elections.

It was said that there were 4.66 crore voters in May, 2001 as against 4.38 crores in 1996 as per the electoral rolls. But the figure in the electoral rolls in May 2001 election was only about 4 crores, since there were large scale deletions by various interested groups and political parties.

- Elections for two-tier system of Panchayati Raj were held in 1984 during Chief Ministership of the late M.G. Ramachandran.
- After 12 long years elections for three-tier system of local bodies was held during the DMK period in 1996, after the introduction of 73rd and 74th Amendments to the Constitution of India.

Enrolment of Voters

The SEC announced that the names of the voters which were missed in the previous general elections could be enrolled and that those who did not have photo identity card could also have their names included in the electoral list. It also allowed the citizens to enroll their names even one day before the last day for filing nomination.

Political Climate

Though it was mandatory to conduct elections for local bodies within 6 months of the expiry of the previous tenure, the political climate prevailing in the state, particularly the relationship between DMK and AIADMK, was not conducive as there were a number of untoward incidents like the disqualification of the former Chief Minister Ms. J. Jayalalitha to contest in the election, the subsequent assumption of office as Chief Minister by Ms. J. Jayalalitha without being elected, this assumption of office being questioned in the court of law, and the midnight arrest of former Chief Minister M. Karunanidhi by the AIADMK Government which resulted in a series of political activities which were mostly violent in nature. Amidst this tense political climate elections to local bodies were announced on 5th September, 2001.

Advisory Committee on Local Poll

The State Election Commissioner had a meeting with higher officials and all the District Collectors to plan for the successful conduct of local bodies elections in Tamil Nadu. The officials were asked to do the preparatory work for smooth conduct of election including imparting training to the election officials.

Printing of Electoral Roll

It was the responsibility of every District Collector to print the voters list sheets required for the conduct of election and for which some officials were deputed. The State Election Commission asked the district officials to look after the printing process and inform it of the particulars about the printing press and the officials deputed periodically for this work.

Display of Voters List

The voters list was to be displayed for verification and confirmation. Those who were eligible to vote but were not included in the voters list could be included upto 27th of September which was the last date for filing nomination. The process of revising the voters list continued till 19th September, 2001.

Talks on Alliance among Political Parties Initiated

Immediately after the announcement of the election dates, the two major political parties in Tamil Nadu—the DMK and the AIADMK— started negotiations for alliance with various political parties with which they had alliance for the Assembly elections held just four months back.

Wall Writing without Party Symbol

Both the political parties in Tamil Nadu started reserving the walls in public places and announced their party candidates but the selection of candidates and allocation of seats among the alliance parties were delayed.

Changes in Alliance for Local Body Elections

- A team of seven senior DMK members held discussions with alliance partners to finalise the arrangements for the local body elections.
- The state unit of Indian National League constituted a five member committee to initiate discussions with the AIADMK.
- Two former state ministers of the DMK and the PMK leader discussed the possibilities of establishing an alliance.
- The TMC led by its chairperson G.K.M. Vasan, son of the founder of TMC, G.K. Mooppanar, held first round discussions with the AIADMK.
- As the AIADMK did not invite the Congress party for seat sharing negotiations for the local bodies election, the majority of the District Congress Committee Presidents urged the Congress party to go it alone or lead a separate front (third front). It was left to the All India Congress President, Mrs. Sonia Gandhi, to take a decision on alliance in Tamil Nadu for the local bodies election.
- The caste based political organisations were very much in a dilemma as to which political party to join with in the local bodies election.

Nomination of Election Officers

The District Collectors made all the arrangements necessary for the smooth conduct of local polls and as part of this they nominated Election Officers at District Panchayat level and Panchayat Union level.

- Project Officers of DRDA and Joint Registrars of cooperative societies at the District Panchayat level and Additional Collectors and other officers in the cadre of Assistant Director at the Panchayat Union level were nominated to conduct the election.
- Commissioners of Municipalities and Executive Officers of Town Panchayats were nominated to conduct the urban local bodies election.

Stay Sought on Local Bodies

An advocate named C. Ponnusamy filed a public interest litigation on 17th September, 2001, seeking a stay on the local bodies elections stating that the State Election Commission has not followed many of the mandatory provisions with regard to preparation of electoral rolls. He also pointed out that there was mass deletion of voters' names during the previous assembly elections. The petitioner also wanted the Chennai Mayor's post to be reserved for a SC woman candidate as Chennai had the largest Scheduled Caste population in the state.

Change in the Reservation for SC Women

The post of District Panchayat Chairperson in Perambalur District was allotted to a SC woman for the present poll. It was the only change made from the earlier reservation schedule.

Non-party Basis Election for Local Bodies

A political party in Tamil Nadu, the Puratchi Thalaivar ADMK, at its office bearers' meeting held in Chennai, suggested to conduct local bodies elections on non-party basis for proper and effective functioning of local bodies.

A Senior Police Officer for Election

The Government designated a senior police officer, Mr. Bholanath, who was till then Inspector General of Prisons, Chennai, as the Inspector General of Police (Elections), Chennai.

Collectors Visited the Counting Centres

The Collectors of the respective districts visited the premises of the counting centres proposed and saw to the arrangements for keeping the ballot boxes safe.

SEC Secretary Transferred

On 25th September, 2001, Mr. Abdulla, the Secretary of the Tamil Nadu SEC, was transferred, 22 days after the announcement of the local body polls. Mr. K. Dhanavel, Joint Secretary, Environment and Forests was appointed in his place.

Communal Rotation for Mayor's Post: Suggested INL

The Indian National League (Tamil Nadu Wing) urged the State Government to revive communal rotation followed earlier for the post of Mayor of the Chennai Corporation.

Time Extended for Inclusion of Voter List

The State Election Commission issued a statement that the voters who had obtained photo identity cards and whose names were included in the electoral lists for the 1999 Parliamentary elections but not in the present list for the local bodies election, could apply afresh till 1 October, 2001.

Police Deployment Sought from Neighbouring States

Mr. V. Balachandran, IG, said that armed police personnel from Andhra Pradesh, Kerala and Karnataka would be deployed in Tamil Nadu for security arrangement in the coming local bodies elections.

Hyper-Sensitive Districts and Pockets were Identified

Five southern districts of Tamil Nadu, namely Tirunelveli, Tuticorin, Virudhunagar, Ramanathapuram and Theni were identified as hyper-sensitive areas by the State Election Commission. In addition to these districts a number of sensitive pockets were also identified where additional *bandobust* was suggested.

Poll Panel Meets with Observers

The State Election Commission held a meeting with Election Observers who were mostly senior IAS officers deputed to the districts.

Non-Party and Party Basis Election

The State Election Commission issued a statement and announced various points.

- Election to Village Panchayats would be conducted not on the basis of political parties. Panchayat Union and District Panchayat elections would be conducted on party basis. Accordingly symbols of the respective political parties could be used.
- Voters in the rural area should exercise four votes (some times five votes).

For rural voters

1.	Village Panchayat Ward Member	—	White
2.	Village Panchayat President	—	Light Red
3.	Panchayat Union Ward Member	—	Green
4.	District Panchayat Ward Member	—	Yellow

Case Filed against the Order of SEC on the Allotment of Symbols

Six registered parties under the leadership of the President of the Congress Democratic Forum, Mr. P. Chidambaram, quoting the order issued by the SEC in 1968 on the allotment of symbols, filed a petition seeking preference for the recognized parties over independents in the allotment of symbols. It was rejected by the SEC on September 19th. As per the Law Commission, there was no such provision. But Mr. Chidambaram, in a fresh petition, sought dismissal of the SEC order. Mr. Chidambaram, as an advocate, argued in court on behalf of the six registered parties.

The court's verdict, handed down a week later, was that the registered parties and independents should not be compared and that the registered political parties should be given preference in the allotment of symbols. The SEC had the power do so. The demand for specific symbols made by the Janata Party and the Janata Dal (United) was rejected.

Recognised Parties

The SEC released the list of political parties registered and recognized in Tamil Nadu. This recognition was given to the parties based on the percentage of votes secured in the previous local body elections and support from the public. Accordingly there were eleven political parties: (1) AIADMK, (2) DMK, (3) Bahujan Samaj Party, (4) Bhartiya Janata Party, (5) Indian Communist Party, (6) Marxist Party, (7) Congress Party, (8) MDMK Party, (9) National Congress Party, (10) PMK, and (11) TMC. Only to the parties mentioned above party symbols were allotted and two copies of the voters list were given. The remaining parties had to contest using independent symbols.

Allocation of Symbols to the Candidates

Though there is a provision for the independent candidates to choose anyone of the symbols printed in the application form, the SEC ordered the Election Officers to allot symbols to the non-party candidates on the basis of lottery. Mr. Rajaram, the former AIADMK minister suggested that the post of Mayor of Chennai should be allotted on rotation basis, as people in Chennai belong to different castes and religious groups. He pointed out that the Justice Party of old had this provision for giving chance to all the castes and religious groups to enjoy the power of Mayor by rotation every year.

High Court Refused to Postpone Election

The Madras High Court refused to postpone the election to the local bodies scheduled for October 16th and 18th though a slight modification was done in the election schedule by the Court. The Court gave the following directions :

- The election process should be commenced on September 14th.
- With regard to the plea of the petitioner on rotation of Mayor's post the Court observed that the Constitution was not specific with regard to the terms of rotation. Hence this was left to the state to decide.
- With regard to reservation for an SC woman as Chennai Mayor the Bench said "we do not see any force in this contention".

All Parties met to Discuss the Poll Arrangements

The District Collectors in every district held discussions with the representatives of political parties on the following points:

- The Goondas Act would be involved against those indulging in casting bogus votes.
- The Collectors appealed for the cooperation of the public and political leaders for the smooth conduct of the election.
- They announced the phone numbers to be contacted by the people to inform the Collectorate of any untoward incident during polling.
- They announced that no cell phones would be allowed in the vicinity of polling centres.
- They also announced the expenditure limit for each level of position as follows :

1.	District Panchayat	-	Rs.	50,000
2.	Panchayat Union	-	Rs.	25,000
3.	Union Chairman	-	Rs.	10,000
4.	Union Ward Member	-	Rs.	2,500
5.	Town Panchayat Member	-	Rs.	5,000
6.	Town Panchayat President	-	Rs.	25,000
7.	Municipal Councillors (first grade)	-	Rs.	10,000
8.	Municipal Chairman	-	Rs.	50,000
9.	Municipal Councillor (above first grade)	-	Rs.	25,000
10.	Chairman	-	Rs.	1,00,000

Binding Rules for Conducting Election

The Election Officers were warned not to indulge in any corrupt activity before or after the election.

Procession Violating the Norms

Following the practice of the Assembly elections, the political parties organised huge processions for filing nominations in the local bodies election. A good number of vehicles accompanied the candidates and halted at several places to garland statues of leaders. Since it was peak hour traffic, the main roads were choked and the traffic had to be diverted and all this took place in the presence of police personnel. What was disheartening was that, when contacted, the police officials said that since it was the ruling party candidate the policemen were quite liberal.

No Clarity in the Responsibility to Control the Procession

It was observed that the duty of the police officials was only to maintain law and order and that it was the task of the Poll Observers to take note of the happenings and initiate action against those who violate the election rules.

Poll Observer Visited the Districts in Person

The Poll Observers were to make sure whether voter lists had been printed properly and sufficiently and kept in a safe place and to identify the sensitive areas in the districts. They have visited the districts and verified with the officials about the poll arrangements made by the officials. The local body Election Observer for each district discussed the arrangements for the polls with the District Collector and the other officials and visited some of the Village Panchayats and urged the officials to ensure peaceful, orderly and fair election. In sensitive areas precaution had to be taken to enable the voters to cast their ballots without any apprehension and adequate police personnel had to be put on duty. Identified sensitive polling booths were given additional police protection. A total of 86,000 police personnel were deployed on poll duty in Tamil Nadu.

A Meeting on Security Arrangements

In the last week of September, there was a meeting to review the security arrangements and precautionary measures to be taken by poll officials. At every Collectorate the duties of the police officers and the guidelines to be followed by the candidates and political parties in the election were spelt out.

- Prior permission of the owners of private buildings should be obtained for wall writings and printing.

- Loudspeakers were allowed from 6.00 a.m. to 10.00 p.m. in urban areas and upto 11.00 p.m. in rural areas.
- Security would be beefed up in sensitive areas at polling centres and counting centres.
- The District Collector were to ensure that all security measures were taken for peaceful conduct of the polls in all the districts.

An intensive survey indicated that there were 4,000 sensitive polling booths in the first phase and 5,100 in the second one. It was planned to deploy police personnel from other states in the areas identified as more sensitive. Over and above there were 4,000 police personnel kept ready to look after law and order and to ensure fair and free election.

The day after the nomination was over the observers started visiting the respective districts and verified weather

- the nominations were scrutinized properly;
- the campaigning activities were conducted peacefully and well within the framework of rules and regulations;
- was there any violation of election rules?

They reported to the Election Commission as and when they detected violation of the election code. In order to conduct peaceful and fair election, the local Inspectors of Police conducted all party meetings where it was decided that no procession should be conducted till the election is over.

Nineteen Proofs can be used as Identity Cards for Voters

Voters could cast their votes by showing anyone of the 19 proofs suggested by the Election Commission, such as: (1) Photo identity card, (2) Passport, (3) Driving licence, (4) Income tax card, (5) Bank pass book, (6) Post office book, (7) Community certificate, (8) Professional identity card, (9) Handicapped certificate and so on.

SEC fixed Deadline for Account

The Election Commission fixed the last date for submitting expenditure account to be within 30 days after the election. A photo copy of the candidates application along with other relevant papers was given to each official concerned.

Date for Election of Vice-President was Fixed

The SEC issued orders to the District Collectors, for the conduct of indirect election to the positions of Vice-Presidents of Gram Panchayats, Chairpersons and Vice-Chairpersons of Panchayat Unions and Chairperson and Vice-Chairperson of District Panchayats on the 31st in the respective districts.

No Need of Security for the *Dalit* and *Dalit* Women Candidates

As there was no complaint by the candidates that they were being tortured or disturbed by the non-SCs in the process of the election campaign and since they did not anticipate any untoward incidents on the day of polling, there was no need for special security for the SC candidates, the Election Commissioner said. In a few places in Madurai district, *Dalits* were not allowed to contest in the election. The Police and the District Administration could not do anything about it. In other places there were problems and they were not brought to light by the affected because of mutual fear.

Additional Security for Sensitive Booths

In the sensitive booths additional security arrangements were made. Thousands of police personnel including AR, TSP, Home Guards, ex-servicemen and NCC cadets were pressed into security duty. Additionally, for immediate access to police during the elections, a control room was opened for district level booths. Also phone numbers to be contacted were also announced in newspapers. The District Collectors after taking steps for the smooth conduct of local body elections, released the voters list for their respective districts and details of the representatives to be elected at different levels.

Order Issued to Surrender Licensed Guns

To be on the safer side and as a precautionary measure an order was issued to those who had licensed guns asking them to surrender their guns at the nearest police station. They were assured that the weapons would be handed back to them on the first day of November. Accordingly the owners of guns surrendered the guns which remained in the police stations till the election process was over.

Order Issued to Close Down Wine Shops

A day before the election, 15th September 2001, the District Administration issued orders to the owners of wineshops to close them for three days, *i.e.* two polling days and the counting day.

Personnel Involved in Election

According to the SEC there were five lakh officials involved in the process of the election. In every district, there were thousands of police personnel deployed with all equipment for controlling any untoward incidents. Apart from police personnel, Tamil Nadu Special Police (one company) Armed Force, Forest Guards, personnel from Fire Service, Ex-servicemen and NCC cadets were also involved.

Order Issued to the Polling Officers by SEC

Two days before the election, the SEC gave instructions to the Polling Officers.

- Officers should go to the polling booth a day before the election by 12 O'clock and check the principal officer, booth agent, polling place and the place were ballot boxes where kept.

- Ensure that there is no mention of the names of leaders or any political parties in the vicinity of the polling station.
- Verify whether the polling place is in a safe location and look for alternatives in case of rain.
- Check the materials needed for voting like indelible ink, stamp ink, ballot sheets and a copy of the voters list.

As a second phase of their activities they should come to the polling booth by 6.00 a.m. in the morning on the day of polling.

- Paste the posters showing the names of the candidates and their respective symbols in front of the booth.
- Sign at the back of 100 voter sheets in advance.
- Verify whether anybody votes against the names of dead persons or otherwise exercises bogus vote.
- Half an hour before the commencement of polling, the booth agents of the candidates have to be examined. Start the polling by 7.30 a.m. and close it by 5.30 p.m. The process of polling should be over by exactly 5.30 p.m. After closing the entrance of the booth ballot sheets should be given to the voters standing in the queue within the entrance.

Ballot Sheets Missed a Day before Election

Ballot papers numbering nearly 15,000 were missing in Theni district from a private printer where they were printed. The printing was started on 5th of October by experts hired from Sivakasi. From that day till they handed over all the printing materials to the election officers, all the workers were not permitted to come out of the press. Food and materials required for printing were supplied from outside. Officials from fire services and 20 personnel from the strike force were deployed in the press under the leadership of four Sub-Inspectors of Police. Generally more ballot papers are printed than the required number. Yet 15,000 ballot sheets printed for Municipal Chairman's post were missing.

Preventive Arrest

The Government resorted to preventive arrest in different parts of the state on the eve of the first phase of the local body election. Only those who were likely to create trouble based on their past records were taken into custody. In this regard leading political parties TMC and DMK, AIADMK had expressed their unhappiness over the steps taken by the Government of Tamil Nadu.

Punishment to Bogus Voter Announced

One year's imprisonment to those who makes attempt to indulge in malpractice in the election was announced by the State Election Commissioner. He also said that if groups stayed in either lodges or any kalyanamandapam, the owners would be booked. These kinds of premises would be checked if they were harbouring groups for political activities.

The Themes of Campaign

It is very interesting to note that the DMK highlighted the major achievements in local bodies when it was in power. But the AIADMK indicated the charges levelled against the DMK for its malpractices and corruption in the functioning of the local bodies. The Congress-I, forming a third front, made a fervent plea that it would provide a clean administration in local bodies if it came to power.

Campaign for the First Phase

For the first phase, the campaign organised by all the political parties and independent candidates came to an end without much anti-social activities and casualties. The campaign started very slowly, electioneering picked up in the last week and ended two days before the election day. There was a good deal of violence during the campaign here and there sometimes leading to the murder of supporters and even candidates (the details are given separately under poll violence).

Tight Security Arrangements

In all the sensitive districts, elaborate *bandobust* arrangements had been made for the peaceful and fair conduct of local body polls :

- Mobile police parties were arranged for being pressed into service on the day of polling.
- Election control rooms started functioning with specific telephones for contact. A local DSP was in charge of the control room which functioned 24 hours a day.

The First Phase Polling — October 16

The details of the posts for which elections were held on 16th October were as follows:

- Corporation 4
- Municipalities 44
- Town Panchayat 307
- The names of the Town Panchayats for which election was held in the first phase were:

Municipalities

1. Mettupalayam
2. Pollachi
3. Nellikuppam
4. Bunruti
5. Viruthachalam
6. Dharmapuri
7. Kodaikanal
8. Dharapuram
9. Sathyamangalam
10. Kancheepuram
11. Madurantagam
12. Kulaichal
13. Kulithalai
14. Karur
15. Melur
16. Nagai
17. Kumarapalayam
18. Rasipuram
19. Thiruchengode
20. Pudukottai
21. Ramanathapuram
22. Aathoor
23. Sivagangai
24. Kumbakonam
25. Tanjore
26. Kunoor
27. Ooty
28. Periyakulam
29. Theni-Allinagaram
30. Thiruvannamalai
31. Tuticorin
32. Thuraiyuir
33. Thiruvallur
34. Mannarkudi
35. Arakonam
36. Aarkadu
37. Ranipettai
38. Vellor
39. Walajabad
40. Villupuram
41. Sivakasi
42. Virudhunagar
43. Aruppukottai
44. Koothanallur

II. UNANIMOUS SELECTION/ELECTION OF CANDIDATES

In the present local body election, there were some strange methods of selection/election of candidates. One such method was the unanimous election of candidates by the village community. In many villages of Tamil Nadu traditional communities were powerful and the social life of villages was regulated by these communities for generations. In almost all the areas these village communities played a crucial role in taking all the decisions taking into account the traditions, customs and practices. This traditional communities have always been more powerful than the elected one which is a formal body and has a fixed duration. The decision taken by the village committee is regarded as the final judgment against which no member from the village can speak or act. The violator will be ex-communicated.

Ex-communication

There was an incident in a village in Madurai district where a man who filed nomination against the candidate already selected by the village committee was ex-communicated. According to this system, the remaining people in the village will have no contact with him. If anyone violates this he/she will also be ex-communicated.

Unanimous Election in a Multi-caste Village

Kamuthi in Ramanathapuram district was one of the caste-ridden areas. Among the multi-caste groups the Nadars and Muslims were dominant communities. Every caste was in the election competing with each other. So the villagers decided to adopt a rotation method in selecting the President. Accordingly, the villagers with different caste groups in a large number assembled under a tree on the premises of the Panchayat on the last day of withdrawal of nominations and selected Ms. Kannammal, a Nadar woman as President and 15 ward members were also selected unanimously for ensuring communal harmony. It is worth mentioning here that

Ms. Kannammal is the only candidate elected unanimously as chairman of Kamuthi town Panchayat along with 15 councillors. The wonder here is that she is an independent candidate.

Selection of Representatives on Rotation Basis

Rajakambeeram is a village near Manamadurai, where adherents of the major three religions, *i.e.* Hinduism, Christianity and Islam live almost in equal number. In order to avoid religious clash over power, the villagers decided to allot the positions of local bodies to all three religions on rotation basis. Accordingly, in the previous election the Village President's post was allotted to a Musalman and the Vice-President's post was given to a Christian. In the present election, a Hindu was given the Village President's post and the post of Vice-President was given to a Christian while the post of Union Councillor was given to a Muslim. After allotting the three posts to three religions, each religious group constituted a committee of 10 members (six elders and four youths). The three committees jointly determined the individuals from different religions for ward members.

Unopposed from Caste-ridden Village

Of all the instances of unopposed selection of representatives the most unexpected and surprising was the selection of a candidate from the Yadava community in Karuvanoor village of Madurai West Union. It was the village where the Joint Secretary of DPI Sri Modakatthanpandi was murdered by a caste Hindus following which there were some caste clashes, mutual damaging of properties and burning of buses and huts. Tension was prevailing as the day for local election was nearing. Foreseeing caste clashes among the various caste groups, the village elders (village committee) convened a meeting to select a candidate for Village President. Accordingly one Mr. Manivannan, a caste Hindu, was elected Village President. Vice-President's post was given to the SC community. Nine ward members were also selected unanimously. It is a good sign putting an end to the caste conflict in the village where SC, Yadava, Mukkalathur and Muslims live together in tension so far.

Ignorance of Competitor Leads to Unopposed Election

In Sivagangai district two candidates were elected unopposed. Of the two, one was the incumbent President against whom a lady filed her nomination but, unfortunately, her nomination was rejected as she did not affix her signature in the appropriate place.

Multi-castes United Against Political Parties

A distinction was observed in a town Panchayat which is a model to be followed. People of different castes and religions live together in this area. For the 15 wards in the town Panchayat more than 50 candidates filed nominations from different caste and religious groups. Each caste group was very particular in capturing the chairman's post, not letting any political party moved in. So different caste groups collectively formed an alliance. The same alliance was also used for selecting the ward members. Accordingly, ward members were elected giving due representation to all the caste groups. The main reason they cited for rejecting the political parties was the wish to create communal harmony and maintain cordial relationship among various caste groups.

Villages with No Nominations

There was not even a single nomination filed in four village Panchayats in the southern districts of Tamil Nadu, i.e. Madurai and Virudhunagar merely because of the fact that all these four village panchayat president posts were reserved for SC candidate. They are: Keeripatty Panchayat of Usilampatty Union and Pappapatty and Nattarmangalam Panchayats of Chellampatti Union in Madurai district and Kottakatchienthal Panchayat of Narikudi Panchayat Union of Virudhunagar district.

A President was Elected Thrice

The same president has been elected thrice successively in a multi-caste village. Kandilan is a Panchayat in Kaddaladi Union of Ramnad district where Thevars, Devendrakula Vellalars and Yadavas live together. The villages around this Panchayat are known for caste clashes and the prevalence of tension frequently created by the two caste groups, Thevars and Devendrakula Vellalars (SC). They elected a member from the Thevar community, Mr. Malaikannan, a B.A. Graduate, as Village President. He has been elected successively for three times just because of his personal character and selflessness and accessibility to the villagers of all hamlets.

Role of Village Committee in the Selection

The village committee's role is a deciding factor in determining the candidates for local bodies in Alanganlauur Union of Madurai district. Four village representatives and two union councillors were selected unanimously. Kodankipatti, Kottaimedu, Manianchi, Anuppatharu and Mettupatti Panchayat Ward members were also elected unanimously. In Kamuthi Union, from 53 village panchayats, 14 village presidents have been elected unopposed. The villages are: Pudukkottai, K.Veppamkulam, Palvaykulam, A.Tharaikodi, Movilangai, A.Tharailodi, Mavilangai, Muthalnadu, Keel Ramanithi, Nagarathar Kurichi, Pammanenthal, N.Kalaissapkulam, Kadamangalam, Erumaikulam, Idivilaki, Aryamangalam.

Better Performance Paved the Way for Second Time President

A gram seva awardee, Ms. Lakshmi Pongaroo Adikalar has been unanimously elected second time as Village President of Melmaruvathur. She was the president elected unopposed for this term. The voters stated that she has been elected by the people because of her unbiased selection of beneficiaries, implementing the Government programmes—both state and central—for which she was awarded 'Gram Rathna Award'. She was also appreciated by the district administration for her achievement in reaching the target fixed for savings in a year.

Thevar Community Produces President for 50 years Continuously

Muthumani Thevar was president during 1960-1970. Aryamangalam Panchayat in Kamuthi Union in Ramnad district has this unique distinction. The post of president has been retained for the past 50 years by one particular family belonging to one community. Ever since elections were held for village Panchayats, it is said that the president has been elected unopposed. The brother of Muthumanithevar Mr. Kottichamy succeeded and was elected three times, and he has again been elected unopposedly for the fourth successive terms.

Two Detained under Goondas Act were Elected Unopposed

What is unbelievable but true is that a person having 18 cases against his name, including three murder cases and has been on the rowdy list of the police since 1992 was elected unopposed from the 15th ward in North Valliyur Town Panchayat. Mr. Ramachandran was said to have been involved in three murder cases including that of the murder of a Policemen, Arulraj, who was hacked to death. Besides, there are three attempt to murder cases, three riot cases and one ganja case against him. He was also detained under the Goondas Act twice in the years 1995 and 1997. Yet another person elected unopposed for the 16th ward in the same town Panchayat was also involved in three cases, including that of the murder of police constable Arulraj. He was also involved in two attempt to murder cases among others. He was also detained under the Goondas Act in the year 1996.

Sister of Detenu was also Elected

The sister of Mr. Ramachandran, Ms. Meena was also elected unopposed from the 19th ward in this town Panchayat. She is not only the sister of a person involved in many anti-social activities, but she is the wife of Mr. Katta Madasamy who was also involved in the murder of the constable and the ex-panchayat vice-president. What is intolerable and disheartening is that one among these three is likely to be elected as the vice-chairman of this Panchayat.

A Family Holding President's Post for 150 years (Generations)

Anoothu is one of the famous villages in Usilampatti Union of Madurai district where the Village President's post has been enjoyed by a single family for 150 years, generation after generation.

During the British period and till the independence one Mr. Moozhi Karuppa Thevar was an important person in the Panchayat. After the dawn of Independence, the family was divided into two groups, *i.e.* Chinna Vallayan group and Periya Vallayan group. Further the family was divided into Veerappan group and Sathan group in which one Mr.Veeranan become President followed by his son Sri Ramasamy Thevar who was the president from 1960 to 1970. He was defeated by Mr. V. Amsukkodi Thevar of the opposite group in the year 1970. In 1985 there was a competition between a former president and Ms.Vijaya the daughter-in-law of an earlier president wherein Vijaya won in 1990. The Panchayat was dissolved. Then the seat was allotted to women. In 1996 the competition was between Ms.Thavamani, the daughter-in-law of ex-president Ramasamy Thevar and Ms. Sinnathayee, wife of the younger brother of Amsukodi Thevar. Mrs.Thavamani won the seat. Though there are 4 hamlets, namely Palanoothu, Rajakkapatti, Paraipatti and Karampatti, yet none filed nomination against her in the current election too. So the incumbent village president Ms.Thavamani has been elected president.

What is surprising here is not only the same family becoming the president for 150 years but the only rival group which has been opposing the ruling group has come to a compromise for unopposed election.

Table 3.1 : Details of the Unanimously Elected Positions in Local Bodies

Sl.	Name	Position	Remark	Place	District
1.	Kannammal	Town Panchayat	Caste ridden area	Kamuthi	Ramnad
			multicaste village rotation	Rajakambeeram Manamadurai	
2.	Women	President	Second time	Chakkanthi Sivagangai	
3.	Women	President	—	Chanarpatti	Dindigul
4.	Ms. Palaniammal	President Vice President	—	Linganwadi Natham Union	Dindigul
5.	Women	Town Panchayat	8 Councillors	Rival Was convinced by village committee	
			Abiramam	Ramanathapuram	
6.	—	6 Ward members	— Ramanatha-puram	Muthukulathoor	
7.	Mr. Murugan	President	—	Vannanparai	Dindigul
8.	Ms. M. Kanagavalli	President	—	Kadayanallur	Tirunelveli
		4 members (1 men , 3 women)	—		
9.	Ms. Banumathi	President	—	Vellakatti Kodaikanal Union	Dindigul
10.	30 Ward members	30 Ward members	—	Padukaipattu Senthankulam union	Tuticorin
11.	A. Chander-sekar	President	Deputy Secy. of Madras Legal Wing	South Alampakka	Villupuram
12.	Ms.Raja-lakshmi ex-president	Wife of AIADMK labour union			
13.	G.Kumar	Ms. Hmalatha	Municipal Councilor	Unopposed	Ramnad
14.	—	President	Unopposed	Kujiliamparai	Karur
		4 presidents		Kallal Union	Sivagangai
		5 presidents		Chekkottai union	Sivagangai

Source : Compiled from Newspapers.

The Largest Number of Nominations

Ward No.1 in Thekkampatti of Karamadai Panchayat Union in Coimbatore district had created a record because 42 persons filed nominations.

Bye-election for Four Village Panchayats

It was announced by the Election Commission that as there was not even a single nomination filed for Village President's posts, bye-election would be held on 19th November for the four villages, *i.e.*, Kottakatchi Eanthal in Virudhunagar district, Keeripatty in Usilampatti Panchayat Union and Pappapatti and Nattarmanagalam of Chellampatti Union (all three from Madurai district).

No Nominations were Filed

There was not even a single nomination filed for the following posts for the local bodies in Tamil Nadu.

Panchayat Presidents	–	4
Panchayat Union Ward Members	–	10
Town Panchayat Ward Members	–	8

No Nomination in the Third Time also

The people in the first ward of the Nellur Town Panchayat in Tuticorin district did not participate in the election for the third time as the ward was reserved for SC woman. Even during the bye-election and the previous Panchayat election no nomination was received.

Rejection of Nominations

Thousands of nominations were rejected and hundreds of nominations were withheld in almost all the districts in Tamil

Nadu. It is here suggested that awareness on the filing of nomination should be created among the aspiring candidate through academic institutes and committed NGOs in the respective areas. It is inferred that in the local body elections aspiring candidates were interested in contesting in the election but they did not bother to know the formalities to be followed for filing nomination. In many places, nominations were rejected just because the candidates had not signed in the appropriate place.

Table 3.2 : Particulars of the No. of posts for which election was held in 2001

Sl.No.	Name of the Posts	No.of Seats	No.of Candidates
1.	Village Panchayat (VP) Ward Member	82,085	2,40,984
2.	Village Panchayat President	12,023	47,809
3.	District Panchayat Ward Member	6,493	25,971
4.	District Panchayat Chairman	654	2,386
5.	Town Panchayat Ward Member	3,349	15,918
6.	Town Panchayat Chairman	602	2,888
7.	Municipal Councillor	3,349	15,918
8.	Municipal Chairman	102	538
9.	Corporation Councillor	474	3,055
10.	Corporation Mayor	6	60
	Total	1,14,819	3,75,380

Source : Compiled from Newspapers.

Tension Created due to Rejection of Nomination

Tension was created over the rejection of nomination on the day of scrutiny. Particularly in Sivaganga district, where the application of an AIADMK party woman candidate and the wife of a former Village Panchayat President was rejected for the reason that her husband was a contractor. There was one more case of this kind in Veersekarapuram Panchayat, where an AIADMK candidate resigned his government job for contesting in the election and against whom a former president of the DMK party filed nomination. The latter lodged a complaint with the election officer that no resignation letter has been received and that therefore his rival's nomination should be rejected. Two nominations in two wards in Vadakudi Panchayat were rejected just because they did not mention the ward number.

Boycotting Election

As in the case of previous elections, in the present election also there were a number of incidents of boycotting the elections for various reasons just to attract the attention of the Government.

Demanding a Separate Ward

Voters from Mottanoothu Panchayat in Andipatty Union in Theni district boycotted the local body election demanding a separate ward for Mottanoothu Village so that a ward member from their village may be elected.

Demanding Fulfilment of Basic Needs

Vellakavi is a village in Kodaikanal Union of Periyakulam Taluk where the public refused to cast their votes demanding the fulfilment of some basic needs like road, electricity and drinking water. But people have elected a body as Village President unanimously. The Election Officer, who walked 10 km to reach the village, returned disappointed because there was no voting.

Fisher Forum Boycotted the Election

Demanding that the Government—both Central and State— ban prawn farms in Tamil Nadu, the Tamil Nadu Fishermens Forum decided to boycott the election throughout Tamil Nadu. They also decided to take out a procession and a stage *dharna* in front of Fort St. George (The Secretariat of Tamil Nadu Government).

Demanding Basic Needs

People from Karthikeyapuram of Thiruthani Union decided to boycott the election demanding the fulfilment of basic needs like road, drinking water and street light. They also pointed to the humiliation meted out to them.

Protesting Against SC Reservation for Successive Election

There were three villages in Madurai district, namely Keeripatti, Pappapatti and Nattarmangalam which boycotted the election because these three villages are reserved for SC. People even in the last election put forth their demand to change the reserved constituency into a general one. In the 1996 local body election, election was held for Nattarmangalam village Panchayat, despite it being allotted to SC community. But in Keeripatti and Pappapatti village Panchayats, people prevented conducting elections only for village Panchayats whereas elections for Panchayati union and district Panchayat were held in both previous and present term. None has filed nomination for village president till the last date for filing nominations.

Peace/Compromise Committee Convinced

In order to arrive at an amicable solution a compromising committee was convened under the leadership of District Revenue Officer (RDO), Mr. Maheswaran, just a month before the actual day of election. People from Pappapatti alone participated while the people from two villages boycotted the committee. People from Nattarmangalam and Keeripatti did not attend the meeting. But elections were held for ward members and councillors of Panchayat union and district Panchayat respectively.

Demanding Drinking Water

The human and the animal population are more or less equal in a village where there is acute drinking water scarcity for years. The problem worsens during the summer season. The only overhead tank available in the village is in a state of disrepair and people demand that it be repaired within 7 days. Demanding drinking water, the people of Mettupati Village in Thevaram Union in Theni district displayed a poster informing that they plan to boycott the local body election. A different reason was given by the people of Sanganakurkulam Village Panchayat in Tirunelveli district for boycotting the election. The reason was very simple. Two persons of different castes from the same village filed nomination for the same post, *i.e.* Village Panchayat President. One nomination was rejected for some valid reasons. People who supported the candidate whose nomination was rejected resolved to boycott the election.

It is disheartening to note here that even after 54 years of independence, people mainly in the rural areas, are not in a position to enjoy the basic needs. They try to request/insist/demand that the Government officials and representatives fulfil their demands but in vain. They find that the only weapon is to boycott the elections. At the same time people also misuse the tool of boycotting even for minor cases like rejection of nomination of their caste candidate. It is a paradox endemic to Indian democracy.

Party Alliance

The local bodies witnessed untold suspenses, and uncertainty over alliance parties, which faced the previous election (Assembly Election) in one umbrella but got split and came out of one group and formed a new alliance with parties against which it contested in the previous election. People (voters) have generally lost their confidence in the ideology of the parties as many parties have alliance with parties with contradictory ideologies. The parties which were part of the AIADMK-led front like, the PMK (Pattali Makkal Katchi), the Congress and the CPI(M) came out of the front and two *Dalit* parties — Pudhiya Tamizhagam (PT) and DPI also walked out of the DMK front. As the date for election was nearing, the Congress party emerged as a third front.

Major Observation in the Election

- The arrest of Mr. M. Karunanidhi, former Chief Minister of Tamil Nadu and the disqualification of Chief Minister J.Jayalalitha did not have any impact on the election campaign for local bodies.
- Both of them did not show keen interest in the election and were not involved directly. Campaigning was not so vigorous and in full swing as expected. It went off peacefully.
- There were a lot of incidents where nominations were filed by the political party members against the official candidate of the party. It created an embarrassing situation to the leading political parties.
- Consensus, supporting and encouraging relative candidates thereby neglecting political parties, influence of local people, caste and village control in electing and selecting candidates were observed.
- No political party took any action or raised its voice against the new methods of electing candidates like auctioning and lottery.
- No steps was taken against those people in the rural areas, particularly of Keeripatti, Pappapatti and Nattarmangalam of Madurai district and Kattanenthal in Virudhunagar district who boycotted the Election.
- Even the bureaucrats, social activists, and NGOs did not take any steps to create social harmony in the villages where caste conflict was observed. *Dalits* were prevented from filing nominations even for the reserved seats.
- The DMK party was very lethargic in campaign in the hope that they could win the election with majority support since during their period the representatives of local bodies at all levels had carried out a lot of activities successfully.

- The candidates who frequently changed alliance compromising on principles found it very difficult to understand the techniques to be adopted to win the election.

There was confusion over allotment of seats among the alliance parties. Many party men refused to withdraw or retire from the contest. The entry of the PT, the New Justice Party and Makkal Tamizh Desam at the last minute further complicated the situation. In some constituencies, the Congress Jananayaka Peravai also setup candidates against Congress nominees. Even though there was no dissidence in the Communist parties, the CPI(M) and the CPI were fighting each other in a few areas. In many Panchayat unions and municipalities the AIADMK fielded candidates in wards allotted to TMC, leading to fierce fight. The major problem in many centres was that the AIADMK men did not allow the TMC candidates to use the wall posters featuring J. Jayalalitha.

III. SYMBOLS, CANDIDATES AND CAMPAIGNING TECHNIQUES

It seemed to be a war of symbols in rural areas of Tamil Nadu since the ward members and village presidents were contesting as candidates without party affiliation. Independent symbols were allotted to them by the State Election Commission ranging from bow and arrow to spear and saw. So mostly symbolic expressions of violence were drawn on the outside walls of almost all the houses particularly on the mud walls of the thatched roof houses. The independents were much more visible this time as their symbols were comb, buckets, key, stove, grinder, glass, tumbler, Doa, screw nail, doll, walking stick, necktie and shirt.

Campaign Techniques

- A candidate in Chennai who was allotted the shirt symbol chose to hang shirts around his vehicle to drive home his symbol.

- Another candidate was seen carrying a lantern to popularise his symbol.
- One councillor aspirant whose symbol was a globe said that it suited him since he had been working on sustainable livelihood practices and there was no better symbol to ensure that his message reached the people.

The most preferred symbols of the independent candidates appeared to be, 'bow and arrow' in the Southern districts and 'truck' and 'lighthouse' in the Northern districts, as several villages sport these symbols. There was a globe, an airplane and a lighthouse right at the doorstep of the villages. An interesting scene till a day before the election was that in the villages where there was not even a single street light there were huge cutouts of clocks and bulbs with airplane symbols. An independent candidate in a remote village made no promises of bringing an airplane to the hamlet. But the village would fly high if you vote for the airplane, he remarked.

A Unique Independent

There were different types of methods for campaigning for votes. Some among them were distinguished and noteworthy. Here are some examples. There is no crowd, nor do any vehicle follows him. A staunch supporter of the DMK, he refused a ticket offered by the party and preferred to contest independently. Mr. Manoharan of Sivagangai was unique in his campaigning technique. His moped had been transformed into a mini-campaign vehicle. The yellow flag sporting his symbol, the coconut palm, was seen flying near the handlebar where he had fixed a loudspeaker. He is dressed in *dhoti* and shirt and he stops at public places and starts his campaign wherever he thinks appropriate and effective. He has a flair for language and is able to give a very interesting speech. He is confident that his youngest daughter Rajathi will become a collector as she wishes. For she has come first in her class upto the VIII standard. He says that, if the people vote for him, he will serve them; otherwise he will do it through his daughter.

Different Types of Candidates

Local elections have become so easy and casual that, in the present election, candidates of different kinds contested. Some of them are listed below.

	Type of Candidate	Position	Place/District
1.	College Student	Mayor-Councillor	Chennai
2.	Blind man	District Councillor	Karur
3.	Village Priest's daughter	Councillor	Chidambaram
4.	Prisoner	Ward member	Tirunelveli
5.	Mother and daughter	Councillor	Kanyakumari
6.	Father and son	Chairman	Srivilliputhur
7.	Elder brother and Younger brother	Town Panchayat Councillor	Madurai
		Town Panchayat Chairman	Theni
		Town Panchayat Chairman	PCpatty,Theni
8.	Mother-in-law and daughter-in-law	Village President	Dindigul
		Town Panchayat Councillor	Kumbakonam
9.	Sisters	Village President	Kanyakumari
10.	President and clerk	Village President	Ramanathapuram
11.	Members from SHG women	Village President	Madurai
		Village President	Dindigul etc.
		Village ward member	Many districts
12.	Dissidents against party official candidate	Except Mayor at all level	Many places
13.	Young unmarried girls/boys	Ward member/ Councillor	Many Places
		Village President	
14.	Member from opposite party	District Councillor	Salem
15.	Dismissed president	Village President	Nagerkoil
16.	TADA detainee	Mayor-Councillor	Tirunelveli
		Ward Member	,,
		Town Panchayat Councillor	,,

(Contd...

	Type of Candidate	Position	Place/District
17.	Local rowdies	Mayor-Councillor	Madurai
		Ward Member	,,
		Town Panchayat Councillor	,,
18.	Friend of local *dada*	Councillor	Chennai etc.
		Ward Member	,,
19.	Sister of local rowdy	Village President	Tirunelveli
		Ward Member	,,
20.	Sourashtra citizen	Mayor-Councillor	Tirunelveli
21.	Mother of six month old baby	Councillor	Kanyakumari
22.	Ex-MLA	Town Panchayat Chairman	Sivagangai
23.	7 Women in a ward	Councillor	Devadanapatty
24.	Man become woman	Village President	Santhankulam
25.	Teacher	Municipal Chairman	Kanyakumari
26.	Husband and Wife	Town Panchayat Chairman	Arcot
		Councillor	Salem
		Village President	Melur
27.	Handicapped person	Mayor	Chennai
28.	Father-in-law and Son-in-law	Municipal Ward	Chidambaram
29.	Scientist	Councillor-Mayor	Chennai
30.	Co-sisters	Town Panchayat Chairman	Pannaipuram
31.	Ex-district ward member	Village President	Muthalai
32.	Same family for 150 years	Village President	Usilampatty
33.	Drunkards association	Town Panchayat Councillor	Kannivadi

Some of these types of candidate were not seen in the previous elections.

Techniques Adopted for Canvassing for Votes

Supporters of a village Panchayat president at Kallipatti near Thuraiyur came up with a 'token' system for distributing snacks and tea to the voters. Accordingly, select voters were given the token after they had exercised their franchise. The supporters were on great demand among the villagers. Many supporters conducted demonstrations with model ballots in front of the polling station.

Due to Cloudy Firmament, the Candidates were in Distress

The candidates regretted that the local body election may be affected by rains. After the election date was announced, the election officers were busy with their duties. Filing of nomination, scrutiny, withdrawal of nomination came to an end. The candidates also willingly engaged themselves in election campaign. Due to drizzling, the candidates were in distress. It did affect the election work.

Campaigning Activities were in Full Swing

The candidates from various political parties contesting for various posts met important persons in the city, elderly people and the committee administrators for support. Party candidates expected the former and the current Chief Ministers of Tamil Nadu for campaigning in support of their party candidates, but both of them didn't oblige. In spite of this fact, local administrators and party members willingly immersed themselves in the campaign. The party candidates started their campaign along with their supporters. Central Ministers and the former Tamil Nadu Assembly speaker also took part in the election campaign for collecting votes. A Congress candidate started his campaign without any dharna and extra expenditure. The Congress party leader also took part in this campaign. Other political parties also actively participated.

The Candidates Hunting Votes by Using the Names of Relationship

The candidates who contested for the post of Municipal Chairman, in Virudhunagar Municipality introduced a new type of election campaign. They were seeking votes by using the names of relationship. One of the candidates, who contested for the post of Ward member, started his campaign even before filing nomination. The women who contested for post in villages and corporations depended upon their husbands. If anybody asked how they would implement the scheme, they simply replied that their husband will give directions. Only the women who had experience in the previous election came with courage to contest in the election.

Woman Conducted Exhibition on Achievements

Kasthuri was already elected member of the 28th ward in 1996 election in Kumbum Municipality. She was to contest in the 2001 election too for the post of Ward member. She adopted a new method to attract the voters. She conducted photo exhibition among the voters, to show her five year achievements. Though she did not post any greater achievements (developmental works) than the other Ward members, the way she expressed it was very amazing.

The Songs of MGR and Rajini used by Contestants

For election campaign, the songs of MGR and actor Rajinikant were used by DMK, AIADMK, Congress and all parties. The famous songs of MGR 'Nerukku Neray', 'Thoonkathe Thambi Thoonkathe', 'Naan Aanaiyittal' were used by the AIADMK. The Congress candidates also used MGR songs for their campaign. Rajini fans, who boycotted the election, played the songs of Rajni 'Raman Aanda Enna, Ravanan Aanda Enna?' By this they expressed their dejection. The political parties used dubbed songs with film song tunes seeking votes from voters. Though it may sound ridiculous to hear, the political party leaders felt that it was their tool of success.

Printing Rate Increased Three Times

The rates for poster printing increased three-fold during the election. The wall posters had their own value. They attracted the voters more than other types of advertisements. So the candidates were very particular to advertise their election symbols. So the wages for printing increased three-fold. There were plenty of distinguished techniques adopted by the candidates which are totally different from the past experience.

Interesting Techniques Adopted for Attracting the Voters

Briyani and Booze to Ture Voters

There were a number of interesting aspects of electioneering during the election held in the year 2001 for local bodies which were not practised by candidates and political parties earlier. Some of them are:

- Different strategies were adopted with impurity and in open defiance of the election code and moral ethics.
- Money, as usual, topped the list of items given to voters. There was an announcement that each voter would be given Rs.50. A candidate from T. Kallupatti, Madurai district said that he urged the people that if they had 4 votes they could come and collect Rs. 200 immediately. His rival went a little further and gave Rs.75 per vote. But a genuine candidate who could not offer such amount told the voters to get the money from both of them but vote for him.

A lady from Usilampatti in Madurai district informed the reporters that she was given Rs.100 for her single vote by a candidate who was contesting for village Panchayat and a day after, she was given Rs.150 by another candidate (rival).

- Some candidates in Melur Municipality offered betel with sandalwood and kumkum to the voters asking them to vote for their symbol.
- Some candidates gave briyani in packets and requested the voters to vote for them.
- Some treated their voters to the spirit that cheers. One from Kalayanallur in Tiruvenlveli district supplied men voters with Indian made foreign liquor (MIFL).
- One candidate from Palani in Dindigul district supplied his own variety of liquor to all men voters.
- Some candidates slaughtered goats and treated their voters to a feast on the eve of the polls along with mini bottles of liquor (mostly Indian made Foreign Liquor).
- Election manifestos were missing in almost all the areas. No plan, promises, and list of problems the candidates intended to solve if they were elected. Just imagine what would be the fate of local administration for the next 5 years.

IV. VIOLENCE BEFORE, DURING AND AFTER POLLING

Before Election

Immediately after the announcement of election dates and the finalization of symbols for the candidates, the election fever reached its peak and cut-throat competition was witnessed in several places. Drawing of symbol on the walls was considered a very important technique in campaigning. Hence each candidate tried to occupy maximum space. In this stiff competition of occupying space violence was witnessed. At Salem, in corporation 39th ward the candidates' husbands resorted to violence, attacked each other and both of them were hospitalized. In another incident, when a party cadre came out against the party decision and contested as an independent, the party candidate and his family members (including women) came as a gang and assaulted the candidate. The injured candidate was hospitalized in Salem.

In Chennai, the DMK candidate of 88th ward went out for propaganda. At that time, the AIADMK candidate and his supporters resorted to violence and assaulted the auto driver. When the DMK candidate interfered in this dispute he too was also assaulted; and, his wife, who came to rescue her husband, was also assaulted. In Nellai, at Pallaipattu Village there were differences of opinion among the people of three hamlets in connection with the election of the president. A representative belonging to Puthia Tamizhagam exchanged heated words during the meeting convened in this connection. Later he was found dead with his throat was cut. Police arrested three men belonging to the man's hamlet.

In Ramanathapuram district, Kadaladi Union, A. Punavasal Village, both DMK and AIADMK party candidates filed their nomination. The supporters of each candidate entered into violent activities during the campaign and one person was butchered and two persons were seriously injured and hospitalized. In Erode Municipality, an independent woman candidate of 22nd ward received a phone call. The candidate was asked to withdraw by an unknown person who threatened over phone to murder her. In Erode, Senthamangalam Town Panchayat, the TMC candidate was beaten when he visited an area for seeking votes. The area people prevented his entry and demanded withdrawal of his nomination. In Dindigul district, Natham Town Panchayat, 4th ward, women candidates, tried to influence one another to withdrawn. As nobody came forward to withdraw, one candidate and her supporters entered into the residence of a rival candidate and assaulted the candidate and her whole family. Three persons were arrested in this incident. In Erode, a woman candidate was attacked with acid and sustained burn injuries. An unidentified person threw a bottle containing acid on her at night and escaped. In Ramnad, an AIADMK candidate's shop was burnt down. His timber yard was completely burnt.

In Virudhunagar during the voting time, DMK and AIADMK supporters entered into a dispute in connection with canvassing for votes. As the wordy dispute became serious four persons received cut injuries and were hospitalized. In Madurai district Nattarmangalam Village Panchayat, the President's position was reserved for SC woman. The dominant community of Nattarmangalam/Keeripatty banned the contest. But a *Dalit* woman bravely came forward to file her nomination. Following this, the dominant caste members grouped together and entered into the habitation of the *Dalits*, pelted stones on their houses and resorted to violence. *Dalit* children were affected in the incident. In spite of filing a complaint with the police, the police failed to take any steps to arrest the culprits.

In Devakotai, when the symbol of a candidate was drawn on his house wall, the owner got angry and abused the culprits. At that time a bypasser argued with the house owner. In a clash between them the house owner was murdered. In Paramakudi, the office-cum-residence of MP Sri Malaichamy was attacked by a gang. In Srivilliputhur the DMK candidate for municipal chairperson Sri Thamaraikani's car was damaged in an attack by AIADMK cadres. The AIADMK party cadres objected to the DMK candidates displaying the photo of MGR and canvassing for himself. The son of the candidate who is the AIADMK MLA was also involved in this incident. The DMK MLA Parithi Ilam Valuthi was attacked by a gang belonging to Johnpandian's group. The MLA complained that he received phone calls saying that he was going to be murdered. So he sought police protection for his life. The High Court ordered to provide police protection to him. A tea shop owned by an AIADMK cadre who contested for the president's position of Periyakulam Panchayat was gutted completely.

AIADMK and independent candidates exchanged words near Tharapuram Ponnapuram Village Panchayat. When the independent candidate's supporters were engaged in canvassing near the polling booth, the AIADMK candidate's supporters objected. Both groups resorted to violence using knives and iron rods. Two persons received knife injuries and were hospitalised. It was reported that the AIADMK candidate compelled the *Dalit* people to cast their vote to a particular symbol and so the independent candidate's supporters quarrelled with him. In Thirupasethi, during the pasting of posters on walls, two groups from the DMK and the AIADMK resorted to violence. One was murdered and another sustained knife injuries. In Dindigul district, Thottanuthu Village an independent candidate's supporters painted his symbol on the wall of individuals house. The house owner objected to the same as the symbol was drawn without his permission. But the supporters of the candidate assaulted the house owner and threatened him also. In Vilampur of Madurathakam area during the poll, the DMK and the AIADMK supporters blamed each other for their mischievous campaign and attacked each other with iron rods and wooden clubs. One person belonging to PMK was murdered.

Polling Percentage

Voting percentage throughout Tamil Nadu according to the State Election Commission was above 66 per cent (63.5). In Chennai it was very low accounting for 36.11 per cent. In some districts, especially Ariyalur, Thirvannamalai and Pudukkottai the percentage of polling was 70-75. For various reasons in the first phase of repolling was ordered in 255 booths. Counting of votes cast in two phases started on 21st October morning in the midst of tight security.

Admissible Persons

Those who were eligible to enter the counting stations were:

Panchayat Ward Member	:	Candidates with only one agent
Panchayat President	:	Candidates with 2 agents
Union Councillor	:	Candidates with 4 agents
District Panchayat Councillor	:	Candidates with 5 agents

Any excess agent was to be sent out by the officials responsible for counting of votes.

Strict Rules and Regulations for Candidates and Agents

There were a number of rules for counting as shown hereunder:

- Candidates and agents concerned should be present at the counting centre at 7.00 a.m.
- Candidates and agents would be permitted only if they came with identity cards. Umbrellas, match boxes, hand sticks, cigarettes, beedis and ink pens were not permitted.

Tight Security Arrangement was Made

- A secret camera and TV was placed in the counting centre.
- Police in civilian clothes were present both inside and outside the station.
- Strict action would be taken against people indulging in violence.

First Phase Poll

It was observed from the total nominations received for the election that except for the panchayat ward members, all other post had drawn a relatively low number of nominations revealing lack of enthusiasm among the voters in local panchayat administration. The final list of candidates against the number of seats was given in Table 3.3.

Election Held

The first phase of polling in the local body election in Tamil Nadu passed off peacefully on 16th. Even in the sensitive areas identified by the police the scene was calm and the polling took place in an orderly manner except for minor skirmishes in some places in some districts. The polling generally started on a low key in most of the areas and picked up later. In some places 70 per cent of the votes had been cast before noon. More women were at the polling booths than men and the women stood quietly, sometimes for hours to cast their votes. The recently included voters, the young boys and girls, cast their votes for the first time very enthusiastically.

Table 3.3 : Final List of Candidates contesting in the election for 2001

	Total Places	Nomination Received	Rejected	Withdraw	Unopposed	Remaining Postings	Candidates
V.P.Ward member	97377	286277	4120	26040	15133	82085	240984
Pt.Un.Ward member	12609	69372	1630	19352	581	12023	47809
Dt.Pt.Ward member	6564	38722	1001	11678	72	6492	25971
Tn.Pt.Ward member	9771	46802	1195	9129	707	9032	35771
Tn.Pt. President	669	5229	249	2085	7	602	2888
Municipal Councillors	3392	21209	633	4616	42	3349	15918
Municipal Chiarman	102	1094	75	481	—	102	538
Corporation Councillors	474	4594	193	1346	—	474	3055
Corporation Mayor	6	116	26	30	—	6	60
Total	431560	9,313	4,77407	76,170	16,544	1,14,819	3,75,380

Source : Release of State Election Commission.

Peaceful in the Sensitive Area

Melavalavu Panchayat which was identified as a most sensitive Panchayat, experienced no trace of disturbance. There were two minor skirmishes in the Piramalaiakallar ward when polling began. Despite the careful steps and tight security there were some untoward incidents during the polling like:

Confusion in the Voters List

- There was incompatibility between the official electorate list and that of the polling agents. Printing errors and gender mix up in some parts of Tamil Nadu marked the first phase of local polls.

- There were complaints of deletions from the electoral rolls including those who had voted in the last six elections and even those who had elector photo identity card.
- There were some printing errors regarding the gender of voters.
- The officials responded that this confusion was because of the SEC order to accept Form 16 for inclusion in the electoral list virtually till the end of the previous month.
- There was confusion at the official level itself. Though the SEC had announced that anyone of the identity proofs (like family card, driving licence, etc.) should be produced by the voters, several voters did not bother to bring any of them. While some officials insisted on the proof and turned away a number of voters some didn't.
- The voter turnout was 56 per cent in the urban areas and 52 per cent in rural areas.
- Chennai witnessed unprecedented incidence of electoral malpractices.

Violence Mars

1. Bogus Voting

- The election officials and opposition parties pointed the finger at the ruling AIADMK as complaints of bogus voting and intimidation of voters poured in from Chennai. Gangs had come to the booths in several autorickshaws and vans and threatened the election agents and chased away the voters waiting to vote.

2. Booth Capturing

- Polling was stopped in 4 booths in the city following complaints of booth capturing.
- A repoll was ordered in seven booths in the Chennai Corporation. The same was ordered in many booths at the district level.

3. *Symbol did not Tally with Names*

- A repoll was also ordered in four village Panchayat wards of which two were in Kancheepuram.
- In one case each in Cuddalore and Virudhunagar districts and 3 cases in Vellore district the symbols did not tally with the names of the candidates.

4. *Police Firing*

- The police fired in the air at two villages, Veeracholam Panchayat in Virudhunagar district and Thayampalayam near Gommudipoondi in Thiruvallur district to disperse clashing groups. But none was injured in the firing according to Home Secretary Mr. Naresh Gupta.

5. *Police Lathi Charge*

- The police opened fire in the air and lathi charged in the Kambar Mallur Panchayat Union to disperse a group which tried to force the voters to vote for a particular party in Dharmapuri.

There was an incident of suspension of polling in a booth at Palamedu, Madurai district following violence and clashes in which a police vehicle was damaged and two policemen were severely injured.

Voters Blocked Roads

Several voters in some districts like Coimbatore, Cuddalore, Tirunelveli, Kanyakumari blocked roads in protest against deletion of their names from the voters list.

Stone thrown at Polling Booth

A group of voters whose names were not found in the voters list started throwing stones at the polling booth at Avudiyapuram in Virudhunagar district.

Complaints were Lodged by Political Parties with SEC

The DMK president and former Chief Minister of Tamil Nadu, Mr. M. Karunanidhi claimed that 353 booths in Chennai were captured. He also commented that the election was not conducted in a free and fair and democratic manner. Mr. Ramesh Chennithala lodged a complaint with the SEC as there was no response from the Police Commissioner Mr. K. Muthukaruppan, stating: "There was widespread intimidation in many booths in Chennai including Thiruvanmiyur, Adayaar and Mylapore.

Opinion of Home Secretary

In response to the complaints lodged by many politicians, the Home Secretary said the polling was peaceful barring, some minor incidents including nine cases of attack and two cases of group clashes.

DGP's View

Mr. B.P. Nailwal stated that there were 28 incidents including two cases of police opening fire, two instances of mild lathi charges, two cases of arson and 12 complaints of assault.

Repolling Ordered in 130 Booths

Due to the unprecedented violence in the first phase of local bodies election, the SEC ordered repolling in 130 booths and instructed the police to resort to firing, if necessary to ensure peaceful polling in the second phase on 18th October.

Second Phase Poll

Dalits were prevented from voting in the premises of Common temple. In some villages in Rajapalayam, the upper caste people had objected to the SCs voting in the booth arranged in the temple premises which led to tension in the village. Receiving information, the officials rushed to the spot and after a lengthy negotiation setup a polling booth in a thatched hut near the noon meal centre where polling took place peacefully.

Disqualified Voters Prevented

In one of the wards in Rajapalayam, about 700 voters, who were not allowed to vote because their names were missing from the voters list prevented the others from voting. The Tehsildar rushed there and allowed the people to vote on the basis of the old electoral list.

Clash over Detention of Genuine Voter Mistakenly

A clash took pace at Palayapalayam in Virudhunagar district following the detention of a voter on suspicion that he had come to cast a bogus vote. But later, on verification, he was found to be a genuine voter.

Women Set Fire to a Ballot Box

A women from Tuticorin district surrendered before the police after setting fire to a ballot box at Kayathar. It was reported that a group of voters went to a booth at Thottampatti village. The presiding officer told the voters that they should go to Sevalpatti booth to cast their votes. Senthurakani, sister of Sermakani who was a candidate for the village president's post, objected to this and asked that they be allowed to vote in the Thottampatti booth. Since the officer refused to budge, Senthurakani seized the ballot box and, poured kerosene on it and set fire to it charring all the ballots in the box. Polling was stopped immediately Senthurakan later surrendered before the Pasuvanthunai police.

Polling Affected for One Hour

Stoppages are very common in many places in every district for various reasons including very minor ones. Some supporters of two candidates clashed at a booth in Kailasapuram in Thuthukudi which affected polling for one hour. In another place two groups clashed with each other over missing names and two persons were injured and a windscreen on a car was damaged. This disrupted polling for an hour.

Mob Ransacked

There was an incident in which a mob ransacked the polling station in Ariyalur where a youth, son of one of the candidates for the village Panchayat was assaulted by the supporters of an other candidate. As the news spread some supporters of the youth ransacked the polling station and took away the ballot boxes. The Collector ordered repolling after the confirmation of the incident from reliable sources.

Firing in Chennai and Virudhunagar

Police opened fire to disperse a mob involved in violence in two important places in Chennai and Virudhunagar.

The Ballot Box was Burnt

In Sukkampatti of Neiveli Village Panchayat in Musiri Union when the polling came to an end, the supporters of AIADMK are said to have cast bogus votes in the polling booth in Iukkampatti allotted for men. Suspected DMK supporters entered the polling booth and took away the ballot boxes and burnt them.

Polling was Stopped as Symbol was found Changed

There was an incident of stopping the poll because the symbol was changed in Meenakshipuram near Mangalam under Madurai district.

New Chief Minister of Tamil Nadu Stood in Queue for Voting

Sri. O. Panneer Selvam, the Chief Minister of Tamil Nadu whose native place is Periyakulam in Theni district, went to the polling centre at R.C. Middle School at 8.25 a.m. He stood in the queue for 15 minutes along with the other voters before casting his vote.

Booth Slips Served as Voter Identification Evidence

According to the Collector in Nagappattinam, more than 50 per cent of the voters exercised their votes only by producing booth slips issued by the supporters of candidates, despite the fact that the State Election Commission announced that voters would not be allowed to cast their votes if they failed to produce any of the 18 specified documents.

Police Arranged Peaceful Repolling in Sensitive Booths

Two booths in Chellampatti Union —Munduvelanpatti and Thathampatti in Usilampatti Taluk of Madurai district— which witnessed unprecedented violence in the first phase of election had peaceful repolling due to heavy police security arrangements.

Repolling

It was reported that the repolling ordered in 306 booths in the state and 6 more in Chennai passed off peacefully in the midst of tight security but the turnout was very low. At the same time, the Director General of Police Mr. B.P. Nailwal, described the polling as reasonably peaceful unlike the first phase of polling for the local bodies election. In general, according to the SEC, of the 80,000 booths less than 500 reported problems.

Total Percentage

The total polling percentage during the two phases stood at 64.66 per cent.

Dalit *Boycott Repoll at Konarkulam*

At the end of the present election, in the second phase of the election, *Dalits* of four hamlets under the Vadavallanadu village Panchayat not only boycotted the repoll held at two booths in Konarkulam but prevented voters belonging to other communities from participating in it. But it did not take a communal twist.

Violence

MLA Supporters Kill a Voter

The following is an incident of poll related violence in the second phase, in one of which a mob is said to have lobbed grenades at voters at Pathinettampadian. It was reported that while polling was in progress at Sivanayakapuram near Muthukulathur, the supporters of an MLA came there in a lorry and tried to attack the polling booth but the local people resisted it. The mob in the lorry then attacked the villagers and threw bombs at them and escaped from the spot. A noon meal organiser, Kesevan, aged 45, was killed.

DMK Candidate Arrested for Serving Liquor to Voters

In Tirunelveli district one Mr. Muthusamy from Kadayanallur Panchayat Union, who was contesting for a ward member, was arrested by the police on charge of serving liquor to voters.

Group Clash

Two groups of persons contesting for village president's post in two Panchayats, *i.e.* Keela Thiru Vallanallur and Pombukovil

Sandhai clashed with each other over a polling dispute. Twenty five shops and a house were damaged during the clash.

End of Polling

At the end of repolling for the second phase, there were skirmishes in some parts of Tamil Nadu and boycott in some villages. Tension prevailed in some districts. The district administration was able to manage them with the help of the police.

Complaints Lodged by DMK and Congress to SEC regarding Violence

These two parties petitioned the SEC that ballot papers with thumb impressions and pencil marks be declared invalid during the counting, particularly in Chennai, where booth capturing occurred.

Counting Process

Once the repolling in 199 booths was over, done the local bodies election 2001 came to an end. The state administration prepared for the counting process which started on 21st of October. The SEC ensured adequate security for counting. Additional observers were posted for overseeing counting which commenced on October 21. The first results were released officially by the afternoon. Apart from that, the SEC had issued instructions that only candidates and authorized persons be allowed entry into counting centres. No one, irrespective of the position he or she held, was permitted inside. Also, even in the case of those allowed, they were checked by the police for possessing weapons or other prohibited materials. The SEC gave the assurance that suspect ballot papers would be closely scrutinized during the counting of votes in the local bodies election. When the opposition pleaded to ensure that bogus votes be rejected, it assured that strict instructions had been given that ballot papers not bearing the signature of polling officers and not stamped by the voters were to be rejected.

Tight security arrangement was made with one head constable and four constables posted at each counting centre.

- Wire mesh fencing was provided to all centres to separate the counting centres and to ensure additional security.
- Entry to the counting stations was restricted to the persons carrying the identity cards issued by the Commission.
- Candidates and their agents were briefed on the arrangements and asked to cooperate with the officials deputed for counting.

Though there was unprecedented violence during the local bodies poll, the SEC stopped that this was not new to any democracy and that as the democratic process is evolving, people who form part of the system will become mature. He cited the USA to substantiate his view. He was optimistic that future elections would not witness the same degree of violence. He also said that it was purely because of lack of adequate security personnel. Though there could be isolated instances of polling personnel colluding with some parties, this can't be generalized. But actually this has occurred in all elections, which cannot be justified.

Violence Mars Counting

There were a number of incidents which occurred during the counting. Some highlights are: In Madurai volunteers of AIDMK and DMK disputed over two votes and so counting was stopped. The DMK wanted the votes declared invalid. But the AIDMK demanded that they be credited to its nominee. The issue was referred to the SEC which ordered resumption of counting process for the votes for Deputy Mayor and to declare the DMK candidate victory. The returning officer, the Corporation Commissioner, fled the counting hall in the face of mob violence. Volunteers of both parties stormed the hall. The police resorted to force to restore order. Police resorted to lathi charge to disperse the crowd which hurled stones on the Panchayat union office of Karur in Dharmapuri district.

V. ANALYSIS OF ELECTION RESULTS

Sixty-seven per cent of the total candidates were elected unopposed. Though the AIADMK alliance won the majority of the seats at all levels, it has not won seats more than what the DMK won during the 1996 elections. The DMK has lost in many places where they had won in the 1996 elections. In 1996 the DMK won the Mayor's seats in Chennai, Madurai, Nellai and Salem and the TMC captured Trichy and Coimbatore. But in the present election Nellai, Coimbatore and Salem went to the AIADMK. The DMK was able to capture only Chennai and Madurai. The TMC was able to retain Trichy in this election too. It was revealed by the politicians that the AIADMK lost Madurai only because the CPI(M) broke the alliance with the AIADMK. The PMK has shifted its alliance with the major political parties in every election. This party, led by Dr. Ramadass, a political organisation originally started as a caste organisation, was badly defeated in the local bodies election. It was defeated in the Salem Mayoral election by the AIADMK with which it had alliance in the Assembly elections. It has lost its influence and power in its own areas.The urgently formed third front party and the independent party MDMK were able to capture two municipal seats each whereby they could maintain their honour. The founder and the leader of PMK Dr. Ramdass cancelled the press meet organised earlier, following the bad defeat of his party.

The AIADMK has suffered an embarrassing situation. In the Chief Minister's hometown, Periyakulam, the DMK candidate won. There were surprising embarrassments and cheer for both the major parties in Tamil Nadu, namely the AIADMK and the DMK. They won where they did not expect and lost there where they were confident of warning. The forts of these parties were broken. For the AIADMK the biggest surprise was that in Virudhunagar district it could not win even a single municipality seat. TMC has not been able to improve its 1996 position. The Congress which went on its own was expected·to finish significantly. But this party was able to finish only a respectable third

Table 3.4 : Seats won by the parties in local bodies

	Held	AIADMK	BSP	BJP	CPI	CPI(M)	DMK	INC	MDMK	NCP	PMK	TMC	Inde
Dt Union and ward member	6489	2582	1	109	83	64	1411	135	130	-	300	503	1171
Dt Pt. ward member	654	369	-	10	12	6	134	11	7	-	33	65	7
Town Pt. Ward member	9023	2178	2	246	83	199	1902	176	185	-	159	538	3355
Town Pt. Chairman	601	198	-	22	4	14	143	20	13	-	7	50	130
Municipal councillor	3346	945	5	102	40	53	952	90	97	-	62	254	746
Municipal Chairman	102	34	1	6	1	1	34	3	2	-	2	9	9
Corporate Councillor	473	169	-	18	5	10	172	7	5	-	3	33	51
Important Mayor	6	3	-	-	-	-	2	-	-	-	-	1	-

Table 3.5 : Comparative Statement on the seats won by AIADMK, DMK, the major political parties

Corporation	Held	AIADMK	BSP/ NCP	BJP	CPI	CPI (M)	DMK	INC	MDMK	PMK	TMC	Inde
1 Chennai	154	67	-	3	1	1	61	2	1	1	14	3
2 Coimbatore	12	23	-	7	3	4	17	3	3	-	4	8
3 Madurai	12	22	-	2	1	5	27	1	-	-	5	9
4 Salem	60	27	-	1	-	-	18	-	-	2	3	9
5 Trichy	60	18	-	4	-	-	26	1	1	-	2	8
6 Tirunelveli	55	22	-	1	-	-	23	-	-	-	5	14
Total	473	169	-	18	5	10	172	7	5	3	33	51

after the two major fronts in most areas. Of the six corporations, where the DMK was mostly expected to win, the AIADMK alliance was able to gain — Salem and Tirunelveli. It established a huge lead in Madurai Corporation but it lost Chennai Corporation by a small margin. As far as municipalities are concerned both the DMK and the AIADMK were more or less equal. They secured 945 and 952 municipal seats respectively. Table 3.4 shows the seats won by the major political parties in Tamil Nadu, *i.e.* DMK, AIADMK at all levels. Table 3.4 shows that independents are more in number than candidates of some of the recognised political parties in Tamil Nadu. It was observed that independents made significant inroads into the territory of political parties in the local bodies election.

In the panchayat ward member category out of 6489 seats, independents won 1171 posts, *i.e.*, 18.04 per cent. As the chairperson has to be indirectly elected for the union council the independents got a price for their vote during the election of chairpersons and vice-chairpersons of the union councils. Horse trading became openly visible in this process. In the scenario of urban local bodies also, independents secured 37.18 per cent of the seats. Out of 9023 town panchayat ward member seats, independents secured 3355 posts. During the election of vice-chairperson of town panchayats the independents demanded huge amounts of money for their votes.

Fear of Abduction of Independents

The time between declaration of the results and indirect election for the Deputy Mayor, District Panchayat President, Panchayat Union Chairman, Vice-president, i.e., the duration, between 21 October and 31 October, was very crucial and thrilling for the independents. In some places, the councillors belonging to one political party were abducted by some other parties. The Cumbum Panchayat Union, the smallest in the state, has only four councillors. Both the major parties in Tamil Nadu, the DMK and the AIADMK, had two each. As there was not enough money and muscle power for the councillors belonging to the DMK to become chairman, the

AIADMK councillors Ms. Maheswari and Ms. Murugalakshmi brought the DMK councillors under their custody. Though there were parleys and intervention of the party district secretary the problem could not be settle solved.

Women SHGs — the New Entrants into the Local Bodies

Formation of women SHGs in rural areas of Tamil Nadu, with the objective of socio-economic development, has not only created social and economic awareness but also oriented women towards the political process. By attending Gram Sabha, the SHG members somewhat understood the structures and functions of local administration at village level and decided to get into the Panchayat bodies and make use of them for the common cause.

Accordingly, the provision of reservation opened an entry gate to them. In the last elections, most of the women candidates were not from the SHGs, but proxies of some elite groups. But witnessing the general performance of women representatives in village Panchayats, the SHGs opted for a better replacement by themselves contesting for presidents and ward member positions. The encouragement and the support rendered by some NGOs and voluntary organisations to SHG women to challenge the so-called, candidates with money, muscle, political and caste affiliations was good. In every district there was a network of NGOs which equipped the women in the elections —from generating awareness to fielding candidates from among SHG members. In Sivagangai district, through a network of Gram Iyakka, in three blocks, 150 positions of ward members and presidents were won by SHG members. In Theni district, under Vaigai network, 122 representatives for ward members, presidents and union councillors were won by SHG members. This phenomenon was noticed in other districts also.

Death of Candidates and Elected Representatives Before and After Elections

There were many instances of death of both candidates and elected representatives at all levels, both before and after the elections. A ward member elected from ward number 3 in Kandamannur Panchayat was found dead in the bus stand a day before taking oath.

Death of Elected Member before Declaration of the Result

Late. Mr. Paraman who contested for Panchayat union councillor from the DMK party, died of heart attack a day after the polling. The next day he was declared elected by a margin of 25 votes. The death of Paraman made the election officials conduct a by-election.

Sworn in with Feast and Boost-thanks Giving

An interesting scene was observed in Kokilapuram Panchayat in Cumbum Panchayat Union where Ms. Pasunkili was elected president. She supplied delicious varieties of dishes to the supporters immediately after taking charge. The total expenditure was equally shared by the elected ward members and district Panchayat president. All the representatives elected for village Panchayat assumed office on 25th October.

Awareness Programme for Village Panchayat at District Level

On a war footing, the state conducted a one day awareness programme on 7th November for all the village Panchayat presidents at the district headquarters under the leadership of the respective District Collector simultaneously throughout Tamil Nadu where they were briefed about the importance of the 73rd Amendment with regard to power decentralization, social justice, preserving bottom level democracy, women and *Dalit* welfare, provision of basic amenities and roles and responsibilities of the president.

The main aim of the one-day orientation was to create a new mindset among the newly elected village presidents. Development perception rather than differences of opinion was the emphasis in the one-day training programme. In addition to the importance of the 73rd Amendment and the concept of decentralization of power and responsibilities to the local bodies, emphasis was given to the presidents assuming more responsibilities rather than waiting for the revolution of power from the State Government. Welfare of *Dalits*, women and delivery of social justice to these marginalised sections were explained to them. Faculty members from Gandhigram Rural Institute, especially from the Department of Political Science and Development Administration, served as resource persons in many districts like Dindigul, Ramnad, Sivagangai, Pudukkottai and Villupuram.

The orientation programme for Dindigul district was conducted in Gandhigram Rural Institute itself with the active support of the Rajiv Gandhi Chair for Panchayati Raj Studies, Department of Political Science and Development Administration, Gandhigram Rural Institute, Gandhigram.

Indirect Election for Vice-President Position

This is the first time in the history of local bodies election that the indirect election of chairman and vice-chairman of the district panchayats etc., has aroused so much enthusiasm for both the major fronts that won almost equal number of seats at all levels. The independents emerged successful in many places. So those aspiring for these posts wooed the independents and kept them in safe custody so as to prevent their rivals from chasing their supporters. The aspirants took the independents to far away destinations, hill stations, tourist spots and Pilgrim centres. Some even found some hill areas on the Kerala-Tamil Nadu border for their 'guests'.

It was also said that the rate for councillors for their single vote in some places reached the level of Rs.2.00 lakhs and even advance amounts were paid to them by the aspiring candidates. Some independents who did not back any party were in the grip of fear that psychosis they may be abducted or kidnapped by the party candidates at anytime. For their own security the independents did not visit the union office till the finalisation of the election.

VI. MAJOR OBSERVATIONS

- Local bodies election has generated a great level of political awareness among the rural people leading to more contestants, both male and female.
- A new trend of auctioning Panchayat president's position was witnessed in several parts of Tamil Nadu like Madurai, Coimbatore, Salem and Sivagangai.
- Lottery method was also introduced in a village mainly for the village president post in Madurai district.
- Village community itself maintained a reservation system for different religious and caste groups on rotation basis by mutual agreement among different groups.
- A rare phenomenon was also observed—the president of village Panchayat has been from the same family for years together (in some places more than 150 years).
- The percentage of polling in rural areas was comparatively higher than in the urban areas.
- The traditional village committee in many Panchayats acted as a powerful deciding factor in selecting the Panchayat president unopposed.
- Consensus among the candidates was observed in many Panchayats with a village committee.
- The number of aspiring candidates who filed nomination for various posts was more compared to previous election, particularly in the case of ward members.
- Caste oriented political parties were sidelined by the people.
- Mayoral candidates were elected not based on their political affiliation but on the basis of their personality.
- Members and councillors were elected based on their personal quality and performance rather than party affiliation.
- Not many proxy candidates were fielded by the so called male dominant section or upper caste people. Women SHGs in the villages motivated and fielded some genuine candidates against the party candidates also.

- There were rivals within the same political party. Such dissident groups contested independently against their own political party candidates and won the election. It shows that people gave importance to individual character rather than political identity.
- Expenditure on election for a candidate for Panchayats ranged from 1 lakh to 4 lakhs, exceeding the official limit of Rs.10000.
- Money was spent for the purchase of individual votes and for maintaining the supporters from the day of nomination till the declaration of the results.
- Outright disbursement of money to the community leaders to influence their community vote bank was also observed.
- Money given by the candidates was spent on common properties like renovation of temple etc., as per the wishes of the village community.
- To reduce the number of competitors through negotiation money was given for the withdrawal of nomination.
- Apart from conventional methods of campaigning like wall posters, bit notices, big banners, cutouts, festoons and decorations, frequent visits to voters using many vehicles were witnessed in the election.
- Contrary to the earlier practice, in the present election women candidates with the support of women groups came out openly and went from visited door to door to canvass for votes.
- NGOs played a crucial role in generating voter awareness and providing guidelines for aspiring candidates and motivated them to win the election. NGOs conducted falicitatious for the elected representatives.
- Rigging during the polling and disturbance during the counting were witnessed in greater degree earlier.
- The leaders of the two important political parties, *i.e.*, Mr. M. Karunanidhi and Ms. J. Jayalalitha did not take much pain for campaigning.
- Two opposition party leaders (AIADMK and DMK) held

similar view with regard to the restoration of two-tier system in Tamil Nadu.

- The major topics that voters assumed would be highlighted by the DMK and the AIADMK during the election. *i.e.* the arrest of the DMK president and the stepping down of Ms. J. Jayalalitha, were not highlighted by both the parties.
- Even among the candidates of the same caste from a village people elected candidates based on characteristics like pro-people and service-mindedness.
- Candidates were close relatives of the majority of the voters in the rural areas (near and dear ones). This attracted all the voters to cast their votes to show their strength.
- In most of the places the polling percentage among women was higher than among man.
- The polling percentage was higher in Panchayat union than in the town Panchayats and municipal limits.
- Violence and even murderous events took place only between the supporters of candidates who contested for village Panchayat president and ward members.
- There was not much political party based violence in the rural areas.
- Though it was the second election for local bodies, rural voters found it very difficult to understand the symbols of independent candidates and the number of votes to be cast. There were too many ballot papers and too many candidates, contesting for the same ward too.
- The whole process was confusing as the rural people had to elect one district councillor for every 50,000 population. In addition to it, they had to elect a Panchayat union level member per 5000 votes. Then there was the village panchayat president. All these three were conducted on political party basis.
- Confusion was prevalent even at the ward level also, where there was a variation in the number of members to be elected from each ward.

- Each Panchayat has a minimum of two wards and maximum of five. The confusion arose because there were double member wards and triple member wards. The voters were confused over the number of votes to be cast and the number of ward members to be elected, various tiers and different colours of ballot papers. Both the Dravidian parties, the AIADMK and the DMK, had been taking about abolishing of the top tier, the District Panchayat Council. Even today voters don't clearly understand the role and functions of each tier.
- A point to be noted here is that earlier an awareness campaign was conducted among rural voters about the election procedures. But in the present election neither political parties nor election officials conducted this type of awareness.
- Till the election date was announced, most of the political parties did not take it very seriously. Even after the announcement of the dates, the court case and disqualification of Ms. Jayalalitha as Chief Minister diverted the attention of all the parties. But the days were running fast.
- All decisions were delayed by negotiation on alliance and seat adjustment among allied parties and allocation of symbols. Once the seat adjustment was over, almost all the parties faced the problem of dissidents, who contested against the official candidates of the same party.
- Since there was no time to sort out the problems and ask the dissidents to withdraw their candidature many contested against the party candidates. Party members at the grassroots level had doné preparatory work with voters in support of their candidature confident that they would be allotted the seat. When it was allotted to an alliance party the number of dissidents began to increase.
- Middle class families generally did not accept the money given by the candidates for voting.
- Though election for village Panchayat is not on party basis,

we could see the mobilization of political parties in support of a particular candidate and in some places a member from a particular party was motivated and party people involved themselves in the campaign activities.

- There were some cases of rejection of nomination just because of the failure to fill up the nomination paper properly following the simple procedure.
- Missing of names in the voters list, error in the mentioning of sex, spelling mistake in the name of the candidates, change of father's name created confusion and the victims had to rush from pillar to post to justify their eligibility/ qualification to contest.
- A large number of voters were unable to cast their vote due to the missing of their names from the list.
- Even those who had voter identity cards could not cast their votes because of their names were missing from the voter list.
- There were some cases of equal votes polled by two contestants the selection decided by adopting lottery method.
- Repolling in both phases of the election was more in number than in the previous election.
- Among the sitting presidents who contested again, the majority were defeated.
- Young contestants were more in number from both the sexes.
- Though in the Assembly election, people rejected caste politics, it was observed that the majority of the independent candidates, unopposed candidates, very particularly the dissidents (member of political party contesting against the party's official candidate independently), who won the local bodies election were backed by their caste people.
- Caste based votes have made the candidates win.
- Political analysts should give more attention to the emergence of such caste based politics to preserve real democracy at the grassroots level.
- Tamil Nadu voters, in general are not mature enough to

vote in local bodies election. It was observed in the election that people voted for a particular party for Mayor and the same voters have selected Councillors or Ward Members from the opposite party or supported independent candidates.

- Voters are not consistent in their decision to support a particular party for both positions, *i.e.* Chairman, Vice-Chairman and Mayor and Deputy Mayor. This created a big problem after the direct election in almost all the areas.
- The majority of the independent candidates were elected because of the direct support of caste based organisations. They will be expected to develop a particular community rather than work for the development of the whole village.
- Violence that occurred during the election process in Tamil Nadu was compared very frequently with that in Bihar by all the media.
- The death of the founder and president of Tamil Manila Congress, Mr. G.K. Mooppanar, rendered the campaign not serious as far as voters and supporters of the TMC were concerned.
- As in any other election even in the local bodies election there were a number of incidents of voters boycotting the election for different reasons.
- At the village Panchayat president and ward member level the good performance of the existing leader, the support of caste organisations, the role of the village committee, the influence of money and muscle power played a crucial role in the (s)election of the candidates.
- New types of election/selection like lottery method, auctioning, rotation were also adopted by the voters in Tamil Nadu.
- The disheartening incidents of preventing *Dalits*, both men and women, from filing nomination took place in the local bodies election in Tamil Nadu.

Prevention of *Dalits* from Filing Nomination

The name may be different, such as boycott or prevention of *Dalits* people from election, but the motive is the same. Three panchayats in Usilampatti Union of Madurai district have not voted in the local bodies election, because no nomination was filed for the post of Panchayat president or member in Keeripatti, Pappapatti and Nattarmangalam and in Kottakachiyendal Panchayat in Virudhunagar district and Katoor in Namakkal district. One of the disturbing incidents which happened in the present local bodies poll was that in some places, particularly in the southern part of Tamil Nadu, *Dalits* were prevented from filing nomination, that too in villages where the posts were reserved for *Dalits*.

In two village Panchayats of Madurai district, Usilampatti Taluk, Keeripatti and Pappapatti, where the existing reservation for local polls was extended for another five years, the local committees ignored the initiatives to hold elections. Talks at the RDO level failed. The adamant attitude of these villagers prevented the administration from holding the local body election in 1996. Subsequently also people did not come forward to file nominations. This is the tenth time that the people did not let the Government conduct the election.

The Main Reasons

- Keeripatti and Pappapatti are among the four important areas of Kallanadu (country of Kallar community).
- Both Keeripatti and Pappapatti are villages where the temple of the dominant community of this are is situated. It is considered to be the 'Thevar Fort' by other villagers. Being a 'Thevar Fort' traditionally they don't accept a *Dalit* as their leader.
- Pappapatti village is the one where the late Mr. P.K. Mookaiah Thevar, the follower of Pasumpon Muthuramalinga Thevar, whom the Thevar community throughout India worships as God, was born.

- P.K. Mookaiah Thevar had been the President of All India Forward Block for long years till his death and he had been MLA and MP for several terms.
- One of the main temple of Kallar community, where they decide their relationships—matrimonial alliances—is situated in this village.
- A Village President has a special role to perform in the village festivals. So, Thevars won't accept a *Dalit* as President as it involves traditional temple honour and prestige.
- Thevars are numerically dominant and SCs are less in number. So they cannot tolerate the dominance of a minority community.
- Unless it is declared a 'general seat' there is no possibility of conducting the local bodies poll.
- Keeripatti has the notoriety of chasing away the official who came to issue voter identity cards in the previous election.
- The District Collector assured them of sanctioning projects/ programmes worth 2 crores if they allow the Government to conduct local bodies election. But the villagers flatly rejected the offer.
- People said that they are ready to undergo any hardships to declare the village a general seat and ready to lose anything for that.
- They feel that the state has done a great injustice to them by reserving their village panchayat for SC. The Government has not changed it to a general seat despite their repeated requests in the last five years.
- They also admit that they find things very difficult because of the absence of Village President.
- They say that the wont prevent *Dalits* from filing nomination, if they want to do so and claim that the *Dalits*, themselves dont have interest in contesting the election.

Opinion of *Dalits*

- The majority of the *Dalits* say that they have been maintaining good relationship with Thevars which they don't want to wreck by contesting the election.
- They also admit that they do not have interest in contesting the election in the village against the wish of the dominant caste.
- They also say that village may be declared a general seat so that their harmonious relationship could be maintained.
- During the temple festival, the village chief is given first respect. But usually the chief would be from 'Kallars'. If anybody from the SC community becomes Village President it would be very difficult and embarrassing situation for the SCs also, the *Dalits* feel.

Just because an SC becomes President the Kallars can't stop worshipping their God and cannot give first respect to the SC in the place of a Kallar chief. So both the communities are not interested in an SC becoming President.

Keeripatti Village

- It is situated 6 km away from Usilampatti.
- 1550 voters are in the 1996 voter list.
- *Dalits* are only 300 voters whereas Kallars are more than 1000.
- Government has committed a blunder of not conducting a survey accurately. Had it collected data from door-to-door during the census it would not have assigned Keeripatti for SC people asserted.
- The government has deliberately allotted this village for SCs just to insult the Kallar community, the village committee felt.
- There is no practice of untouchability in both the villages despite the fact that SCs are in minority.

- Most of the SCs are landless labourers depending fully on the lands of Kallars for their livelihood.
- Preference has been given to SCs in the celebration of the Kula God in the village for generations.
- When there was a caste clash around Usilampatti, wherein other caste people tried to attack SCs it was this village people who saved the lives and properties of SCs.
- It is the Kallars in Keeripatti who have allotted their land for the construction of group houses for SCs.
- SC people, it seems, have some intention and interest to file nomination but they show reluctance just because the dominant caste group, the Kallars whom rely on for livelihood want it to be declared a general seat and have fought for it.
- Both of them want it to be a general seat so that their relationship could be properly maintained.
- They don't want any programme/project for the welfare or development of the village unless it is converted to a general seat.
- No matter how many years they are firm that they will not accept an SC as their leader.
- SC people will also not be able to contest the election against the wish of Kallars.
- The procedure followed for allocation of SC reservation was not made clear to the people (Kallars).
- People unnecessarily believe that the Government has reserved the seat for SCs deliberately to insult the Kallars.
- Government officials don't perform their duty in such a manner as to convince the people.
- Political parties and Government don't have commitment or interest in it.
- Collector/RDO talks of this topic with people only when election comes, then forget it. So people has developed an anomaly against the Government.
- People don't want any media people to expose the dispute in village to the world unnecessarily.

Mr. Narasingam of Pappapatti Panchayat, an SC, came forward to file the nomination with the support of the District Collector. But because he was half an hour late on the last date of filing nomination, an AIADMK supporter in Karayampatti hamlet who belongs to SC community tried to file nomination against the village control. Though all the officials including the SP supported him, he failed in his attempt. One report said on the last day for filing nominations when he proceeded to file his papers, he was told that the Collector had asked him to meet the DSP and an attender was assigned to take him on foot to the DSP. That resulted in 15 minutes' delay and he was late for filing nomination. Narasingam, a farmer, had been provided round the clock police security for just attempting to file nomination for President of Pappapatti in the local bodies polls. Saraswathiammal has been summoned to appear before the local committee for defying the village decree.

Here the previous election was held despite its being reserved for SC. Having tolerated 5 years of SC releadership, this term, on seeing the other two villages nearby, *i.e.* Keerpatti and Pappapatty, people of this village also started protesting against SC reservation. SCs of Nattarmangalam feel that if any one files nomination against the wish of Kallars, this village will also become like Melevalavu in Melur taluk where 6 *Dalits* including the Village President were murdered. So the SCs there expressed their fear of filing nomination.

Virudhunagar District

Kottachineanthal Village, near Aruppukottai of Virudhunagar district, has 500 voters. It was declared a reserved seat for SCs based on the 1991 census where it was found that out of the total population of 582, SCs are 346 and other caste people are 236. Since SCs account for more than 50 per cent of the total population, it was reserved for SC. Following this announcement people, particularly the non-SCs, started protesting against the reservation. None from SC came forward to file nomination for the reserved post. It is mainly because they don't want to develop any enmity with the upper and dominant caste. So there was no election for local bodies in 1996.

Followed by talks in the villages, the Government was able to conduct by-election to the village, but no SC came forward to contest for Village President post. But the non-SCs elected their ward members and decided to elect a candidate from the non-SCs as vice-president so that the village administration could be made possible. Accordingly, 4 were elected unopposed. There was not even a single member from SCs. A non-SC member became Vice-President. They spent 5 years without village president but with the vice-president. In the present election too none from SC came forward for filing nomination. Instead the technique used in the previous election, *i.e.* running village Panchayat with vice-president was adopted. Though the village is situated in a remote area without basic facilities like road, water etc., they dont want an SC president.

They will not allow an SC to file nomination. But now, according to non-*Dalits*, the equations have changed and the *Dalit* population is less than 10 per cent. There are only 100 families in the village, of which only 10 are *Dalit* families and hence there is no reason to keep it still reserved. The officials expressed helplessness as the reservation can be revised only in 2006. Most of the SC people have migrated to other areas in search of employment.

No Election for the Third Time

For the third time, the people in the first ward of Nallur town Panchayat have refrained from filing nominations as the ward has been reserved for women belonging to the SC. It was observed that even during the by-election nominations were not received. It shows that protest against reservations for SC has been made in almost in all the southern districts of Tamil Nadu. It may be because of the caste riots which frequently occur in the region.

Dalit Woman was Prevented from Filing Nomination

Ms. Saraswathiammal, a *Dalit* woman attempted to file nomination for the Nattarmangalam Panchayat president post in Chellampatti

Union. Coming to know of this a strong mob comprising members mostly from a dominant caste group—Piramalaikallar— stormed the *Dalit* area and resorted to stone pelting for having violated the village discipline. It is said that the non-SC people took her to an undisclosed destination, before chasing away the mob. The inmates of the huts and all the *Dalits* fled the village. In the meanwhile, Dr. K. Krishnaswamy, the leader of Pudhiya Tamizhagam, called for the intervention of the Chief Minister of Tamil Nadu. He also said that if elections are not held in these villages, the Pudhiya Tamilzhagam will conduct the election and if the Government fails to take action immediately, they will mobilize the people and enter the villages for solution. Reliable sources confirmed that two houses belonging to Saraswathiammal and Mr. Pattar Payakaruppan were partly damaged when a mob pelted stones at Nattarmanagalam in the night. Tension prevailed in the area following the incident. Police pickets were posted at sensitive points as a precautionary measure. This measure would be taken only up to the election. What about the security after the election and for how long is the question every *Dalit* asks. The widow of a police constable who underwent a course in teacher training is apprehensive of the future of her family with children. She said that she wanted to live peacefully there and she was not interested in filing the nomination.

What was observed here is that:

- Only *Dalits* concentrated in one particulars place think of enjoying power.
- Education motivates women to violate village discipline.
- Local committee is more powerful than education, law and constitution.
- Economically dependent *Dalits* can never contest the election against the wish of the dominant group in the area.
- *Dalit* consider an attempt to file nomination by themselves a grave sin.
- *Dalits* are not cooperative enough to enjoy the power. They lack training and suffer from financial backwardness.
- There were some persons, ready to file nomination if the District Collector and the SP gave enough security, no

matter what would happen to the remaining people of their caste living in the village.

- There is going to be tension in these areas if the District Collector, the SP and other Government officials try to encourage SCs to file nomination in the by-election.

Reactions

Mr. E.V.K.S. Elangaovan, the TNCC President, described it as a disgraceful situation which prevailed not only in Tamil Nadu but in many parts of the country also for the past several years. He also said such attempts ran counter to the country's democratic ethos. Various social fora urged the Government to initiate action against those who "created an atmosphere" in which *Dalits* were not allowed to file nominations for the reserved Panchayats. Creating fear among the *Dalits* should be viewed as a major social crime and the persons responsible should be brought under the provisions of the Prevention of Atrocities against SC and ST Act.

Anticipatory Implication if Government Compels to Hold Election

- If the number of votes is the only criterion for allocation of reservation a considerable percentage of the SC people would be chased away by the upper caste.
- Upper caste people will not provide them land for construction of new houses in the SC area.
- Non-SC people will prevent SCs from getting employment on their land which is the only means of livelihood, which may force the SCs to migrate from the village on their own.
- The inter-caste relationship prevailing over centuries will disintegrate.
- An attitude of enmity would develop between SC and non-SCs which may create perpetual tension in the rural area.
- The incident of Melavalavu has been imbibed in the minds of all the villagers which is an indirect expression of a violent attitude.

Observation

- When *Dalits* are badly in need of food and employment (which is being provided by the non-SCs) in these villages, it is not wise for the Government and *Dalit* based parties to make a statement likely to disturb the cordial relationship prevailing between SCs and non-SCs.
- It is to be strongly condemned that some leaders of *Dalit* based parties encourage the *Dalits* to contest the election and assure that the party will enter the village and conduct the election. It is merely for political gain, cheap popularity and caste development. The leaders want to gain cheap popularity by making such a statement without knowing the ABC of the ground reality.

Suggestions

It is not political power that the SCs are in need of. But what is urgent is economic independence through guaranteed employment without depending on the lands of the upper caste people in their own village. It is social security which they receive from the non-SCs of the village and the same has been affected due to the announcement of SC reservation and the attempt of some SCs to file nomination against the wish of the non-SCs. Till recently SC people were saved by the local non-SCs from any atrocities and violence from non-SCs of other villages nearby during the caste conflicts. When the local saviours—socially local employers, economically and culturally relatives—become enemies the very survival of the SC community in their native village will be a big question.

Lack of Commitment on the Part of Government

Imposing Government's polices and principles in the caste ridden villages all of a sudden will disturb the peaceful social life of the villages. The Government and NGOs should have studied the ground reality before declaring the reservation. Had the villagers been slowly informed of the forthcoming reservation and the criteria followed for allotting reservation much earlier than the formal declaration, the people would have prepared their minds to accept the Government norms and procedures.

Contrary to this, Government officials, all of a sudden, declared in some caste riden villages that they were reserved for SC while, till that time some members from non-SCs the numerically dominant group, had prepared themselves to become president by spending money in thousands and lakhs for years. And the people were also ready for selecting some particular person as their president. When the announcement came without any prior information people were shocked and protested against the reservation.

If we go deep into every reason uttered by the people and observed by the social activists, we can understand that people in Keeripatti are not against the *Dalits* and have not prevented *Dalits* from filing nomination. But they express their anger towards the Government by boycotting the election for denying their right to become leader of their own villages. They are claiming their rights and are not against *Dalits*. If anyone from SC files nomination election will be held. Then the non-SCs cannot regain their rights. In the process of claiming their rights from the Government the Kallars seek the support of SCs also. It is in support of Kallars that the SCs don't come forward to file nomination. Of course, reservation for SCs is like a fortune knocking at their door to enjoy power in the politics. SC people may have some intention to become leaders of their village. But taking into account their number, financial, cultural, educational dependence, awareness level and the protest of the non-SCs against reservation, the SC people dropped the idea of contesting and becoming village president. It is the media, Government and NGOs which made the problem serious.

- More exposition of such sensitive stories in the media.
- Press people frequently held interview with the people who are already tense.
- Students edged on by the caste based political parties in the name of encouraging *Dalits* increased the tension between two castes.

- Government invited only limited, unspecified VIPs from the village to the headquarters to hold a peace/compromise/ consensus talk with Collectors, RDOs.
- The officials went to the people only after date for election was announced. These steps will not bring about any change in the minds of the people. It needs much more practical measures for which NGOs, academicians, Government officials and social workers, leading political leaders should take the lead with social concern and commitment.

Implications of *Dalits* being Prevented from Filing Nomination

Where the *Dalits* were prevented from filing nominations, the *Dalit* community is losing interest and faith in the New Panchayati Raj System.

- Due to lack of proper action against the lawful activities of the upper caste people they further consolidated their supremacy through Panchayati Raj. Here the very objective of Panchayati Raj is defeated.
- Out of three villages, in one village, Nattarmangalam, a *Dalit* attempted but failed to file his nomination due to delay in time. Upon learning of this the caste Hindus attacked the SC people and damaged the houses and properties belong to SC. A case had been registered and is pending in court. The enmity which existed unnoticed has come into the open and has disturbed the communal harmony which prevailed earlier.
- Based on this reality, the caste based associatiosn and political parties working among the *Dalits* and the Piramalaikallars of local area, a sub-caste of Mukkalathores (Thevars), exploit the situation by blowing up the hatred between them with vested interest.

4

PANCHAYATS AND SOCIAL DEVELOPMENT

Introduction

In terms of democratic practice India is in the ninth place and in terms of human development it is in the 124th place and more specifically it fell from the 113th place in the previous year (UNDP, 2002), which poses a paradoxical situation in the process of socio-economic transformation of the Indian society through democratic governance. It is axiomatic that freedom enhances human capability and opportunity for human energy and skill and ensures adequate power and authority to the people to decide their destiny since human beings mature gradually. But, in India, the development scenario presents a dismal picture despite the concentrated and centralized efforts of the federal and state governments with a strong bureaucracy through a multiplicity of development schemes and programmes. It is beyond doubt that the overall performance of the Government in terms of human development has improved significantly between 1981 and 2001 (Planning Commission, 2002). But a wide disparity prevails across the states, districts and even across the Panchayats. The disparity and the dismal performance in development by the initiative of the Government is attributed to a set of causative factors of which the most important and the foremost is the wide gap between the people and the Government (World Bank, 2000-2001). In the process of administering development people have been perceived as beneficiaries or receivers of benefits from the Government and the Government machinery has been perceived as the provider of benefits to the people. Efforts have been made since 1991 to bridge the gap between the Government and the people, re-define the concept of Government as facilitator rather than provider and make the people stakeholders in the process of administering development.[1]

The new efforts in empowering people would restore the self-respect and self-confidence of the people. It would enhance the capability of the people to manage their affairs on their own. The whole process of administering development by the involvement and participation of the people would make the people understand the process of development and governance. By deepening democracy local development issues would be left to the community to be addressed (G. Palanithurai, 2001).

Statement of the Problem

Tamil Nadu has witnessed considerable economic development and social progress since independence. It has enjoyed positive economic growth every year since 1950. It has achieved a per capita income of Rs. 9180 during 1994-95, almost 10 per cent higher than the national average and this state is ranked next only to Punjab, Haryana, Gujarat and Maharashtra. Tamil Nadu has done well on many indicators of social development. Yet there are areas where its performance lags behind that of many of the poorer states (UNICEF, 2000).

For example whereas 28 per cent of Tamil Nadu's rural habitations were fully covered with access to safe water, the proportion was 77 per cent in Bihar, 54 per cent in Rajasthan and 49 per cent in Madhya Pradesh. Only 57.5 per cent of households had toilet facilities, almost the same as in Bihar. Close to 48 per cent of children under four were moderately and severely underweight in Tamil Nadu, the proportion was 42 per cent in Rajasthan. Another issue of Tamil Nadu's social development is the persistent inequality between the rural and urban areas across districts and between communities. In general communities classified as belonging to Scheduled Castes and Scheduled Tribes fared worse than the rest of the society on most

---

[1] When Manmohan Singh presented the annual budget in the Parliament, he made it clear that the time has come to redefine the concept of Government and thereby Government takes a new shape as facilitator instead of provider.

indicators of human development. From the human development perspective the balance sheet of Tamil Nadu shows many achievements and also several challenges.

Two features are striking about Tamil Nadu's record in social development. The state has not been able to consistently translate its record of economic growth into sustained improvements in the quality of people's lives. Another striking feature is the large gap that persists between the state's commitments and actual achievements (Tamil Nadu People's Forum for Social Development, 2000). Most of the goals for the year 2000 remain unattained. Against this background the new declaration of the Government of Tamil Nadu "making Tamil Nadu number one in development in the whole country" and its subsequent development programme named "15-point programme" have to be observed (Government of Tamil Nadu, 2002). For women and children, the Government of Tamil Nadu introduced another "18-point action programme". The present write up makes an attempt to analyse the role of the community in achieving social development through the Panchayats as a result of an action research project which has been carried out in ten Gram Panchayats with the support of the Population Foundation of India (G. Palanithurai, 1999).

About the Action Project

It is assumed that the RCH Programme will cover the following elements at the Gram Panchayat level: basic ante-natal, natal and post-natal care services, immunization of children, contraceptive services and related social developmental efforts, particularly an organised programme for raising the age at marriage for girls and enrolment of all children in the age group 5-14 in schools and ensuring that they continue their education up to middle school.

In all the above areas, the indicators for monitoring should be simple, easy to measure so that it can be done by local people after some basic training and be indicative of the progress and impact of the programme on fertility, mortality and health levels of the population. The conventional measures of fertility, mortality, health and education are defined, which could be used by demographers and administrators.

A more acceptable procedure would be monitoring of all births, pregnancies and children in the school going ages with regard to the selected characteristics and specific services provided to them. Indicators based on the so-called numerator analysis or characteristics of events should be the basis for monitoring of programmes at the village Panchayat level. With regard to reproductive and child health, the birth based or event based approach will lead to the following programme elements and related key indicators:

1. The programme's field activities will be centred round currently pregnant women (CPW) and recently delivered mothers (RDM), *i.e.* those who have delivered a child within the last 12 months, rather than all women in the reproductive ages.
2. The cycle starts as soon as a pregnancy is detected and will include antenatal care, **TT** and **IFA** tablets to mothers, safe delivery procedures, post-partum care and advice on infant feeding, immunization, use of dehydration therapy, nutritional status, growth monitoring of children and contraceptive advice, services and supplies to mothers including advice on full breast feeding of children by mothers at least up to six months after delivery.
3. It has been estimated from a number of empirical studies within India and outside that recently delivered women are self-selected for higher potential fertility and hence for the same contraceptive prevalence level, protection offered among such women (excluding the post-partum amennorhea periods), will have a greater demographic impact on the population.
4. Such a procedure would promote use of spacing methods, increase their efficiency of use by focusing on those most in need, and integrate functionally and in a more meaningful manner family planning and maternal and child health services.
5. Family planning services will be offered not just as a demographic measure to control the aggregate fertility levels of the population, for the purpose of intangible

macro-economic benefits, but as a measure of promoting the reproductive health of the mother and the health and survival status of the recently born children. Since the impact of the quality of care provided to the mother and child will be tangible both to the fieldworkers providing these services and to the mothers, the continuity of contraceptive use is likely to improve and the impact on fertility on the most vulnerable groups of the population will be higher.

In essence and substance the "Birth-Based Strategy to Family Planning Programme" is similar to the traditional post-partum approach to family planning with one important difference, namely that attention is focused on all currently pregnant women (CPW) and all recently delivered mothers (RDM), unlike in the post-partum approach wherein the focus has been only on those women who deliver in hospitals or who are already registered in an institution for ante-natal services at the time of their pregnancy.

The level of demand and utilization of RCH services depends to a considerable extent on the empowerment of women and education of children. Hence, monitoring of marriages in the village on age at marriage with a need to raise the marriage to legal levels and ensuring attendance of children in school in the age group 5-14 should be ensured.

Information will be collected on the following variables based on the above approach:

1. Identify all pregnant women in the village/Panchayat. This can be done either by house to house visit or by the women Panchayat members meeting and discussing from their respective knowledge of pregnant women in the village. This number generally should be broken up into those of below 3 months of pregnancy, 3-6 months and above 6 months and by birth order.
2. Arrange to provide ante-natal services including basic check-up of the pregnant woman, giving her iron and folic acid tablets, arranging for TT injection and informing her

of proper nutrition and safe delivery procedures either at home or in a nearby institution, if available.

3. Arrange to identify all *dais* in the village and request the ANM of the village to give the *dais* necessary training in MCH and supply them with Disposable Delivery Kits (DDKs). *Dais* should be informed of the details of all the pregnant women in the village and requested to provide necessary care after delivery.
4. Arrange to transport high-risk pregnant women or complicated cases of delivery to nearby institutions (PHCs-CHCs) for which the Panchayat should spend from the funds available for the benefit of the pregnant women.
5. Recently delivered mothers (RDM) (those who delivered within the last 12 weeks) should be given post-natal care as needed and the newly born infants should be given required immunizations at periodical intervals. This should be arranged by the women members of the Panchayat in consultation with the auxiliary nurse mid-wives and ICDS workers.
6. Recently delivered mothers (RDM) should be advised on contraceptive methods and be motivated to use either IUD, oral pills or condom and also encouraged to continue breast-feeding, including colostrums, which is extremely useful in developing the immunity status of the newly born child.
7. The women or their husbands who do not want any more children should be advised to undergo sterilization and arrangements for the same should be made by the women members of the Panchayat in consultation with ANMs.
8. All children in the age group 5-14 should be identified and a list of those who are not enrolled in school should be prepared. The Panchayat members should visit their houses and ensure that their children are sent to schools and if they have any genuine difficulties, they should be helped to the extent possible using various Government subsidy programmes available to them. This should be monitored closely, especially for the girl children in the village.

9. All marriages in the village should be registered by the women members of the Panchayat in relation to age at marriage with a plan to have within the five years all marriages of girls above the age of 18 and boys above age of 21.

If the above programmes are to be taken up and monitored, it is necessary that one woman member of the Panchayat from the village, especially one who is educated, should take primary responsibility for the above tasks. She should be provided with some basic training on the above issues. The enclosed proforma can be used by her to prepare a profile of the village with regard to RCH and for monitoring the type of activities indicated above.

It is necessary that the educated women members of, Panchayats are identified from each village and they are brought together at Samiti level by the ANM and the Medical Officer at the Primary Health Centre and given needed information and education on the above topics. The type of assistance and support from the governmental system that could be available for recently delivered mothers or currently pregnant women or to the school age population should be made clear to them. The proforma could be completed by these trained Panchayat members, and even be presented on a black board in the village with figures updated once a month or once in three months, as feasible.

Basic Objectives

The action project has the following objectives:

(a) To improve the quality of life of people by ensuring adoption of appropriate community processes;

(b) To enable the community to set achievable development goals in the areas of school enrolment, literacy, immunization, pre- and post-natal care, family welfare, nutrition, sanitation, child care, water supply and environment;

(c) To assist communities to develop their agenda of development; and

(d) To give the required professional assistance to the community in its efforts to achieve the above said objectives.

The Approach

The Gram Sabhas in the identified Gram Panchayats were assisted to develop their agenda of development through participatory learning and action (PLA) techniques. The Panchayats were encouraged to develop the capacity for the application of PLA techniques. The agenda of development focused on areas outlined in the second objective. The Panchayats were responsible for motivating various Government agencies to cover the developmental programmes/schemes at the community level. Specific responsibilities for achieving the set goals were fixed with specific groups and individuals from amongst Gram Sabha members. Based on the requirements and the social situation, community based groups for development and maintenance of community assets were formed. The Population Foundation of India encouraged the Panchayats in performance in the areas of social development indicated above by providing an incentive of Rs. 8000 per year per Gram Panchayat. It also assisted each Panchayat by providing an animator at a token honorarium of Rs. 100 per month to help the Gram Panchayat President. The action project commenced in the year 1999 and carried out the activities in ten Gram Panchayats of Dindigul District.

Before starting this project in the Panchayats, the Panchayat Presidents and animators had been taken to Kerala for field visits. They visited Erattupettah and Poonjar Therukkara Gram Panchayats and had discussion with the leaders and other functionaries on the performance of the Panchayats on the issues of social development (G.Palanithurai, 1999). After the two day visit to Kerala an orientation programme was given in Gandhigram on social development issues for the Panchayat Presidents and animators.

The programme was carried out in the following Panchayats of Dindigul district:

Sl. No.	Name of the Panchayat	Name of the Panchayat Union
1.	D.Gudalore	Gujiliamparai
2.	Vadugampadi	Gujiliamparai
3.	T.Pudupatti	Reddiyarchatram
4.	Karisalpatti	Reddiyarchatram
5.	Palayamkottai	Athoor
6.	Munnilaikottai	Athoor
7.	N.Panjampatti	Athoor
8.	Veriyapur	Athoor
9.	Komberipatti	Vadamadurai
10.	Sukkampatti	Vadamadurai

Of the ten Panchayats, four Panchayats are headed by women Presidents. Activities were initiated in all the ten Gram Panchayats. In all the target villages the project objectives and activities were explained through Participatory Rural Appraisal and voluntary groups of youths and women were organised. Initiative was taken for the effective functioning of the parent-teachers association. Meaningful rapport was established with the field health staff for the successful implementation of RCH activities. Statutory committees were formed among the members of the Panchayat council.

The action project was launched in the month of May 1999 and it was evaluated every year and incentive money was disbursed to all the ten Panchayats. Final evaluation was done in 2002. The tables appended to this article are illustrative of the achievements made by the Panchayats. (See Table 4.1)

School Enrolment

From Table 4.2 it is clear that eligible children who did not go to school in the ten Panchayats were in two digits in the year 1999-2000 and it has been reduced to single digit in the third year. This was done with the help of the SHG members and youth groups. Both the Panchayat Presidents and the animators were conscientised on the importance and implications of primary education and thereby they worked for cent per cent school enrolment. Though they could not achieve 100 per cent enrolment, they have increased the enrolment of children in the schools.

Table 4.1 : Details of Population

Sl. No.	Name of the Panchayat	Population											
		1999-2000				2000-2001				2001-2002			
		Male	Female	Total	6-14 Yrs.	Male	Female	Total	6-14 Yrs.	Male	Female	Total	6-14 Yrs.
1.	T. Pudupatti	1696	1574	3270	652	1628	1691	3319	340	1631	1710	3341	378
2.	Karisalpatti	1342	1324	2666	348	1559	1574	3133	696	1531	1559	3090	516
3.	Palayankottai	1832	1950	3782	416	1970	1902	3872	612	1968	1935	3903	469
4.	N. Panchampatti	2753	2926	5679	662	3057	3105	6162	1145	3441	3331	6772	1698
5.	Munnilakottai	1318	1260	2578	316	1414	1448	2862	587	1607	1519	2116	493
6.	Veriappoor	1421	1439	2860	321	1455	1405	2856	358	1444	1493	2937	340
7.	Vadugambadi	1381	1486	2867	497	1463	1624	3087	615	1582	1716	3298	516
8.	D. Gudalore	1816	1810	3626	287	2426	2560	4986	396	3193	3146	6339	574
9.	Komberipatti	1750	1528	3278	542	1820	1881	3701	540	1937	2051	3988	536
10.	Sukkampatti	3230	3040	6270	1178	3253	3065	6318	1137	3321	3090	6411	1116

Source : Computed.

Table 4.2 : School Enrolment

Sl. No.	Name of the Panchayat	School Enrolment											
		1999-2000			2000-2001			2001-2002			No. of Children not going to school		
		Boys	Girls	Total	Boys	Girls	Total	Boys	Girls	Total	1999-2000	2000-2001	2001-2002
1.	T. Pudupatti	363	270	633	183	145	328	222	158	380	19	12	2
2.	Karisalpatti	176	141	317	368	312	680	292	221	513	31	16	3
3.	Palayankottai	225	163	388	336	263	599	220	245	465	28	13	4
4.	N. Panchampatti	302	332	634	546	583	1129	855	842	1697	28	16	1
5.	Munnilakottai	153	127	280	333	234	567	254	237	491	36	20	2
6.	Veriappoor	150	147	297	180	163	343	183	154	337	24	15	3
7.	Vadugambadi	214	243	458	254	244	598	279	235	514	39	17	2
8.	D. Gudalore	146	114	260	206	182	388	293	280	573	27	08	1
9.	Komberipatti	250	260	510	255	272	529	271	260	531	32	11	5
10.	Sukkampatti	586	514	1100	617	537	1154	596	513	1109	78	17	7

Source : Computed.

Providing Toilets to Schools

All the Gram Panchayats of the project area have provided toilets to the schools with adequate water supply. Teachers have been oriented to bring about toilet culture among the students. The Health Committee supervises the functioning of the toilets in the schools.

Providing Water Supply

All the ten Gram Panchayats have achieved the supply of safe drinking water to all the families of the Gram Panchayat areas. Periodically overhead tanks are cleaned and water is chlorinated. Adequate water is supplied to all the residents of the Gram Panchayats. The Gram Panchayat Presidents regulate the water supply to all the families in the Panchayat area.

Ante-natal, Natal and Post-natal Care

Pregnant women are registered properly. (See Table 4.3) Health personnel who visit and attend to the pregnant women are made to perform their duties properly and thereby T.T. injections are given and IFA tables are provided to the pregnant women. Details regarding ante-natal care and post-natal care are being printed as pamphlets and they are being circulated among the people. Likewise details regarding immunization have been printed as pamphlets and they are being distributed to all families. The concept of family welfare is known to the people. Giving birth to a third child is very rare even among the poor families as family planning methods are familiar to them. Family planning methods are being adopted by the people but it is unfortunate that whether it is temporary or permanent, they are being used by the women and not by men. It could be inferred from Table 4.4, that very few men are using the methods. Though steps had been taken for the use of condoms, men are reluctant to use it as disposal of the used condom is difficult in the rural areas. Steps have been taken to ensure institutional delivery. Very few are yet to come under this purview. All the recently delivered mothers are conscientised on the importance of breast feeding. Almost all the recently delivered mothers are having the habit of breast feeding. All children are being given immunizations such as BCG, DPT I, DPT II, DPT III, Polio I, Polio II, Polio III and measles. Table 4.5 shows that all the children in all the ten Gram Panchayats have been given immunization. Only in the year 1999, a few individuals reported that they had not been provided with the immunization. There is yet another work done in all the Gram Panchayats, namely sensitizing the people on the age of marriage for men and women. Further the Village Panchayat leaders took steps to create awareness about RCH among adolescent girls in the villages with the help of Gandhigram Rural Institute staff. School going children were sensitized on good health practices such as trimming the nails, washing hands before taking meals and using the toilets in the schools. Youth club members were assigned the task of trimming the nails of the school students. SHG women were sensitized on burning the used napkin by other women. It helps a lot to keep the villages clean and neat. All the Gram Panchayats have conducted health camps with the assistance of the Health Department as the Government of Tamil Nadu has introduced a new scheme called "Varummun Kappom" (Preventive Action). All the children were medically examined and cases of ailments were referred to the Government hospitals. The above mentioned activities have been compared with those in other nearby ten Panchayats in the same district with a view to understanding the factors responsible for the success of this project. The comparative study was conducted in the following Gram Panchayats: Karungal, Ulliyakottai, Morepatti, Paganatham, Kalanjipatti, Pillauarnatham, Vakkampatti, Bodikammanvadi, Dhrmathupatti and Panniapatti (G. Palanithurai, 2001). It is inferred from the study that the people and their leaders in those Panchayats are not conscientised on social development issues so far and hence no such activities have been carried out. Even the Gram Panchayat Presidents are not aware of the existing schemes for social development. They are not conscious of social development whereas in the project Panchayats, the Panchayat leaders are repeatedly sensitized on the issues of social development.

Table 4.3. : Information of Pregnant Women

Sl. No.	Name of the Panchayat	Infomration of Pregnant Women																				
		Registered			TT Injection			IFA Tablets			No Complication			Ceasarian			Maternal Deaths			Infant Deaths		
		99-00	00-01	01-02	99-00	00-01	01-02	99-00	00-01	01-02	99-00	00-01	01-02	99-00	00-01	01-02	99-00	00-01	01-02	99-00	00-01	01-02
1.	T. Pudupatti	54/68	63/70	64/64	54/68	63/70	64/64	54/68	63/70	64/64	58/68	65/70	63/64	6	3	1	2	1	-	2	1	-
2.	Karisalpatti	52/81	78/90	93/93	52/81	78/90	93/93	52/81	78/90	93/93	62/81	81/90	93/93	14	7	-	2	-	-	3	2	-
3.	Palayankottai	68/83	79/89	94/94	68/83	79/89	94/94	68/83	79/89	94/94	78/83	84/89	92/94	3	4	2	1	-	-	1	1	-
4.	N. Panchampatti	46/67	43/56	34/34	46/67	43/56	34/34	46/67	43/56	34/34	56/67	49/56	34/34	7	5	-	2	1	-	2	1	-
5.	Munnilakottai	79/93	60/78	58/58	76/93	60/78	58/58	76/93	60/78	58/58	89/93	73/78	58/58	4	4	-	-	-	-	-	1	-
6.	Veriappoor	58/72	49/58	51/51	58/72	49/58	51/51	58/72	49/58	51/51	68/72	52/58	51/51	2	5	-	2	1	-	-	-	-
7.	Vadugambadi	78/99	84/97	69/69	78/99	84/97	69/69	78/99	84/97	69/69	90/99	95/97	69/69	7	2	-	2	-	-	-	-	-
8.	D. Gudalore	32/48	27/36	43/43	32/48	27/36	43/43	32/48	27/36	43/43	42/48	34/36	43/43	5	2	-	1	-	-	-	-	-
9.	Komberipatti	24/38	31/39	42/42	24/38	31/39	42/42	24/38	31/39	42/42	28/38	34/39	40/42	5	3	1	3	1	1	2	1	-
10.	Sukkampatti	32/54	35/42	39/39	32/54	35/42	39/39	32/54	35/42	39/39	42/54	38/42	38/39	5	3	1	4	1	-	3	-	-

Source : Computed.

Table 4.4 : Family Planning Particulars

Sl. No.	Name of the Panchayat	Permanent Methods									Temporary Methods								
		1999-2000			2000-2001			2001-2002			1999-2000			2000-2001			2001-2002		
		Male	Female	Total	Male	Female	Total	Male	Female	Total	Male	Female	Total	Male	Female	Total	Male	Female	Total
1.	T. Pudupatti	-	20	20	-	25	25	-	32	32	2	21	23	8	34	42	16	36	52
2.	Karisalpatti	-	32	32	-	24	24	-	36	36	1	26	27	15	38	53	21	45	66
3.	Palayankottai	-	28	28	-	29	29	-	26	26	2	19	21	14	28	42	19	37	56
4.	N. Panchampatti	-	27	27	-	41	41	-	29	29	3	40	43	12	40	52	21	48	69
5.	Munnilakottai	-	31	31	-	37	37	-	28	28	4	32	36	14	31	45	26	49	75
6.	Veriappoor	-	30	30	-	32	32	-	32	32	6	34	40	16	33	49	31	52	83
7.	Vadugambadi	-	29	29	-	35	35	-	37	37	7	26	33	19	26	45	27	56	83
8.	D. Gudalore	-	27	27	-	33	35	-	39	39	4	21	25	21	37	58	30	53	83
9.	Komberipatti	-	17	17	-	37	37	-	18	18	5	17	22	23	22	45	27	39	66
10.	Sukkampatti	-	19	19	-	34	34	-	17	17	3	12	15	24	21	45	29	41	70

Source : Computed.

Table 4.5 : Immunization of Children

0-12 Months			12-24 Months			BCG			DPT-I & Polio-I			DPT-II & Polio-II			DPT-III & Polio-III			Measles			Number of infants not immunized		
99-00	00-01	01-02	99-00	00-01	01-02	99-00	00-01	01-02	99-00	00-01	01-02	99-00	00-01	01-02	99-00	00-01	01-02	99-00	00-01	01-02	99-00	00-01	01-02
36	45	70	42	104	42	76	104	112	75	104	112	73	104	112	73	104	112	73	104	112	5	-	-
28	43	63	46	57	62	70	100	125	70	100	125	70	100	125	70	100	125	68	100	125	8	-	-
33	34	43	47	64	16	76	98	59	76	98	59	76	98	59	76	98	59	76	98	59	4	-	-
38	22	142	42	27	152	77	49	294	77	49	294	77	49	294	77	49	294	77	49	294	3	-	-
37	31	34	35	31	11	67	62	45	67	62	45	67	62	45	67	62	45	67	62	45	5	-	-
41	78	50	38	65	54	68	123	104	68	123	104	68	123	104	68	123	104	68	123	104	11	-	-
39	39	42	41	50	16	78	89	58	78	89	58	78	89	58	78	89	58	78	89	58	2	-	-
27	14	69	46	27	105	68	41	174	68	41	174	68	41	174	68	41	174	68	41	174	5	-	-
29	24	89	43	21	77	62	45	166	62	45	166	62	45	166	62	45	166	62	100	166	10	-	-
30	15	113	41	22	134	59	37	247	59	37	247	59	37	247	59	37	247	59	37	247	12	-	-

Source : Computed.

From the beginning the Panchayat leaders were oriented on social development issues. Further they were taken to Kerala for exposure to Panchayats and in order to know-how Panchayats are working on social development issues. Every year, while distributing the incentive money, a review was made through a review workshop. Further the funding agency (Population Foundation of India, New Delhi) organised two workshops to share the experiences of the ten Panchayats with ten Gram Panchayats in Dharmapuri district where the same exercise was being carried out by Satyamoorthy Centre for Democratic Studies and all the twenty Panchayats' experiences were shared with those of another ten Gram Panchayats of Pune District of Maharashtra (G. Palanithurai, 2002). This kind of experience and exposure made the Panchayat Presidents conscious of the social development issues.

REFERENCES

Government of Tamil Nadu, 2002 *Address by the Governor of Tamil Nadu in the Legislative Assembly,* Chennai : Government Central Press, 2002.

G. Palanithurai, (1999) *Community Action for Social Development for through Panchayat,* Gandhigram : Rajiv Gandhi Chair for Panchayati Raj Studies, 1999.

G. Palanithurai, (1999) *Report of the Interface and Interact Programme organized in Karalla for Gram Panchayat Presidents of Tamil Nadu,* Gandhigram : Rajiv Gandhi Chair for Panchayati Raj Studies, 1999.

G. Palanithurai, (2001) *A Comparative Analysis of the Performance of Panchayati Leaders in Social Development Issues,* Gandhigram : Rajiv Gandhi Chair for Panchayati Raj Studies, 2001.

G. Palanithurai, (2001) *Towards Decentralization of Powers (Mono),* Gandhigram : Rajiv Gandhi Chair for Panchayati Raj Studie, 2001.

G. Palanithurai, (2002) *Report of the Interface Programme,* Gandhigram : Rajiv Gandhi Chair for Panchayati Raj Studies, 2002.

Planning Commission, (2002) *National Human Development Report, 2001,* New Delhi : Planning Commission Government of India, 2002.

Tamil Nadu People's Forum for Social Development, (2000) *Tamil Nadu Social Development Report 2000,* Chennai : Tamil Nadu People's Forum for Social Development, 2000.

The World Bank, (2001) *World Deveopment Report 2000/2001 Attacking Poverty,* New York : Oxford University, Press, 2001.

UDNP, (2002) *Human Development Report, 2002,* New Delhi : Oxford University Press, 2002.

UNICEF, (2000) *Tamil Nadu Social Sector Priorities and Strategies,* Chennai : UNICEF, 2000, p. 5.

5

DEVELOPMENT ROLES REVERSED

Introduction

This article presents the lessons learnt from the experiments in micro level planning initiated by the six Gram Panchayats headed by women leaders of Sivaganga District of Tamil Nadu for widespread dissemination. Dominant academic and administrative perceptions indicate that planning is an exercise to be carried out at the federal and State Government level and that planning activities are to be undertaken by the Departments of Governments with the participation of the people, if necessary, and thereby Rural Development Departments have been made highly target oriented and rural development activities are carried out in a supply driven mode, leaving the felt needs of the people unattended to as Government schemes do not have the potential to meet the location specific demands of the people. Sporadic exercises in decentralized planning have been carried out intermittently over a period of time and yet a dominant implementable view could not be distilled from all these exercises (T.M. Thomas Issac with Richard W. Franke 2000, 21-29). It is increasingly felt that the existing mode of activities not only shelves the felt needs of the people but also creates a gap between the people and the Government and thereby the people are driven out of the orbit of governance, making space exclusively for officials, which results in large scale corruption and takes away the self-respect of the people by making them beneficiaries and not participants of the development process (N. Narayanasamy, M.P. Boraian and M.A. Jeyaraju, 2000). In many of the developing countries it is a difficult task to bridge the gap between the people and the government (Commonwealth Foundation, 1999). To bridge the gap and to reverse the trend and the roles, the historic 73rd and 74th Constitutional Amendments provided scope for the people to take the initiative for planning at the grassroots to achieve development with the active participation of the people and the support of the departments of governments. The question now is to what extent this provision has been used in the new context and what the implications of this provision in the rural development scenario are. To understand the significance and the implications of the new provision in the Constitution for decentralized planning, an attempt is made here to study and analyse the initiative of the Gram Panchayats in preparing plans for the development of their respective areas.

General Assumptions

Planning initiatives at the grassroots alter the very paradigm of development. Primarily they give power to the institutions at the grassroots to decide upon the course of action through planning for development and administering social justice. Indirectly they give confidence and self-esteem to the people when they involve themselves in the planning exercise. The supply driven and target oriented rural development activities are replaced by demand driven, participatory and sustainable rural development activities. The concept of beneficiary is changed to that of stakeholders in development.

The perception of state initiated rural development through scheme based activities with the participation of the people in implementing the activities will be reversed and replaced by people initiated rural development programmes with the participation of the Government. It will enlarge opportunities for the citizens to participate in decisions affecting their lives. It will draw on local knowledge and preferences about development. It will also create interest among the people at lower levels by instilling a greater sense of ownership of development projects (James Manor, 1999, pp. 36-38). Further it will enhance the accountability of bureaucrats, elected representatives and political institutions. It will equip the people with skills at representation and bargaining. It will empower women and the marginalized. These are the broad assumptions with which the whole decentralization process was initiated.[1]

After ten years of decentralization in India and after the passing of the 73rd Constitutional Amendment, an attempt is made here to study the process of decentralized planning by Panchayats. The people's planning model experimented with in Kerela has revealed the opportunities for Panchayati Raj Institutions in developing a local plan with the participation of the people (T.M. Thomas Issac with Richard W. Frank, 2000). The Kerala model of people's plan was an outcome of the political commitment of the Left Front Government. To a great extent it was state sponsored and designed at the state level. Once the Left Front Government was replaced by a Government with a different ideological orientation, the model was derailed.

However, the Kerala experiment has immense value in developing models of participatory decentralized planning in Panchayats. The limitations of a state sponsored initiative have been exposed by the Kerala experiment. Against this background the significance of people centred initiatives in the area of decentralized planning can be fully appreciated. The Rajiv Gandhi Chair for Panchayati Raj Studies closely studied the working of the Kerala model from its very inception with the intention of trying out a similar experiment in a few Village Panchayats of Tamil Nadu. Around 60 Panchayat leaders from Tamil Nadu were taken to Panchayats in Kerala on an interface programme. The Panchayat leaders from Tamil Nadu acquired first hand knowledge of the process of participatory decentralized planning and evinced great interest in taking such initiatives in the Panchayats of Tamil Nadu. Particularly women Panchayat Presidents showed a special interest in using the methodology in the area of social development. Six women headed Gram Panchayats of Sivaganga district came forward to experiment with the people's planning exercise. Out of the six village Panchayats three are headed by *Dalit* women.

In the whole of Tamil Nadu the six Gram Panchayats of Sivaganga district have made a breakthrough by developing perspective plans for their Panchayats and presenting them before the Gram Sabha and the Panchayat Council. After that the plan documents were presented in a development seminar organised by Gandhigram Rural Institute for widespread dissemination and for critical inquiry by administrators, officials, academics, plan experts, media representatives and representatives of the people. After the critical review the plan document was perfected by plugging the loopholes and correcting the shortcomings pointed out by the experts in the development seminar.

Case Studies

Before presenting the cases, it is not out of context to briefly indicate the basis for the selection of the six Gram Panchayats for this study. Primarily the six Gram Panchayat Presidents are pioneers in the whole of Tamil Nadu in taking up the planning exercise seriously and making the Government aware of the legal and development implications of planning at the grassroots. These six Panchayat Presidents are drawn from self-help groups and they are highly conscientised on the issues of social development and social justice. The six Gram Panchayat Presidents were identified during the voters awareness campaign conducted by Gandhigram Rural Institute in Sivagangai district with the collaboration of an NGO, Rural Welfare Trust, during the time of the Panchayat elections.[2]

During the time of the elections it was decided that at least 100 representatives from SHGs should be drawn towards Panchayats either as ward members or Presidents of Gram Panchayats. It was a surprise that in Sivagangai District alone 35 Gram Panchayat Presidents and 132 ward members of Gram Panchayats were elected from the SHGs (G. Palanithurai, 2002). Of them 12 were *Dalits*. This surprise victory provided the needed momentum to the women collectives and so they offered their services, subjecting themselves to any new experiments and innovations in Panchayats, and they made a declaration in the meeting organised to felicitate the victorious candidates in the elections that they would take many innovative measures in their Panchayats, for which they sought the help of the NGOs, academics and officials. It was suggested at the function that Panchayat leaders could take up the planning exercise at the Gram Panchayat level by which the supply driven rural development activities could be replaced by demand driven and participatory rural development activities. Of the 35 women leaders the following six Gram Panchayat leaders spontaneously came forward to take up this assignment, knowing fully well that it is a highly challenging task.

Table 5.1 : Details of the Panchayat Presidents

Sl. No.	Name of the President	Community	Name of the Gram Panchayat	Name of the Panchayat Union
1.	Veerakalaiarasi	SC	Veppankulam	Kallal
2.	A. Pushpam	BC	P. Nerpuhapatti	Kallal
3.	K. Rakku	SC	Vadavanpatti	Singampunari
4.	Y. Nagajothi	BC	Kozhikudipatti	Singampunari
5.	C. Chinnammal	SC	Urathupatti	S. Pudur
6.	S. Gomathy	BC	Manalur	S. Pudur

Source : Computed.

Methodology of the Plan Preparation[3]

Before commencing the actual work, an intensive training was organised for three days to build the capacity of the leaders including the men and women who were all committed to this exercise. The training programme was organised from the 27th to the 31st May, 2002 in Gandhigram Rural Institute as a fully residential programme. Experts were drawn from different institutions including the Government to conduct the programme (G. Palanithurai, 2002). All the six Gram Panchayat Presidents wanted to have a common workshop to sensitize the panchayat ward members, community leaders, SHG leaders, members of the youth groups and opinion makers on the importance and the implications of grassroots planning. The lead NGO, Rural Welfare Trust, agreed to help the Panchayats to organise the workshop and do the needful for planning also. The Hunger Council of Tamil Nadu has agreed to share some of the responsibilities. As a result on 17th August, 2002, a workshop was organised at Tirupathur for all the six Panchayats and around 210 members from all the Panchayats participated in the programme (G. Palanithurai, 2002). The whole exercise was on planning at the Gram Panchayat level and the discussion was on the steps to be followed in the planning. It was agreed that the planning exercise would be completed before October 2002 and that the Panchayats and the NGO should take up the responsibility. Further it was decided to identify what could be done by the leaders and people of the respective Panchayats. What could not be done by the Panchayats would be done by the Hunger Project.

The next step was to collect basic data about the people and their conditions. This could be collected by the Panchayats. Before starting the exercise the statutory seven committees had to be constituted so that the number of members in the orbit of governance would be increased. For the data collection a well developed schedule prepared by the State Planning Commission was used. After collecting the data from each village a PRA exercise was carried out with the help of the staff of the Kottayam based NGO,[4] Centre for Rural Management (CRM) to assess the needs of the people and to prioritise the needs. This exercise was done extensive and the staff of the CRM prepared a plan. Simultaneously the representatives of the people in the Panchayats also prepared a plan based on the PRA exercise. Finally, both were synthesized and brought out in the form of a document. In the whole process the concept of development was critiqued, the role of the Government was criticized and people expressed their willingness to participate in the whole process as the Panchayat leaders provided ample scope for people to participate in the planning exercise. When the document was ready for presentation in any forum for critical evaluation, the Hunger Council of Tamil Nadu organised a development seminar with a set of objectives, namely, of making this document legitimate, to sensitize the Government on planning at the grassroots and to motivate other Panchayat Presidents to start this kind of exercise in their Panchayats also. On October 26 and 27, 2002, the development seminar was organised in Gandhigram Rural Institute by inviting the State Minister for Local Bodies, secretaries, directors, planning officials, experts, representatives from the media, MLAs, community leaders, Panchayat leaders and women and youth groups from the six Gram Panchayats and women Gram Panchayat Presidents from all over Tamil Nadu numbering around six hundred.

The perspective plan document of the six Gram Panchayats contained a brief history of the Panchayats, details about the former Panchayat Presidents who held office during the pre-73rd Amendment era, basic data about agriculture, source of irrigation, veterinary facilities, land utilization, land ownership, landless families with social background, facilities available in schools, admission in schools, drop-outs in schools, status of women and children, energy utilization, non-conventional energy sources, environmental conditions, skills available in the village, housing facilities etc. After projecting all these the document projected the needs and prioritized them. Further it stated how these prioritized needs are to be met (Veerakalaiarasi, 2002; A. Pushpam, 2002; K. Rakku, 2002; V. Nagajothi, 2002; C. Chinnammal, 2002 and S. Gomathi, 2002).

Responsibilities were fixed on individuals and groups to take steps to meet the needs indicated in the plan document. Achievable indicators were fixed to monitor the activities of the Panchayats. It was stated unequivocally that the Panchayat would concentrate on 100 per cent school admission, ensure the normal weight of new born babies, institutional delivery, attention to pre-natal and post-natal care, reduce malnutrition, concentrate on family welfare etc. Thus this plan document became a vision document. Responsibility was not fixed on the Government alone. Activities were classified and accordingly responsibilities were fixed by which partners were identified for administering development and social justice.

Reactions and Responses to Plan Document

Officials from the State Planning Commission and the Project Office of the District Rural Development Agency of Sivaganga District first examined the document and offered their comments. They found certain deficiencies in the process of data collection. Apart from the basic data all other data were collected through PRA exercises and prioritization was also done through the same exercise. This was not approved of by the officials. The activities envisaged in the plan document could not be carried out under the available schemes of the Government. The Panchayats had not identified the individual beneficiaries for the

Government schemes. While putting the activities in the plan document, the Panchayats had to indicate the source of funding to carry out all the activities. Further they questioned the legitimacy of the plan document in the absence of a planning exercise at the Block level and the District level. On certain issues such as agriculture, veterinary care, non-conventional energy and environment, the people in the villages had not consulted the Government departments while projecting activities in the plan document. These subjects were highly technical in nature, but the Panchayats had taken the opinion of the people in deciding upon the activities. On the whole it was an expression of cynicism. It is to be noted here that in the inaugural function, the Minister for Panchayati Raj and Rural Development, Government of Tamil Nadu, showered encomium on the women leaders for their exercise and he said that despite the implementation of a variety of schemes and programmes of the Central and State Governments, people's felt needs could not be met. This kind of micro level plan would reverse the trend and the felt needs would be met and thereby wasteful expenditure could be avoided. He further informed that this kind of exercise would trigger a movement for people's planning. He appealed that in each district this kind of exercise should be initiated.

Despite the remark of the Minister, the officials recorded their negative remarks about the whole exercise. Following the reaction and response of the officials, some of the experts from the audience came forward to express their opinion. Prominent among them were B.S. Raghavan, retired Chief Secretary of West Bengal and adviser to FAO, A.K. Venkatasubramanian, retired civil servant specializing in Public Distribution System, Dr. Rajagopalan of the M.S. Swaminathan Foundation, Mr. Vallinayagam, retired Additional Director of Rural Development, and Mr. N.S. Chidambaram, retired Additional Director of Rural Development.[5] First, all the experts appreciated the effort in taking up this cause and facing all the problems in collecting data and putting them in a plan proposal and getting the approval of the people in the Gram Sabha and the Panchayat Council. It is a plan of the people prepared by the people and not a plan prepared by officials. It is their vision. They have chalked out their activities on the basis of their felt needs. It is true that they have not chalked out activities to implement the schemes of the Government and hence there will be a gap between the available schemes and the activities envisaged in the plan document of the Panchayats. The plan document is not a petition prepared by them to get sanction from the Government. It is their plan and they seek to be partners in governance to administer development. They have indicated the possibilities to generate employment opportunity with the resources and skills available in their respective Panchayats. Further it is to be noted that social development issues have been projected in the plan document and it is indicated that they will take up the responsibility to achieve sustainable results in development in the social sector. While appreciating the efforts of the Gram Panchayat leaders, they addressed a few questions to the Government officials and a few suggestions to the Gram Panchayat leaders.

In fifty years of democratic governance in India, no such document was prepared for village development by the Government. Even after the introduction of the 73rd Amendment and the Constitution of the District Planning Committee, no systematic effort was made at the micro level despite planning officials working at the district level. Having failed miserably in discharging duties and responsibilities at the Government level it was unfair on the part of the officials to criticize the efforts made by the women leaders for their small technical lapses. Further it was characteristic on the part of the officials to denigrate the people's efforts as unscientific. Since the officials have been oriented to act in the supply driven mode of development activities, they look at everything from the supply side and not from the demand side. While evaluating the proposal, officials had looked for proposals for the government schemes and programmes and that was why they were not in a position to suggest ways and means to meet the demands which could not be fulfilled by the government schemes and programmes. The experts said that the officials could have offered their suggestions rather than criticizing the plan. Even the model plan prepared by the officials in some of the villages in Tamil Nadu did not include social development issues.[6] The model plans prepared by the officials have not seen the light of day.

It is a unique exercise in fifty years of governance because every segment of the rural community has been involved in this exercise to make a declaration that their destinies are going to be decided by their efforts only. Now owners have been found for the rural development activities. They have realistically projected their needs as felt by the community without looking into the supply side of it. Hence it is the responsibility of the officials to help in identifying the institutions to be involved in the process of fulfilling the needs of the people. The existing schemes of the Government could be utilized for many of the demands and for some of the demands a slight modification is necessary in implementing the existing government schemes for which the District Collector as Chairman of the DRDA and Inspector of Panchayats can make use of his discretionary powers. Demands which could not be met through Government schemes could be taken to various financial institutions for financial support with a viable action proposal prepared by professionals for which the Panchayats have to seek the support of NGOs. It is fortunate that the Rural Welfare Trust is working with all these six Panchayats. The same organization can be involved in preparing such proposals and approach CAPART, DST, NABARD and other agencies. For the social development issues targeted, achievable and quantifiable indicators have to be fixed. For instance school enrolment of students, birth weight of newly born babies, institutional delivery, reduction of school drop-outs, providing safe drinking water supply to all families, ensuring sanitation facilities to all families, eradication of plastics and so on have been identified as activities and responsibilities have also been fixed to look after all the above said activities. The seven statutory committees in the villages have to be activated to involve themselves in all these activities. What is required now for the Gram Panchayats is partners to carry this task further.

After making these observations the experts again requested the officials directly dealing with planning at the grassroots to give their feedback again. The officials from the State Planning Commission and the District Rural Development Agency informed the audience and more specifically the Panchayat Presidents of the possibility of making use of many of the

Central and State Government schemes and programmes to meet many of the issues projected in the plan document. For other issues and demands the nodal agency, the NGO, Rural Welfare Trust, was to prepare and send proposals to NABARD, CAPART and other agencies. Achievable indicators have to be explicitly entrusted to the committees of the Panchayats and their activities have to be monitored every year. This was the assurance given to the Panchayats by the officials.

Finally, the Panchayat Presidents concluded their presentation by assuring the officials that they would take up the responsibilities to achieve many of the achievable indicators on social development. Further they informed that they would meet all the sectoral departments to seek their help to fulfil all the demands of the people mentioned in the PRA meetings while preparing the plan for the Gram Panchayats. The women leaders, while expressing their gratitude to the officials, explained their struggle to make use of the power devolved to them.

The whole exercise and the presentation of the plan in the development seminar provoked the women leaders assembled in the seminar to think on the social issues highlighted by the women Presidents of the six Gram Panchayats. The women Presidents who assembled in the seminar from all over Tamil Nadu under the banner of the Tamil Nadu Federation of Women Leaders prepared a charter of activities and declared it a charter of activities for the next year. The charter is presented hereunder.

Declaration

We, the elected women representatives who are gathered here at Gandhigram Rural Institute on this 27th day of October, 2002, declare that we will address the following issues in the next one year:

1. All the eligible children (girls and boys) will be enrolled in schools.
2. We will strive to remove malnourishment amongst children in the age group of 0-5 years. As elected representatives we shall ensure that no underweight

babies are born in our villages. The mothers will be given proper nourishment before and after delivery.

3. Better anti-natal and post-natal care will be provided for all the women in our Panchayats.
4. Any injustice against women in our Panchayats will be dealt with firmly. As a collective we will fight against domestic violence and also any other form of violence against any women in our Panchayat.
5. We will ensure that child labour is abolished in our Panchayats.
6. We will ensure equitable access to and distribution of Panchayat resources among all the people in the Panchayats and guarantee at least the provision of the basic minimum requirements for the poorest. The PDS system will be improved with our intervention.
7. Problems faced by the women Panchayat leaders and women in general will be addressed collectively by making alliance with supportive institutions and organizations.
8. The newly implemented sanitary complexes meant for women will be effectively managed by women's groups with the support of the Panchayats.
9. Our Panchayats will not suffer from lack of drinking water. Everyone will be entitled to safe drinking water.
10. We will ensure that Gram Sabhas take place regularly and more and more people take part in these meetings. We will ensure that a minimum of 50 per cent of the total women in the Panchayat attend the meetings and that their issues are properly heard.
11. We commit ourselves to the implementation of the 15-point programme prepared by the Tamil Nadu Government and request the State Government to devolve necessary powers to the Panchayats and local bodies for the same.

Following the presentation of reports and the declaration of the charter of activities for women Panchayat Presidents, the Pudukkottai District Project Officer, DRDA, representing the Pudukkottai District administration, pleaded that this kind of exercise be undertaken in the whole of Pudukkottai district for which he sought the help of NGOs and Gandhigram Rural Institute. Women leaders from Pudukkottai district who attended the development seminar expressed their willingness to undertake this kind of exercise in their Panchayats. Thus the micro plan exercise done in six Gram Panchayats and the presentation of all the six plans in the development seminar in the presence of the Minister for Panchayati Raj and Rural Development, Government of Tamil Nadu, officials of the State Government, experts on Micro Level Planning and six hundred Gram Panchayat Women Presidents created an awareness among the minister, the officials and the local body leaders on the importance of micro level planning and, as a result, the State Planning Commission started the exercise of giving training to the local body leaders on planning exercises to be done at the grassroots.

Integrated Analysis

Primarily, though it is a constitutional mandate that the planning exercise has to be initiated at the grassroots, beyond the State Governments and the Central Government producing documents on decentralized planning, nothing has been done on the ground in the 9th and the 10th Plans. These six Panchayats, under the leadership of women, have sensitized the minister and the higher officials to the implications of micro level planning.

Secondly, while carrying out this exercise, it could be seen at what level devolution of powers has taken place in the state as the Panchayats faced problems in getting the support of the sectoral departments. Empirically this proved the extent to which powers have been devolved to the Panchayats.

Thirdly, in the process of interacting with the officials and hearing views of the officials on the plan proposals of the Panchayats, the official attitude to this new dispensation and the exercise has been exposed and they have been sensitized to the legal and social implications of micro level planning.

Fourthly, the other women Presidents have gained confidence that this kind of exercise could be done in their

Panchayats also as they heard the methodology adopted in six Gram Panchayats for planning at the micro level.

Fifthly, social development issues came to the limelight because of the micro plans of the six Gram Panchayats. These six Gram Panchayat leaders gained this insight while they were in self-help groups and thereby they quickly grasped the social development issues and fixed achievable indicators for the Panchayats. This kind of exercise motivated the other Panchayat leaders to take up this issue. As a result the women Panchayat leaders published a charter of activities to be undertaken by the Panchayats on the social development sector.

Sixthly, in the recent past people have been mobilized by various agencies for participation in the implementation of various schemes and programmes brought from above. But the position "we govern you participate" has not altered. By doing the planning exercise by the people, people's demands and priorities have been prominently projected in the plan document and thereby the old position "we govern you participate" has been replaced by "you govern yourselves and you participate".

Seventhly, the six Panchayat Presidents have started negotiations with officials, representatives of the people like MLAs and MPs and NGOs for fulfilling the requirements of the plan. They have developed skills of negotiation.

Eighthly, the hidden potential of the leadership has been exhibited through this process. Class, caste and political organizations have their own roles in the activities of the rural society. While mobilizing all the groups cutting across these differences, the women leaders have exhibited a high degree of democratic leadership. Even the traditional Panchayat leaders have extended their fullest cooperation to the efforts of these Panchayat Presidents.

Ninthly, the conventional mode of looking at issues and demands from the supply mode has been done away with and instead issues are being looked at from the perspective of the people and thereby a sense of ownership has been cultivated among the people for the development of the community.

Tenthly, so far the Panchayats negotiated for schemes and programmes of the Government. Now the trend has been reversed and they ask for the Government's participation in their schemes and programmes. Petitioners have changed their role to that of negotiators because of this new exercise.

Eleventhly, the Panchayats have started mobilizing partners for their evelopment activities. They have gathered many organizations to their support in implementing their schemes.

Twelfthly, the leaders have built a vision document through this exercise. They have gained rich input on vision building from the training undergone elsewhere by the Presidents. While doing so they are critiquing the very concept of development. They move around the skills and the resources available at their disposal.

Though they are women and, that too, three of them are of the Backward Class and another three are *Dalits,* their leadership is recognized, appreciated and supported by even traditional Panchayat leaders. The women leaders, by their performance, have won the recognition of the community. Since initiatives are taken jointly by the leaders, the administration becomes transparent and it reduces corruption to the maximum extent. The planning exercise has made the people volunteers in the development initiative.

Conclusion

Planning at the grassroots for administering development and social justice has long range implications in the paradigm of development. It alters the entire process of development. The roles of the Government and the community have been reversed. All the loopholes in the development process in the existing paradigm have been exposed and people have developed a new perspective to look at issues and now plans of activities are chalked out on the basis of their demands and needs as prioritized by the people and not on the basis of the available schemes and programmes of the Government. The concept of: "we govern you participate" has gone and the new concept "you govern and you participate" has been ushered in. Social development issues have drawn the attention of the people because of this exercise and achievable indicators have been fixed on social development issues and people have taken up the responsibility of achieving the target. People have developed a sense of ownership as this plan document carries the demands of the people as schemes and programmes. Now the Government finds itself in a tight spot as to whether this is to be allowed or not. There is no other option except to allow and continue the new practice. Over and above, at the earliest, the entire state has to take the initiative to plan for development from the Gram Panchayat to the District Planning Committee. The new paradigm will gain momentum and it will ultimately end a movement for decentralized governance for development and social justice.

Acknowledgement : I record my thanks to The Hunger Project for its support to transport the women from the SHG to Panchayat which enabled them to undertake this exercise.

NOTES

1. For more details refer to K.V. Sundaram's work.
2. In this district the SHG members decided to contest in the election among themselves to avoid the competition of the political party candidates. After the election the defeated candidates came to the victorious candidates and congratulated her and offered her their support in initiatives and activities.
3. The Government of Tamil Nadu through the State Planning Commission has formulated guidelines for the preparation of plans at micro level and the same guidelines have been adopted in all these Gram Panchayats. This process had been explained to those involved in the plan exercise in the training programme itself.
4. The Centre for Rural Management is an NGO based at Kottayam with a good number of experts in micro level planning, helping Gandhigram Rural Institute in its interface programme and hence experts were drawn from this agency. The experts knew Tamil.
5. They are supporters of Panchayati Raj and they help Panchayat leaders in many ways to overcome their problems and to enhance their skill to perform better in Panchayats.
6. The State Planning Commission has conducted some pilot exercises in select Gram Panchayats with the help of the officials of the District Planning Committee and yet the documents could not be projected as models to be emulated.

REFERENCES

Chinnammal, C., (2002), *Perspective Plan for Development of Urathupatti*, Tirupathur: Grama Iyyakkam.

Commonwealth Foundation, (1999), *Citizens and Governance : Civil Society in the New Millennium*, London: The Common Wealth Foundation.

Gomathy, S., (2002), *Perspective Plan for Development of Manalur*, Tirupathur: Grama Iyyakkam.

Issac, T.M. Thomas and Franke Richard W., (2002), *Local Democracy and Development*, New Delhi: Left Word Books.

Manor, James, (1999), *The Political Economy of Democratic Decentralization*, Washington D.C: The World Bank.

Nagajothi, Y., (2002), *Perspective Plan for Development of Kozhikudipatti*, Tirupathur: Grama Iyyakkam.

Narayanasamy, N., Boraian, M.P. and Jeyaraju, M.A. (eds), (2000), *Corruption at the Grassroots: The Shades and Shadows*, New Delhi: Concept Publishing Company.

Palanithurai, G., (2002), *Report of the Pre-Election Voters Awareness*, Gandhigram: Rajiv Gandhi Chair for Panchayati Raj Studies.

Palanithurai, G., (2002), *Report of the Training on Multi Level Planning*, Gandhigram: Tamil Nadu Council for Sustainable Livelihood.

Palanithurai, G., (2002), *Report of the Workshop on Multi Level Planning*, Gandhigram: Tamil Nadu Council for Sustainable Livelihood.

Pushpam, A., (2002), *Perspective Plan for Development of P. Nerpuhapatti*, Tirupathur: Grama Iyyakkam.

Rakku, K., (2002), *Perspective Plan for Development of Vadavanpatti*, Tirupathur: Grama Iyyakkam.

Sundaram, K.V., (1997), *Decentralized Multi Level Planning : Principle and Practice*, New Delhi: Concept Publishing Company.

Veerakalaiarasi, (2002), *Perspective Plan for Development of Veppankulam*, Tirupathur: Grama Iyyakkam.

6

TRADITIONAL PANCHAYATS AND FORMAL PANCHAYATS

The 73rd Amendment to the Constitution of India has created space for decision-making by involving all social groups at the grassroots in the rural areas. This new dispensation has been imposed on communities which had their own structural arrangements to manage their community affairs by following the norms evolved over a period of time by the elite of the society, which is characterized as feudal, elitist, patriarchical and caste based and unchallenged (Medha Kotwal Lele, 2001, p. 4702). When the new formal institutions, with their earmarked responsibilities and powers, started functioning in the rural areas, they were confronted by the traditional Panchayats (G. Palanithurai, 2001). Wherever the traditional Panchayat is weak, the formal panchayat establishes its sway and wherever it is strong the formal Panchayat cannot make inroads and, as a result, conflicts between the two Panchayats are visible. In Tamil Nadu, due to the Dravidian movement, the caste hierarchy had been diluted to some extent to the advantage of the backward classes (Indhu Rajagopal, 1985) but not to that of the *Dalits*. Wherever the Dravidian movement established its impact the traditional structure has been weakened. In the same way wherever the Left movement registered an impact, the caste hierarchy has been dismantled even up to the *Dalits* and discriminatory practices have been mitigated if not eradicated*. This, however, is not uniform in all areas in Tamil Nadu. There are a few places where a synergy between the traditional Panchayat and the

---

* In certain districts, namely Nagapattinam and Thiruvarur in Tamil Nadu, the discriminatory practices have been totally eradicated.

formal panchayat has enabled the formal Panchayat to perform very well. Karisalpatti, a Gram Panchayat in Dindigul district, secured the second prize in Tamil Nadu State and the first prize at the district level to draw the attention of all as it performed well by synergising the two panchayats.

This study makes an attempt to analyze the dynamics of the systemic fusion of the two panchayats for the effective delivery of services to the people and to maintain harmony among the people in this panchayat area. Before investigating the problem, it is necessary to take a look at the backdrop of the problem.

How power relations in the rural areas are to be analysed is a major area of focus for academics in Anthropology. Political scientists focus much attention on state politics and federal polity but rarely touch upon the formal panchayat system under the caption of administration. Power and authority are vested with communities and community leaders to take decision which affect the life of the people. As power relationship changes at a snail's pace, it cannot be matched with the village economy and the state politics in terms of quantum of change. Power relations vary from place to place and region to region.

Studies on communities are available in plenty on the aspects of economy (Mukherjee, 1959), social structure and conflict of village communities (Amrita Basu and Atul Kohli, 1998). But little attention has been paid to the power relationship between groups and communities in the villages (Andre Beteille, 1965) on the assumption that the communities are far from the power relationship and operate outside the purview of state and central politics. Though village dynamics are different and distinct, there are linkages between the village and the wider political system. These linkages are intensive only during the time of elections. Yet power relations are strong on deciding things which affect the life of the community. The political process can be examined from the perspective of the relationship between the formal panchayats and the local elite, popularly called *grama nattanmai*. The formal panchayats are vested with specific political functions and they are to play an influencing role in deciding things which affect the life of the people. At the same time the *grama nattanmai*, with his own council, has got legitimacy from the community to decide things in the community either in the presence of the formal panchayat or in its absence. No matter what quantum of power the formal panchayat enjoys, the traditional panchayat has established its grip on the society. The manner in which power is distributed leads to the division of the village community into different categories. There are hierarchical arrangements in the traditional system. The traditional panchayat has its own role in the electoral process of the formation of the formal panchayat. Sometimes the role of the traditional panchayat is vital in determining the victory of the candidates and sometimes the role of external political influence, particularly from the state politics, is vital in determining the victory of the candidates in the elections.

In the context of shifting power relations how the formal panchayat manages the affairs of the community while facing the traditional panchayat and the problems of the people is the major area of concern in this work.

Methodology

To study the power dynamics in Karisalpatti Village Panchayat, the formal Panchayat leaders, the traditional Panchayat leaders and the Panchayat functionaries were contacted with the objective of eliciting their opinion of the success of the formal panchayat in the context of the presence of traditional panchayat. Formal panchayat leaders, informal community leaders and leaders of social and cultural institutions were asked questions relating to the success of the panchayat. Their reactions and observations are presented in this work.

History of the Village

Karisalpatti Gram Panchayat is a multi-caste village panchayat situated on the northern side of the Kannivadi Hills which is a part of the Western Ghats range. Karisalpatti is the main village and along with it there are two hamlets, namely Pazhaya Kannivadi and Karamadai. Karamadai is a new habitation coming up on the Palani-Sempatti State Highway.

Christian Vanniars are the dominant caste group in this panchayat. There are Hindu Vanniar families also living in the panchayat area. It is stated that the Vanniars of this area had their origin in the Chozha kingdom. The present Thiruchirapalli was once under the Chozha kingdom. A zamindar in the Chola kingdom ruled over a small area around Lalgudi. The above said Vanniar community lived in the Lalgudi area. Once the zamindar went out for hunting. He commanded the Vanniar community men who accompanied him to carry his shoes when he had to cross a river. The Vanniar menfolk took it as an insult to the community and refused to do so and started a dispute with the zamindar and in the ensuring encounter the zamindar was killed. Fearing the wrath of the zamindari administration, the majority of the Vanniar families escaped from the Lalgudi area and proceeded south to seek a new habitation for their settlement. In this way their kith and kin settled here in Dindigul district. It was stated by the old men and women of this village that this incident occurred in the fifteenth century and that during the British period most of them converted to Christianity.

The Vanniars on the hillocks of Kannivadi are brave enough to domesticate wild elephants. The word *kari* means elephant and the word *patti* means shed. Karisalpatti is the place where the wild elephants are domesticated by the brave Vanniar community. The community has lived cooperatively and faced the elephant menace successfully. Hence the village is called Karisalpatti.

Caste and Religious Composition

Christian Vanniars are the dominant caste group. There are 500 families belonging to the Christian Vanniar community. The Hindu Vellalars are the next in numerical strength, with 150 families. People belonging to the SC number about 100 families. They are of the Parayar sub-caste. Chettiyars are a minority community and there are only ten families in Karisalpatti Village.

Christianity is the main religion practised by 70 per cent of the population. Karisalpatti has been a Christian Parish since 1976. A primary school started in the year 1985 is run by the

Parish. Now it is functioning with eleven teachers and four hundred students. To cater to the educational needs of the higher class students, in the year 1960, a high school was sanctioned to Karisalpatti at the initiative of the community leaders. The Karisalpatti Village community donated four acres of land and Rs.10,000 cash for starting the high school.

Religious celebrations by the Christian families bring about a feeling of oneness among them. There are seven Crusadies, that is, places earmarked for the fixing of the Holy Cross in seven streets. The families living in each street organize flag hoisting during festivals and distribute free meal to all. A car procession is also an event during the celebration. These religious activities make the people work together.

The Parish priest exercises a moral authority over every Christian family. From birth till death a number of ceremonies have to be observed with the help of the Parish priest as done by the Hindus with the help of a Brahmin priest. The Parish priest explained during the interview that there are seven types of religious ceremonies called Sacraments which must be observed by each Christian family. They are as follows:

1. Baptism of every child at the age of one month.
2. Orientation in Christianity and Holly Communion at the age of ten.
3. Confirmation of faith at the age of ten.
4. Confession.
5. Anointment of the sick (Extreme function).
6. Solemnizing marriage (Matrimony).
7. Burial of the dead.

These Holy Sacraments create a sense of oneness among the Christians and create a conducive environment for undertaking any activities benefiting the community under the moral authority of the Parish priest. The Parish priest further explained that the sermons delivered by the Church authorities during the ceremony of the Mass includes guidance for day-to-day life also. The Church involves itself in creating awareness among the people about the importance of sanitation, childcare, women's development and public health.

Role of Traditional Heads

When the Parish priest explained the social dynamics of the Christian community in Karisalpatti, he brought to light the power and authority of the traditional panchayat leaders and their committees. In spite of the moral supremacy of the Parish priest over the Christian community, the Parish administration has to adjust with the traditional community system in Karisalpatti Village.

The traditional panchayat committee consists of three members. The *Nattanmai* is the head and the *Maniam* and the *Chinna Nattanmai* are his deputies. For any social activity or religious activity, the traditional panchayat committee has to be consulted. This system has further cemented the solidarity among the communities. In villages traditional panchayat committee members are mostly drawn from a set of families. It is observed that through the traditional panchayat committee social control is imposed on the people of Karisalpatti. But the people of this area view this control as moral in nature.

Community mobilization among the Hindus is also being done through temples. The temples of Lord Vinayaka, Goddess Kaliamman, Bhaghavathiamman and Muthalamman are the institutions through which the Hindu community generates the feeling of unity. Vinayaka Sathurthi celebration is now becoming a Hindu community celebration as all the castes, Vellalars, Chettiars and *Dalits* join together in observing the same.

Among the Hindu families castewise traditional committees are also functioning. Any dispute not settled by them is brought to the notice of the traditional panchayat committee of the Christian Vanniars as it is the supreme body. The judgment delivered by this committee over the dispute between the members of other castes is final and accepted in general by all. Any violation or breach is treated as an anti-social activity. The first respect is always given to the traditional committee of the respective castes. At the same time the Christian Vanniars' panchayat committee is considered supreme. It is said that the participation of women is generally not permitted during the meeting of the traditional panchayat.

There are specific places earmarked for each caste where the traditional committee or any other common meet is organized. The village ground is earmarked for the Christian Vanniars, the temple campus for Vellalars, the Chavadi for Hindu Vanniars and the *Dalit* community has a separate place. People celebrate religious functions and spend a lot. The Christians celebrate New Year, Saint Antony's day, the Pascha, St. Sebastian's day, Holy Yatra to Velankanni, Karamadai Matha day, Resurrection day, and Christmas. Hindus celebrate Pongal, Muthalamman temple festival, Vinayaka Sathurthi, Adi Perukku and Deepavali.

Collecting donations, planning of celebrations and organizing of various events by Hindus and Christians, though done separately, generates much socialization among the villagers. Both religious groups mutually admire and participate in the religious functions. Hence it is said that inter-caste and inter-religious marriages are common in Karisalpatti Village. Three marriages between Hindu Vellalars and Christian Vanniars and two marriages between Hindu Vanniars and Christian Vanniars have been solemnized recently. There is no conflict among the caste and religious groups due to these inter-caste marriages since these marriages are accepted by the traditional panchayat.

Consolidation of Womenfolk

Harmony in a society can be disturbed if there is any eruption involving women in the rural areas. Women in general have been less oriented in social life. Now the trend is getting changed slowly. Activities relating to mobilizing women, initiated by the Church authorities as well as Government departments, have brought about a new climate in rural areas. Self-help groups have brought together women of different communities. Though they deal among themselves in micro credit and micro finance activities, a number of other social activities are introduced to them. Awareness has been created among the women on education, health, sanitation, reproductive and child health and child welfare along with economic activities. There are five vibrant self-help groups working in Karisalpatti. With the help of an NGO the self-help groups got loan for their micro finance activities. In addition to the above mentioned women related activities, nurses from the Christian Convent used to meet the womenfolk periodically and offer counsel to them. Awareness about health is being created by the nuns of the Convent where the nurse trainees used to go for their training placement. Yet the women have little role in the traditional panchayat system.

Youth and the Community

There is a Youth Committee constituted by the formal panchayat for promoting sports and games. The youth of all castes are making use of this forum. In the name of V.O. Chidambaram (a freedom fighter), the youth belonging to the Vellalar community formed a group and the SC youth formed an Ambedkar Youth Association. The Christian youth have formed a Youth Club to undertake religious activities. Both religious and sports activities have brought the youth of different castes together. They stage dramas and cultural programmes during Christmas. The youth of Karisalpatti sustain the harmonious relationship among themselves and so far they have never entertained any illwill or hatered in the name of religion or caste. The community leaders never misguide the youth. Hence a smooth and congenial atmosphere prevails among the youth of Karisalpatti. Both the formal and traditional panchayat leaders orient the youth properly for maintaining peace and communal harmony.

Common Property Resources

Drinking Water Resources

There are five wells meant for drinking water, of which three are in use and the other two are not in use as the water in the wells has dried up. The drinking water has been brought under the comprehensive village water supply scheme of the Government. It is meant for two village panchayats, namely Karisalpatti and Kasavanampatti. The sharing ratio of water between these two panchayats is 5:3. There are two overhead tanks and one ground level reservoir to supply water to 39 public taps and 130 individual taps in individual houses. A deposit of Rs.1000 each for all the 130 individual tap connections has been collected by the panchayat. The monthly water tax of Rs. 30 per household is also collected regularly. Centper cent water charges collection has been ensured till July 2002.

There are five handpumps, of which four are functioning well. In one bore well, a mini pump has been fitted with the financial assistance of TWAD. The water points are properly monitored as the social groups of the concerned street ensure proper and equitable distribution of water and prevention of any misuse. Moreover if any unexpected failure occurs, spare parts are kept ready in the panchayat office to replace the defective ones. The village community cooperates in the maintenance of water supply points. In all collective action, the traditional panchayat helps the formal panchayat.

During the current season of severe drought due to the failure of the monsoon, in consultation with the community, a system of public water supply at one point was arranged for the continuous and equal distribution of water to all. In the meantime, the deepening of a well meant for drinking water was undertaken by the panchayat. In the midst of a financial crisis, the panchayat decided to draw money from the deposit money collected for individual tap connections. The President informed that the decision was intimated to the higher officials of the Department and, after the receipt of the grant from the Government, the money would be repaid to the water supply account. This decision of withdrawing of money is contrary to panchayat rules. Yet, because the community insisted, the panchayat took such a decision. The members unanimously resolved in this regard and if any action was initiated against the panchayat, the village community as a whole would stand up to rescue the panchayat. Being transparent in his transactions, the President commands respect and confidence and support among the public. The President said that a local youth could be given training in handpump mechanism by which means the dependence on the panchayat union mechanic could be avoided.

Streetlight Maintenance

There are seventy-seven tubelights in Karisalpatti. Sodium vapour lamps are not fitted anywhere in Karisalpatti. Though the

Government of Tamil Nadu allowed the panchayats to purchase sodium vapour lamps, the Karisalpatti Panchayat President declined to do so as it would increase the electricity bill. This decision was taken after consulting all concerned. The traditional panchayat leaders are aware of the implications of the excess use of electricity and water and hence they always support the energy conservation activities. To them natural resources are the lifeline of the community. Now, when all Panchayats are facing financial crunch, Karisalpatti maintains its finances very well. Moreover it is noted that the village community does not demand sodium vapour lamps as they witness the successful handling of any failure in the streetlights in the present system. Maintenance work is carried out properly by the Panchayat. A ceiling of Rs. 22,000 is fixed for the head streetlights maintenance. The Gram Panchayat has never spent more than Rs.15,000. The Panchayat used to switch on the lights from 7.00 p.m. to 5.30 a.m. only. The Village Panchayat is remitting the Electricity Bill regularly and the community has extended their cooperation in the maintenance of streetlights.

Maintenance of Graveyard

There are five locations earmarked for graveyard. The extent of the site is as follows: 1 acre, 0.30 cent, 0.10 cent, 0.15 cent, and 0.05 cent. The approach roads to two sites were improved by the Panchayat. Half a kilometre of BT road and half a kilometre of mud road were laid. With the support of the community, a shed at a cost of Rs.15,000 was erected in the graveyard meant for the Christian community. When the demand for the provision of the shed came during the Gram Sabha, the Panchayat explained its inability but agreed to undertake road improvement. Hence the community happily came forward to meet the expenditure of the erection of a shed for funerals. In each and every activity of the formal panchayat, the traditional panchayat takes responsibilities including contribution in monetary terms.

Road Maintenance

The Gram Sabha decided which roads were to be converted to cement concrete. The village community listed six roads as having priority. Further the community decided to lay a BT road to the high school. Normally decisions are taken only after a prolonged discussion. On most occasions, the President used to take time to explain and convince the members and then only decisions are taken. The strength of the Panchayat is the prevalence of communal harmony and broad understanding among the caste groups. People are oriented by the traditional panchayat in participating in the meetings of the community. In the community meetings all the participants have equal opportunity to speak and hence they conduct meetings for longer durations. The same practice has been extended to the Gram Sabha also.

Community Tanks and Maintenance

A tank under the category of Manthai remained unutilized for several years. When water was available, villagers used to take their cattle there. During 1997-98 the tank was desilted and deepened properly by the Panchayat after a decision was taken in the Gram Sabha meeting to augment resources through tree-plantation on the banks of the tank.

The Manthaikulam, with an extent of 2 acres, is now maintained properly. Seventeen coconut trees, 50 silk cotton trees, 50 bamboo trees, 50 tamarind trees and 10 vaagai trees have been planted on the banks of the tank. Before the growth of the trees an inter-crop was proposed by the community and flower plants were cultivated. In the next two years Rs.10,000 was earned through the auction of these flower plants by the Panchayat. The community cooperated with the Panchayat in the maintenance of this tank. Fencing was done by the Panchayat. The youth helped to protect the tank. After the successful venture in the Manthaikulam, it was decided to undertake the planting of 400 silk cotton trees in another tank known as Kanakkankulam, which is four acres in extent. Three years after plantation, the silk cotton trees would yield Rs.10,000 per year. The maintenance of these tanks is possible for the Panchayat as the villagers have witnessed the utility of the common properties under the management of the Village Panchayat. Moreover any encroachment is dealt with seriously by the Panchayat irrespective of the community of the encroachers.

Recently an individual erected a shed on a Village Panchayat land. He was asked to remove the encroachment. As he failed to remove it, a notice was issued. Besides, a complaint was registered with the police station by the Panchayat. In the meantime the leaders of all communities were told about the proposed action against the particular encroacher. Understanding the role of the Panchayat in the maintenance of common property resources, the community leaders agreed to support the Panchayat administration. To verify the ownership of the disputed site, the village revenue officials were contacted and the records available were verified. After ensuring that the site belonged to the Village Panchayat, with the help of the police, the erected shed was removed and the materials are still kept in the Village Panchayat office. There was no tension as the community supported the Panchayat. In the meantime the concerned individual agreed to a compromise and it was decided to settle the dispute by imposing a fine on him. All these activities are possible only because of good understanding between the community and the Panchayat. In many Gram Panchayats in Tamil Nadu eviction of encroachers is a tough job and the Panchayat leaders find it very difficult as the community leaders do not extend any cooperation. But in Karisalpatti the traditional Panchayat leaders help the Panchayat to retrieve the property from the encroachers.

Maintenance of Orchards and Social Forestry

The campus of the Village Panchayat office is vast. When the Gandhigram Rural Institute students proposed their camp in Karisalpatti, a village meeting was held to discuss the plan for utilising their camp days fruitfully. In that meeting a proposal was made to lay a garden in the campus. It was said that the plants could be irrigated as drain water is available from the nearby community hall. During 1998-99, the students' camp was organised. The village youth joined hands with farmers and reclaimed the land lying waste for many years. Now, a garden of nearly sixty banana trees, fifty coconut trees and six tamarind trees has come up in the campus. Marriages are conducted in the nearby community hall. For each marriage banana trees are needed as they are considered an auspicious welcome festoon. Hence, at the rate of Rs. 75 each, banana trees are sold to the public. Since 1998-99 Rs. 9000 has been credited to the Panchayat account from the sale of banana trees.

Claim over the Entitlement to Tamarind Trees

The Sempatti-Palani State Rural Highway runs through Karisalpatti and Dharmathupatti Villages. Each Village Panchayat is a separate one but under the jurisdiction of one revenue village. So far the roadside tamarind trees were under the enjoyment of Dharmathupatti even though the rural highway runs through Karisalpatti Village Panchayat limits. When the Panchayat approached the Highways authorities to hand over the tamarind trees of Karisalpatti they asked to prove the entitlement of Karisalpatti. Hence the revenue authorities were contacted and, after duly verifying the survey number of the highway, the Village Administrative Officer certified that the land came under Karisalpatti Village Panchayat. It was found that there are 6 tamarind trees within the Karisalpatti Panchayat limits. Now, after paying the prescribed fees to the Highways, the Panchayat of Karisalpatti has got six tamarind trees. The village elders helped by accompanying the Panchayat President to meet the Highways officials. The village community's level of consciousness and interest in common property resources is very high and it is an example of an organized community. The community has realised that the trees are yielding revenue to the Panchayat and so the community is coming forward to join hands with the panchayat in managing the common property resources.

The Categories of Common Buildings

Apart from sites, trees, ponds, and tanks a number of buildings are also listed as common property resources of the Panchayat. A look at the list of items under the head buildings in the register maintained by the Panchayat will make the visitor wonder.

There are different types of buildings, all put to proper use in Karisalpatti Village and the maintenance of these buildings is also taken care of by the Panchayat.

It is a common sight in any village that the public toilet is lying unused in spite of a *pucca* building constructed for the purpose. In Karisalpatti it is a different story. Two community toilets, one for males and the other for females, were constructed and both are used by the villagers. Awareness is created about the proper use and maintenance of these toilets by the Panchayat. Witnessing the successful use of the community toilets, an additional public toilet (a sanitary complex) was allotted and construction was completed. Women groups are entrusted with the responsibility of looking after these public toilets. Cards have been issued to the families and a nominal amount is collected for maintenance.

The Panchayat office building, the health sub-centre, the veterinary hospital and the community-cum-marriage hall are located in one campus. There are toilet facilities in the Panchayat office as well as the community hall. The toilet at the community hall was constructed from the incentive money given to Karisalpatti for the community's involvement through the Panchayat in the activities of a project on social development sponsored by Population Foundation of India.

An old building was renovated and a part-time library is now functioning in it. The Annai Velankanni Pilgrimage Association donated folding chairs to the library. The villagers use this library. There are three TV rooms and the television sets are functioning well. The village volunteers are looking after these properties.

A ration shop is functioning in the Panchayat in its own building. The maintenance of the same is also done whenever necessary by the Panchayat. There is a chavadi, a common place maintained by the Village Panchayat. The villagers make use of it as a place for rest and community meets. A *balwadi* is also functioning in an independent building owned by the Panchayat. There is a primary school run by the Panchayat Union. The maintenance work in the primary school is periodically done by the Panchayat. These common buildings are put to use effectively in Karisalpatti Panchayat. The Ward Members are asked to look after the buildings located in their respective wards. The youth are asked not to spoil the walls of these common properties. They help the Panchayat to maintain these buildings. Consciousness of the community in maintaining common properties is visible in Karisalpatti Village as all buildings are in proper use.

Poramboke Lands

Among the poramboke lands entrusted to the Village Panchayat there are roadside poramboke, canal poramboke and footpath poramboke. There are eight areas of roadside poramboke to the extent of 3.79 acre, 12.72 acres of canal poramboke and 8.08 acres of roadside poramboke. The President informed that there is no encroachment on these poramboke lands.

Community Initiative in Digging a New Tank

Due to scarcity of irrigation water the farmers of Karisalpatti felt very badly the unexpected fall in the level of their ground water sources. Understanding the importance and necessity of creation of a new water storage tank for their farm land, the farmers expressed their felt need for constructing a new tank in their area during the Gram Sabha meetings. The Panchayat President informed the community of the non-availability of any common land to spare for digging a new tank. Further, during the discussion on the subject, a few farmers suggested that there was a site of an extent of 4 acres owned by the Parish of Karisalpatti which could be the fittest site for the construction of a new tank. Its topography was suitable to serve as a catchment area and a channel was also running on the other side, which could be made use of for outlet of water if necessary during the monsoon. As the suggestion attracted all it was decided to make efforts under the leadership of the Panchayat to get the particular land from the Parish of Karisalpatti.

The Anthoniar Tank Renovation Committee was constituted to take up this assignment. The President of Karisalpatti Village Panchayat served as adviser to the Committee. There were eleven members in the Committee. Village elders, community leaders and farmers used to attend the meetings of this Committee.

The Committee met the Parish priest and the traditional panchayat committee members and shared the idea of construction of a new tank for the benefit of the villagers in general and the farming community in particular. The factor of non-availability of any other common land was duly highlighted. After considering the plea of the villagers, the Parish came forward to spare the land of 4 acres. The value of the land was Rs.1.5 lakhs. The Church authorities permitted the villagers to dig a new tank there. The Committee appealed to all farmers whose lands were spread around the land earmarked for the tank to join in this endeavour. Though the property belonged to the Parish, cutting across religions, farmers of both Christian and Hindu religions contributed money. Rs.1.0 lakh was collected and digging was undertaken. The villagers requested the Panchayat to help in the construction of a check dam across the channel running along the tank. A resolution was passed in the Panchayat Council meeting and the District Panchayat was contacted for funds. At a cost of Rs. 0.70 lakh the check dam-*cum*-outlet sluice arrangement was constructed.

Some individuals failed to appreciate the good efforts of the public. A few individuals reported to the higher authorities that the Panchayat misguided the District Panchayat and that the Village Panchayat showed the patta land as poramboke. Due to this complaint the allocation of funds was delayed. Then the records were verified and it was proved that the site identified for the check dam-*cum*-outlet sluice was of the category of odai poramboke as per the village revenue records. Hence an extent of 5 × 10 metre land was put to proper use where the check dam was constructed. As a token of appreciation of the community the local member of the Legislative Assembly took part in the ceremony organised jointly by the Anthoniar Tank Renovation Committee and the Village Panchayat during 2001-2002. It is said that the Parish authorities consented to give in writing to the Anthoniar Tank Renovation Committee that the tank could be utilised by all the people though the Parish owns the legal title to the land. The important principle of local dynamics operated during the whole process of the dialogue between the Church and the Anthoniar Tank Renovation Committee. The Panchayat leaders clearly understood the local dynamics and so facilitated the interaction between the Tank Committee and the Church.

The Status of Revenue Poramboke in Karisalpatti

There is a total extent of 15 hectares of poramboke land in the following categories:

Road poramboke	—	5 hectares
Odai poramboke	—	5 hectares
Natham poramboke	—	5 hectares

The Village Administrative Officer (VAO), when interviewed, informed that there is no land available in the Karisalpatti Panchayat limits for assignment, except the above rementioned road, odai and natham porambokes. Under natham poramboke, apart from the existing houses, the front yard of each house also comes under the natham account. Hence it could not be assigned to others as the households themselves kept these lands in their possession.

He suggested that memos under 'B' form, challenging any encroachment, should not be issued for the forest and hillside lands. These lands come under non-cessable land and so they could not be made available for assignment to any individual. But, at the same time, when 'B' memo is served, the encroacher used to take the issue to court and continue to enjoy these lands without paying any compensation to the Government. Moreover the encroachers of this type are usually not small farmers or landless labourers, but mostly rich and wealthy individuals. The VAO suggested to constitute a joint committee consisting of Panchayat, Forest, Revenue officials and representatives of the general public to look after these common property resources for their proper maintenance, protection if need arises, for the distribution of these lands to the community or to individual beneficiaries. Now vast extents of non-cessable lands are under the clutches of rich people in the hillsides of Kannivadi. He maintained that if the Panchayat and Revenue administration joined together a more successful management of common property resources would be possible.

To generate additional income to the Panchayat, enhancement of house tax was proposed by the Ward Members during the Panchayat Council meeting. The proposal was discussed during the Gram Sabha meet held on 18th May 2002 and it was resolved to enhance the house tax slab from Rs.11 to Rs.22 and Rs.22 to Rs.33 and the licence fee collected from the shops was enhanced from Rs.50 to Rs.75. Further it was decided to increase the rent of the community hall from Rs.500 to Rs.750. These proposals did not cause any problem during the Gram Sabha meeting. The participants approved of the enhancement unanimously.

A deadline was fixed to collect the cable TV tax from the cable TV operator, and, after this, the cable TV operator paid the tax for 55 connections at the rate of Rs.10 per connection till April 2002. The operator promised to pay the balance tax amount at the earliest. The deposit of Rs.10,000 as per the Government Order has also not yet been paid by the operator. This was informed to the public during the Gram Sabha meeting.

Regularization of Drinking Water Supply

The habitations in Karisalpatti Village are situated on an undulating landscape. Hence distribution of drinking water needed regularization. With public cooperation, 12 gate valves were fixed in the pipeline. During the summer, considering the scarcity of water in the sources as well as interrupted power supply, distribution of water was properly planned and equal distribution to all, both upland habitations and low level dwellings, was ensured. The public adjusted to the system of getting water at different times.

Community Sanitation

During 1999-2000, under JVVT, a public toilet for women was constructed. As the women failed to use it, an awareness programme was conducted with the help of nuns and trainee nurses. Now it is in full use. It is observed from the village that any facility that is being provided by the Government through schemes, will not be utilized by the people for their benefit unless they are conscientised. In this Panchayat, the Panchayat leader takes the services of the Church and the traditional panchayat. The Panchayat transforms every facility which comes through schemes into a demand driven one from a supply driven one. During 2000-2001, as demanded, a public toilet for men was constructed along the graveyard road. Menfolk are using this toilet.

Under the new scheme of sanitary complex, during 2001-2002, an integrated sanitary complex for women and children was constructed. In addition to Rs.1.75 lakh earmarked under the MLA area development fund, Rs.0.35 lakh from Panchayat funds was also spent for providing facilities in this sanitary complex. Now 102 families are enlisted as beneficiaries of this complex. A sum Rs.10 per month is collected and a committee of beneficiaries is constituted to administer the complex. Two women among the committee members have opened a bank account and they jointly operate the account.

Milk Producers Cooperative Society *vs.* Panchayat

In Karisalpatti, the majority caste of Vanniars consolidated their unity through their caste association of Vanniar Sangam during the statewide mobilization-*cum*-movement initiatives under the leadership of Dr. Ramdass. It was reported that the State high command of the Vanniar Sangam misguided the Vanniars and instigated them to resort to violence. The Karisalpatti experience was otherwise. Of course the Vanniars of Karisalpatti too were sensitized and organized themselves like the Vanniars of other parts of the State during the movement. At the same time, they developed a positive mental attitude through this process. The Church played a predominant role in culturing the community rather than instigating the community to resort to violence. They organized a cooperative society for milk producers along with the caste organizational activities during the 1980s. In the year 1988, the Karisalpatti Milk Producers' Cooperative was formed with 700 members. It is said that the society brought about a basic change in the lifestyle of the Vanniar community. The menfolk engaged in rearing milch animals and so they used their time and energy constructively. Otherwise they would have often engaged in disputes with others or among themselves and lost peace in their life. Rearing of milch animals became a full time job for those families who were landless and the landed gentry also spared their time and energy for this avocation as it was one of the allied activities of agriculture. The Milk Producers' Cooperative created an impact on the socio-economic life of each family in Karisalpatti.

The pioneers who formed the Society sustained their leadership in spite of the curse of political interference in the cooperative sector. The Society initially functioned well. But recently there have been maladministration and benami transactions. When credit facility was given to procure milch animals for the members, the President of the Society released loan amounts in the name of six members who were his kith and kin. Rs.1.70 lakh fell due from their account and in the meantime he sold all the milch animals also. Being a defaulter himself, the President could not command the other members when they failed to bring milk to the Society. The actual sufferers were those who regularly supplied milk to the Society. About Rs. 5 lakhs, due to those who regularly supplied milk, could not be paid. After registering complaint with the District Registrar of Cooperatives, the members sold their milk to private vendors and they too started defaulting.

Intervention of Panchayat

The President of Karisalpatti Panchayat happened to be the Vice-President of the Milk Society. All the members of the society asked him to take necessary action against the culprit. A team of villagers and the Panchayat President met the concerned officials and the cheque power of the board of the Society was withdrawn so that further misappropriation could be prevented.

The traditional panchayat meeting was convened and the president of the Society being the *Chinna Nattanmai* of the community, the suggestions of the Panchayat President in this regard were accepted. The accused person sought one month's time to settle the loans and, with the witness of Police officials, time was given. But he failed to repay as promised and so an Action Committee was formed under the leadership of the Panchayat President. A proposal for road *roko* was announced. The Police and the Revenue officials swung into action and they warned the accused that he would be arrested. He undertook to pay Rs.25,000 within 10 days and the balance amount within a month. He paid Rs.25,000 to the Society but he failed to pay the balance. Again the Committee announced an agitation and Rs.20,000 was paid by the accused. Time has been given to pay the balance.

The Panchayat President said that most of the members of the Society belong to the DMK party, whereas he belongs to the AIADMK party. But all of them unanimously resolved to make him the chairperson of the Action Committee. They repose faith in his leadership, not because of his party involvement, but because of his leadership in the Panchayat. The village community considers him their common leader. Thus the Panchayati Raj System has brought about a new trend in local leadership.

Panchayat Income and Expenditure

House tax, professional tax, licence fees, building licence fee, rent from Panchayat buildings, auction of fish ponds and trees, entertainment tax, cable TV tax, advertisement tax, stamp duty share, land tax share and grants from Government are the major sources of revenue. The State Finance Commission grant, matching grant for house tax, grant for the funeral expenses of poor SC families and other grants are also received. On the expenditure side, the following items of expenditure are recurring ones and the expenditure cannot be avoided as if the statutory responsibility of any Village Panchayat: salary to panchayat staff, maintenance of roads and streets, maintenance of drinking water supply system, payment of electricity bills for streetlights, Panchayat buildings and water supply pumps, maintenance of streetlights, maintenance of environmental sanitation, sitting fee to Panchayat Ward Members, stationery and postage expenses and TA to the clerk and the President. Further the doles to Panchayat staff as per the Government direction have to be given by the Panchayat and all these items of expenditure have to be met from the income of the Village Panchayat.

Scheme funds allotted by both Centre and State cannot be diverted to the above mentioned activities. The scheme funds have to be spent for the specified work as per the direction of the Central and State Governments. Most of the time the funds are tied up. Even the felt needs prioritized by the people could not be taken up under the scheme funds. In this context augmentation of the Panchayat's own resources becomes an urgent necessity. Karisalpatti Panchayat felt the need and took steps to improve its income sources through common property resources. A review of the income and expenditure of Karisalpatti since the introduction of the New Panchayati Raj System will give a lot of information on the efforts taken by the Panchayat in resource mobilization as well as activities initiated for the betterment of the public.

During the year 1996-97

Table 6.1 : Income and Expenditure of the Panchayats during 1996-97

Sl. No.	Income	Rs.	Expenditure	Rs.
1.	Stamp duty	40918.00	Maintenance of water supply	2985.00
2.	House and professional tax	5884.00	Salary of staff and TA	21397.00
3.	Auctioning of trees	2350.00	EB charges	24096.00
4.	Matching grant for house tax collection	1012.00	Streetlight maintenance	365.00
5.	Opening balance	5667.00	Closing balance	7753.00
	Total	55831.00	Total	56596.00

Source : Computed from Karisalpatti Gram Panchayat records.

It is observed that 40 per cent was spent for establishment, 5.64 per cent for water and sanitation and 45 per cent for payment of electricity bills during the period 1996-97.

Table 6.2 : Income and Expenditure of the Panchayats during 1997-98

Sl. No.	Income	Rs.	Expenditure	Rs.
1.	House tax	4100.00	Establishment	37410.00
2.	Professional tax	9900.00	EB charges	28811.00
3.	SFC grant	53445.00	Water and sanitation	13103.00
4.	Other grant (Matching grant)	24860.00	Common property management	3453.00
			Streetlight maintenance	4285.00
			Road repair	500.00
			Other expenses	1877.00
			Balance	2788.00
	Total	92305.00	Total	92227.00

Source : Computed from Karisalpatti Gram Panchayat records.

The expenditure during 1997-98 is observed to be 40.60 per cent for establishment, 31.27 per cent for electricity bills, 14.22 per cent for water and sanitation, 3.74 per cent for common property resource management and 4.65 per cent for streetlight maintenance.

Table 6.3 : Income and Expenditure of the Panchayats during 1998-99

Sl. No.	Income	Rs.	Expenditure	Rs.
1.	Comprehensive water supply scheme	26652.00	Establishment	54151.00
2.	Auction of flowers	400.00	EB charges	37885.00
3.	Community hall rent	750.00	Water and sanitation	22269.00
4.	Building licence	950.00	Construction of new buildings TV room	48044.00
5.	Stamp duty share	46373.00		
6.	House tax matching grant	21864.00		
7.	SFC grant	53557.00		
	Total	150546	Total	162349

Source : Computed from Karisalpatti Gram Panchayat records.

Table 6.4 : Income and Expenditure of the Panchayats during 1999-2000

Sl. No.	Income	Rs.	Expenditure	Rs.
1.	House tax and matching grant	34251.00	EB charges	74808.00
2.	Professional tax	16740.00	Sanitation	25534.00
3.	Dangerous objectional trade licence	4260.00	Maintenance of street light and drainage	45559.00
4.	Community hall rent	9500.00	Bank balance	9686.00
5.	Tree auction	3919.00		
6.	Stamp duty share	34726.00		
7.	SFC grant	109034.00		
8.	Comprehensive drinking water supply	26485.00		
9.	Other grants	10586.00		
10.	Auction of wastage and scraps	284.00		
	Total	249785.00	Total	155587

Source : Computed from Karisalpatti Gram Panchayat records.

Table 6.5 : Income and Expenditure of the Panchayats during 2000-2001

Sl. No.	Income	Rs.	Expenditure	Rs.
1.	House tax	15900.00	Establishment	76221.00
2.	Matching grant	15150.00	EB charges	72744.00
3.	Professional tax	16150.00	Sanitation	32109.00
4.	Building licence	3080.00	Maintenance of streetlights and other properties	67338.00
5.	Income from community hall	9250.00	Purchase of sports materials	2850.00
6.	Income from common properties, trees and flowers	4938.00	Bank balance	179661.00
7.	Stamp duty share	44295.00		
8.	SFC	81150.00		
9.	Comprehensive water supply scheme	15046.00		
10.	Award money	200000.00		
11.	GRI grant	8000.00		
	Total	412959.00	Total	430923

Source : Computed from Karisalpatti Gram Panchayat records.

Scheme Funds
Receipt Details

Sl. No.	Year	Scheme	Amount (Rs.)
1.	1996-1997	JVVT	68,000
2.	1997-1998	JVVT	50,692
3.	1998-1999	JVVT	70,660
4.	1999-2000	JGSY	51,623
5.	2000-2001	JGSY	53,539
6.	2001-2002	JGSY 1st instalment	54,100

Source : Computed from Karisalpatti Gram Panchayat records.

There were many items of income during the year 1998-99. As house tax was increased the incentive given by the State Government also increased under house tax matching grant. Professional tax collection also increased. The drinking water supply was through a comprehensive rural water supply scheme which included another nearby Panchayat.

Activities Undertaken under Scheme Funds:

1. Adi Dravidar colony improvement, TV room, Chavadi, Cement concrete roads, threshing floor, were provided at a total cost of Rs. 92,105.
2. Culverts, retaining wall, kitchen room for community hall, drainage were provided at a cost of Rs. 89,530.
3. Community toilet for women, CRSP toilet, community toilet for men were constructed at a total cost of Rs. 91,305.
4. CC road was provided to main streets at a cost of Rs. 16,104.

An allocation of Rs. 59,446 was made for the construction of a toilet in the SC colony. Due to inadequate space, the families did not want a toilet. Hence the amount was refunded.

From this analysis it is observed that, without tapping additional sources, the Village Panchayat cannot meet the recurring expenses under various items like establishment, payment of electricity bills, water and sanitation expenses, maintenance of streetlights, roads, streets, buildings and other common property resources.

In Karisalpatti an attempt was made to generate additional income through growing trees in the Panchayat tank and

Panchayat premises, claiming entitlement to roadside trees and improving the facilities in the community hall so that it could be rented for functions. Further, with the involvement of the community, the administration of the Panchayat was able to enhance the taxes, collect the taxes and avail of the matching grant from the government. Moreover it got the award money of Rs.2.0 lakhs and Rs. 8,000 from the Government and Gandhigram Rural Institute respectively for its good performance in carrying out its functions. This could be achieved only with the support and cooperation of the community. We can understand the synergization of the Village Panchayat with and the traditional panchayat. It is understood that the Karisalpatti Village community realizes the significance of the power, authority and function of the Village Panchayat under the New Panchayati Raj System and so the community make proper use of the Panchayat for its development. And the Panchayat leadership understands the strength of the community and so gives due recognition to the community, duly holds consultation with the community, and, avails of its opinion and guidance whenever necessary for smooth and successful administration in the Panchayat.

Conclusion

The New Panchayati Raj System was introduced with the twin objective of bringing about economic development in rural areas and ensuring social justice. Further, to strengthen the grassroots democracy, the participation of the people is encouraged through Gram Sabha meetings. The earlier system of Panchayati Raj did not provide for the involvement of the community and so a gap developed between the community and the Panchayat which destroyed the community initiatives through the Panchayat. These drawbacks have been removed in the new system. In Karisalpatti Village Panchayat, after the introduction of the New Panchayati Raj System, the leadership is capacitated and the community is informed well about the Panchayati Raj System. Stress is given to mobilizing the community through the Panchayat. Community based organizations are properly linked with the Panchayat. Against this backdrop this study has been made of the involvement of the community in the management of common property resources in Karisalpatti through the Village Panchayat. The findings are as follows.

A capacitated Panchayat leadership comprehended the ways and means of development. Linkages with community based organizations helped the Panchayat to strengthen its power and so delivery was qualitatively good. If common property resources could be improved, income to the Panchayat would be augmented in which the traditional panchayat plays an important role. Special funds are needed to improve common property resources. Expenditure on establishment, electricity bills and maintenance is always high. Prudent counsel provided by the traditional panchayat helped the Panchayat to manage its finances. The Panchayat must be enabled to promote awareness on Panchayati Raj, sanitation and public health. Instead of tying up grants, the Panchayat should be permitted to make use of scheme funds for felt needs.

Mobilization of the community is the prerequisite for any developmental activities and it is not easy for the Government machinery to mobilize the people. The Village Panchayat, under the New Panchayati Raj System of governance, has ample opportunities to interact with the people for a better orientation of the community to plan and work for the better utilisation of common property resources. In circumstances wherein the traditional community understands the power and responsibility of the New Panchayati Raj Institutions, the Panchayati Raj leadership should be proactive. The leadership of the traditional panchayat and its strength have to be understood by the President and Ward Members of Panchayati Raj Institutions. It is expected that, for any development, pooling energies is required in the context of resources crunch as well as the erosion of democratic values in the governmental system. The stakeholders could be mobilized for the better management of common property resources by the Panchayat if the Panchayat leadership is proactive and well-oriented in the art of managing the Panchayat. In the case of Karisalpatti, the President who served during 1996-2001 was Mr. Irudayam. He was the pioneer who organised the Annai Velankanni Pilgrimage Association, one of the religion based community organizations in Karisalpatti. His proactive role in various public activities was observed by the community. His religious catholicism was appreciated even by people belonging to the Hindu community. Hence he won in the elections and successfully managed the Panchayat. The Government of Tamil Nadu, after evaluating the performance of Karisalpatti Panchayat, awarded the second prize at the State level and the first prize at the District level to Karisalpatti. Mr.Irudhayam got his training and intensive orientation through the Rajiv Gandhi Chair for Panchayati Raj Studies of Gandhigram Rural Institute.

For the next period of 2001-2006, Mr. Joseph Irudhayaraj Soodamani has been elected President. He is a traditional leader as he was a *Chinna Nattanmai* in the traditional committee of Christian Vanniars. Moreover he belongs to the AIADMK Party. He is an active member of that party. In spite of that he has ensured fairness in his administration.

It is a rare phenomenon that in Karisalpatti both the ex-President and the current President work together for the development of their village. The ex-President frequently visits the Panchayat office, helps in the day-to-day administration, accompanies the current President whenever necessary to various places in connection with public assignments and also gives encouragement to the President in the Panchayat administration. This rare phenomenon helps in the management of common property resources in Karisalpatti which motivated the present researchers to undertake a study of this process for dissemination.

REFERENCES

Basu, Amrita & Kohli, Atul, (1998), *Community Conflicts and the State in India,* Delhi: Oxford University Press.

Beteille, A., (1965), *Caste, Class and Power: Changing Patterns of Stratification in a Tanjure Village*, Berkeley: University of California Press.

Lele, M.K., (2001), "Local Government: Conflict of Interests and Issues of Legitimisation," *Economic and Political Weekly*, Vol. No. xxxvi:51 (Dec 22).

Mukherjee, P.K., (1959), *Economic Survey in Under Developed Countries,* Bombay.

Palanithurai, G., (2001), *Problems Faced by the Leaders of Gram Panchayat*, Gandhigram: Rajiv Gandhi Chair for Panchayati Raj Studies.

Rajagopal Indhu, (1985), *The Tyranny of Caste*, New Delhi: Vikas.

7

BUILDING ALLIANCES AND CAPABILITIES AMONG THE ELECTED WOMEN REPRESENTATIVES

Introduction

It is beyond doubt that steps have been taken systematically from the enactment of the Constitution to empower women and that the condition of the Indian women has also improved since Independence in terms of literacy, life expectancy and maternal mortality. Yet their position has not improved on par with that of men and, till date, they occupy only a subordinate position in political, economic and social life. Even the improvements achieved are not uniform among different categories of women[1]. In some cases the condition has worsened among a few categories of women.

In a positive move, women have now started organizing themselves to create awareness among women and to work for the development of women through different strategies, organizations, associations and institutions. Yet the process is not quite smooth or free from barriers and hurdles.

In the meanwhile, the globalization of the economy has exerted different types of impact on the Indian women at different levels with differences of intensity and nature. Likewise the localization of the political process is going to make an impact on the life of the women[2]. The negative impact of the globalization of the economy could be overcome through the localization of the political process if the women are properly oriented, trained, capacitated, conscientized and associated. The localization of the political process has brought one million women with varying social economic backgrounds to different levels of political institutions. This was facilitated constitutionally by amending the Constitution of India. The 73rd Amendment to the Constitution of India is a milestone in the history of women empowerment in India. How the constitutional provision of reserving seats for women in the grassroots institutions is going to be used will surely determine the process of empowering women in Indian society.

The globalization process has driven a variety of social groups into the poverty basket and poverty alleviation task has become quite complicated. Further, all the routes to access to resources for women, particularly poor women, have been closed as the market driven approach has taken away all the common resources. In the competitive market process, the rights of women and the marginalized sections are the casualties. How to protect their rights enshrined in the Constitution and secure their livelihood are the major issues being faced by the women who are in the thick of the women's movement.

The decentralization process has opened up opportunities for women and other marginalized groups to influence the allocation of Government and community resources in their favour and protect and promote their human rights[3]. However, there are a variety of barriers to women hailing from marginalized sections exercising their powers[4]. Really it is a challenge to work for the social, economic and political empowerment of women, particularly those from marginalized sections. No doubt it is necessary to work for the goal of empowering women for which the oppressive power of the existing gender relations is to be exposed and challenged. Further the gender relations have to be reshaped[5]. This exercise could be started at the level of the elected women representatives of rural local bodies as they constitute a critical mass since one-third of seats have been reserved for women. The critical mass will be able to perform the critical function only if they are oriented, conscientized and trained in the methodology of de-construction and re-construction of gender relations.

Institutional Intervention

The Rajiv Gandhi Chair for Panchayati Raj Studies in Gandhigram Rural Institute has fixed the major objective of building the elected women leaders' capabilities to make use of the reservation made available to them for better delivery of services by conducting continuous capacity building exercises and performing the facilitating role in removing the barriers in their way to wielding power. A series of training programmes have been organized exclusively for Gram Panchayat women leaders with the support of the Ministry of Rural Development, Government of India. Capacity and capabilities cannot be built into an individual overnight. It is a slow and continuous process by which the leaders can enhance their capacity while practising what they have learnt in the training programme. While managing the institutions and tackling the issues women leaders face a lot of problems and they are also to be tackled.

It is to be taken note of that the barriers and obstacles for the women to take up power in the political process are formidable and that they require a powerful support structure beyond the training programmes to build up their skills to manage the institutions effectively and efficiently.

New Initiative

An action project was undertaken with the following objectives: to build an alliance of women leaders; to conscientise them on the issues which affect the life of women; and, to orient them in the methods and nuances of tackling the problems. This initiative was a demand driven one. It was taken up by the Rajiv Gandhi Chair because of the repeated requests made by the elected women representatives who came to Gandhigram to attend the training programmes[6]. The question was whether Gandhigram Rural Institute would serve as a supportive resource centre for the elected women representatives facing problems in the Panchayats while managing the affairs of the Panchayats and the people. The capacity building programmes were organized mostly in class rooms and the leaders were taken to the field for brief exposure visits. Certainly this helped them to build up their skill and capacity. However, the rural socio-political scenario varies from region to region and hence the women have to face a volley of problems. While facing problems on the ground who will extend support to the women leaders is the major question.

Gandhigram being a nodal centre for women empowerment from the beginning, the Rajiv Gandhi Chair accepted the challenge and took the initiative.

Sensitized and conscientised women leaders were keen on certain issues in the Panchayats after attending the training programmes, namely, ensuring entitlements to the poor and the needy, evicting the encroachers from the encroached common properties and creating awareness among the women about their problems and the remedies for the same. But the prevailing conditions were not conducive for the elected women representatives to tackle all those issues and they had to face a lot of problems in the Panchayat administration[7].

At this juncture, the idea of creating a network among the institutions working in different South Indian States with the same commitment to the issues of women struck the minds of development workers. The Singamma Sreenivasan Foundation, Bangalore, under the leadership of Devaki Jain, a well known woman activist and development economist, agreed to be a coordinating agency. Partners were found in Kerala and Andhra Pradesh. Thus this activity was initiated simultaneously in four States, namely, Kerala, Karnataka, Tamil Nadu and Andhra Pradesh. The Ford Foundation agreed to help these agencies in their work for women empowerment.

Environment

Tamil Nadu politics has its own significance in Indian politics from the perspective of social transformation due to the impact of the Dravidian Movement. In the Dravidian Movement, under the leadership of E.V. Ramasamy Naicker (Periyar), women emancipation was an important area of political action which trained the leaders to internalize the concept of women liberation and empowerment of women[8]. After the emergence of the Dravidian political parties in the electoral politics of Tamil Nadu, the issues of women captured the central stage. A series of legislations were enacted to liberate and empower women after these political parties assumed power in the State. Along with the left movement, the Dravidian Movement created an impact in the process of social transformation in Tamil Nadu. It does not mean that Tamil Nadu has come out of the clutches of patriarchy. It just means that the position of women in Tamil Nadu, compared with that in North Indian States, may be better. Despite all these progressive legislations, a variety of problems affecting the life of women, namely, female infanticide, foeticide, denial of access to common properties, atrocities against women, dowry deaths continue to haunt the womenfolk in Tamil Nadu. Even though women are elected to State Legislative Assembly and National Parliament from the Dravidian parties, their powers are severely restricted and they are being used by their husbands and the official machinery of the party as proxies. This is being extended to local bodies too. But in local bodies a large number of the women are from the sections below middle class and they will, by nature, assert themselves provided they are given the needed wherewithal.

In Tamil Nadu, women leaders in local bodies at the level of Gram Panchayats, from their experience with men leaders, thought that it was necessary to form an association of elected women representatives to sort out their issues. They formed associations locally at block or district levels but these associations did not have any structure and standing. The women leaders used them as platforms to meet the officials collectively and individually to represent their problems and get them redressed. In this new exercise the women leaders obtained some positive response from the officials. On seeing the response of the officials the elected women representatives wanted to continue this kind of practice in the management of institutions. Upon seeing this development it was perceived that the elected women representatives' need was only facilitation. Since the Rajiv Gandhi Chair for Panchayati Raj Studies has the same objective of facilitation, the Chair perceived the women leaders' need as an appropriate opportunity for intervention.

The primary objective of the Chair is to activate grassroots democracy by conducting action research and extension programmes. It has to work with the Panchayat leaders for the regeneration of the rustic folk and to create awareness among the people about the new system of governance through the new institutional arrangement, namely, Panchayati Raj System. The Chair will work at different levels. It will also act as a nodal centre to offer training to the elected local body leaders in governance, particularly in administering development. Further it will act as a coordinating agency for NGOs for people oriented participative action for sustainable development and good governance. This approach emanates from the basic premise that people are capable, honest, sincere and committed in deciding their destiny and hence all the issues will be visualized from the perspective of the people.

Against this background it was planned to adopt the following as objectives and activities of this project: to enable the elected women representatives to be courageous and self-confident and not to be intimidated by atrocities or yield to pressure in carrying out their role and responsibilities; to empower the elected women representatives to assert their rights; to facilitate the sharing of experience among the elected women representatives not only within districts and states but also across states; to build a movement of women political leaders to address issues on their own; to make the Government listen to the collective voice of the elected women representatives; and to institutionalize a gender perspective in decision-making.

Developing an Approach

With these objectives, reputed action oriented feminists, gender specialists, lawyers, representatives from NGOs and academics were invited to deliberate upon the strategies and the approaches to be adopted for a transformation process through the women's organizations. The elected women representatives were invited to share their experiences with the feminists and gender specialists. On 26th August, 2000, they deliberated upon the prevailing environment in the rural society for the functioning of the local bodies under the leadership of the women drawn from different socio-economic conditions.

In this consultation exercise, the following actions and approaches were evolved[9]. As a first step, the loosely organized associations have to be federated into a cohesive movement to address the issues of the women and the marginalized. To do this, regional meetings have to be organized and zonal or regional units have to be created for furthering the activities of the federation. While organizing such regional meetings, the problems faced by the women leaders have to be properly documented for policy advocacy and they have to be published through the media. Leaders from different regions are to be gathered for periodical meetings and they have to be sensitized on the basic issues of development like food security, livelihood security and more specifically on the issues of women. While sensitizing the women, these issues are to be discussed contextually and futuristically. To gain confidence, they need hands on experience for which meaningful interface programmes could be organized on demand by taking these leaders from Tamil Nadu to Kerala and even from one region to another region within Tamil Nadu where success cases are reported.

An annual Elected Women Leaders Convention has to be organized where the documented problems of different regions have to be discussed in front of dignarities and the media for popular dissemination and corrective action. The discussed issues have to be taken to the policy making level for lobbying for which Gandhigram Rural Institute should take up the responsibility. Through the regional outfits, needed information has to be provided periodically to the Panchayat leaders. The elected women representatives who are struggling in the Panchayat administration to deliver services should be given a helping hand by which it can be demonstrated to the other leaders that they are not alone and that there are thousands of leaders behind them and very many civil society organizations. To develop this movement the elected women representatives have to be trained in Panchayat management. They should be provided with needed skills and capability. Further the leaders of the Association in different regions are to be oriented in providing leadership to other elected women representatives. To adduce visibility to the issues of women and the organization, a proper media tie up has to be established. The media has to be sensitized on women in governance and the issues of women. The media's role in the movement is felt to be imperative. There are certain issues which are to be fought only through legal means for which the leaders are to be oriented for such an eventuality. To push forward the movement the strong support of the NGO network is required. It is to be underlined that the NGOs' activities should always be at the back of the Women

Leaders Association and not *vice versa*. After finalizing the strategy, approach and action programme, another meeting was organized to create an NGO network to support the women's organization. It was held on 23rd October, 2000[10]. The NGOs who have been working on the issues of women development were invited to participate in the meeting. The NGO representatives participated and deliberated upon the strategies and approaches evolved in the previous meeting. It was almost a workshop for women's solidarity activities and expressed their commitment to this work. They agreed upon the objectives and offered to extend their support in carrying out the activities as partners. It was decided to divide Tamil Nadu into five zones. The activities had to be carried out in all the five zones through the NGOs and the NGOs had to act as nodal agencies and resource centres for the activities of the elected women representatives.

Following this commitment of the NGOs, regional meetings were organized at Madurai on 21st December 2000, at Thiruvarur on 2nd February, 2001, at Chengalpattu on 16th February, 2001, and at Karur on 21st March, 2001. In all the regional or zonal meetings, the problems faced by the elected women representatives in administering development were discussed and they were documented. The documents were published and circulated among the representatives of the media for wider dissemination. The problems had to be taken to different levels for redressal. So they were classified and they were taken to the Block Development Office and to the State Legislative Assembly for redressal. On 5th August, 2001 an annual convention of the women leaders was organized at Gandhigram and it discussed the basic issues of the women, strategies to overcome the problems and the problems faced by the Panchayats[12]. As they discussed the issues thoroughly all the issues were fully covered in the media which brought visibility to the women's federation.

Interface Meetings

After the zonal or regional meetings and the annual convention, it was decided to undertake the interface programme under which the federation leaders were to be taken to Kerala to visit some of the Panchayats and hold discussion with the leaders and functionaries on the issues of development. They concentrated more on the issues of social and economic development. Almost all the federation leaders got an opportunity to visit Kerala to have a glimpse of the social and economic development activities of the Gram Panchayats[13].

The elected women representatives tried to bring the Minister for Rural Development, Government of India, to their programme and succeeded in their attempt. On 20th February, 2002, Mr. Venkaiah Naidu participated in their programme wherein the elected representatives discussed their issues with him and appealed to him to intervene at the appropriate level to redress their grievance. Along with the Minister, State level officials also participated and they were all asked by the Rural Development Minister to give replies to the questions raised by the representatives[14].

They organized the Second Annual Meet in Gandhigram on 3rd May, 2002. In the second annual meeting, they discussed the 15-point programme of the Government of Tamil Nadu. In the course of the discussion they pointed out that, out of the 15 points, about 13 come under the purview of the Panchayati Raj institutions. They went on to clarify at what level they can work and to what extent officials have to work to achieve the target. They compiled guidelines by which the details of the earmarked responsibilities could be identified[15]. For the annual meet they invited the Director of Rural Development, Government of Tamil Nadu, Mr. S. Ayyar, I.A.S. They made a powerful plea that in each and every district the District Collector has to convene a meeting of Gram Panchayat women leaders and redress their problems in the management of the Panchayats. He agreed to do so and promised to issue an order in this regard[16]. They further decided to form an advisory council consisting of retired officials, representatives from NGOs, academics and representatives from the media to facilitate the functioning of the federation. Subsequently, based on the deliberations of the Second Annual Convention, a regional leaders' meet was organized on 9th May, 2002 to make an in-depth study of the 15-point programme and the problems faced by the women leaders[17] and consolidate their demands to be presented to the Government of Tamil Nadu.

Implications

So far the sequence of events has been presented. But the implications of the activities have to be explained. One should not assume that the federation met once a year and deliberated only in Gandhigram. They organized several meetings in several places with the help of other NGOs also. They met political party leaders and officials for presenting their charter of demands. They used to meet the press periodically and express their opinions on vital issues which affect the life of the people, particularly women, children and *Dalits*[18]. Based on the training programme, we have collected the problems faced by the Panchayati leaders generally, and women and *Dalit* leaders specifically, and those problems have been documented by our centre. These documents have been used by this Federation for policy advocacy. It was very difficult for them to get information regarding Government orders, rules and schemes. But now they are being received from Gandhigram Rural Institute and so they regard it as a resource centre. Contacting Minsters, higher officials, MPs and MLAs is no more a problem for them. Women leaders who are in this federating arrangement are highly sensitized on the issues of social development and more specifically on the issues of women and children. When the State Government's proposal to introduce cheap liquor came as the most unkindest cut of all for the women heading village Panchayats, the women Presidents reacted sharply that they were let down by a woman Chief Minister. They unequivocally argued and made it clear that they would launch an agitation if the Government refused to drop the proposal. When the regional leaders of the Federation met at Gandhigram, they discussed this issue at length and spoke to the *Hindu* Special Reporter Mr. S. Annamalai that they have been fighting at the village level for the past five years to eradicate illicit liquor, but now the Government itself seeks to introduce liquor to make money. Subsequently the move was withdrawn in the rural areas. It was considered a victory for the Women Panchayati Leaders' Federation.

Subsequently, in 2002, in the month of December, when they met at Gandhigram, they made a plea to the Government of Tamil Nadu to increase the revenue of the Panchayats. The Women Panchayati Leaders' Federation suggested that the State Government can hand over the common properties to the Panchayats. They indicated that quarries, tanks and trees which were now under the control of the Government's agencies and individuals would fetch adequate revenue to make the local bodies self-reliant. They projected an alternative model of resource mobilization for Panchayats.

As they attend periodical meetings of the Federation, the restrictions imposed on them have been gradually removed. Without the assistance of the males of their family they travel to Chennai, Madurai and Trichy to attend the meetings of the Federation. Further their communicative ability has improved to a surprising level as the grassroots women leaders have developed their own style of communication which has been accepted as a formal mode of communication. Their bargaining capability has been enhanced to strike a deal with officials, MLAs, and MPs for the benefit of the people. The feeling of isolation that prevailed among the elected women representatives has gone as they meet frequently and share their joys and difficulties. When the elected women representatives face problems in administration, the Federation leaders take the issue to the District Collector and to the level of the Director for Rural Development. They get their problems redressed, failing which they go to court and get suitable legal remedy which has raised the morale of the women leaders. Frequent sharing has built up the idea that this kind of exercise is necessary for their success. Their media contact is frequent and its implications are also positive.

Though Tamil Nadu has a District Panchayat Presidents Association, a Block Panchayat Association, and a Gram Panchyat Association, only the Federation of Women Panchayat Leaders Associations is visible and reacts sharply on many of the vital issues. Even though the elected women representatives have a charter of demands, they are more keen on getting reservation of seats for women for ten years, retrieving common properties from encroachment, and, ensuring the entitlements of the poor through the public distribution system. Active leaders in the Federation are very much sensitized on these social development issues after visiting the Kerala Panchayats. During the first period the women leaders were harping on transfer of power, finance and functionaries. Now they speak about issues and problems. They have gained voice and bargaining power.

One major achievement that they have scored through their work is getting the reservation of seats for women in local bodies extended for one more term. It is unique in the whole of the country. Another important achievement is that the Federation has made the State Government withdraw the plan for cheap liquor. They pleaded with the Government that every month higher level officials at the district level should convene a meeting of the women Panchayat leaders and solve their problems. The Director, Rural Development, Government of Tamil Nadu, issued an order immediately to District Collectors to convene such meetings and solve the problems of the women leaders.

Because of their repeated pleas and activities, the Federation of Women Leaders Associations is visible to the policy makers and 33.3 per cent of seats have been reserved for women even in cooperatives societies also. Likewise an order has been issued that in all statutory committees one-third reservation should be provided for women. Some of the women Panchayat leaders were in deep trouble. It was only the Federation which saved them. Menaka, the President of Oorappakkam, was murdered in the Panchayat office due to her stern action against encroachment. No FIR was filed till the Federation leaders went to the Panchayat. It was only because of this Federation that the culprits were booked. Another interesting noteworthy feature is that more number of office bearers in the Federation are now from the *Dalit* community and the Federation has focused its attention on *Dalit* issues.

Learnings

Elected women leaders are of different categories. They are educated, uneducated, highly sophisticated, rich, poor, wage earners, *Dalits* and others. There are leaders with political orientation and party background. They look at issues only from their party perspective. There are leaders without any political background but under the clutches of their husbands or the males of their families. There are leaders who have commitments and values but no awareness and information. There are leaders with high political aspirations. It is to be noted that the leaders who are deeply committed to the issues of the people without political background continue to be active members of the Federation. The Federation attracts more number of Gram Panchayat women leaders as the Gram Panchayat is freed from the party fold and the problems focused on in the Federation are mostly the problems faced by the Gram Panchayat women leaders. One layer of elected women representatives is alert and they are oriented and conscientized but the other segments are not so well oriented. When oriented and motivated leaders take up the development issues, they face a volley of problems. To tackle all these problems they require a support structure. They demand periodical sensitization on vital issues affecting women and other marginalized groups. They require periodical update on Government orders and new schemes of the Government. They are in need of periodical interface programmes. The Federation of elected women representatives does not include all the women leaders of rural and urban local bodies. Those who have come out despite obstacles and barriers and those who are struggling with determination have joined together. A large number of elected representatives have not come out of their houses and have not even visited their offices. The Federation is slowly moving towards them. Even now some women leaders are asked to remain inside their houses and the males of their families operate their offices. One positive aspect is that when the successful women leaders are being appreciated and covered in the media, the males of the families of the elected women representatives develop an aspiration that their women leaders should also get such appreciation. The Federation has created such a mindset. There is a potential danger in that potential leaders who can mobilize the masses at the grassroots level are lured by the political leaders. There are women leaders who look at issues from the perspective of the people and want to serve the people at the cost of their own prospects and hence they tend to toe the line of the ruling party in the State Government purely with the intention of getting things done for the people.

Summing Up

Women have started realizing the potential of the Associations and the Federation. Political parties have started identifying the potential leaders from Gram Panchayats and enlisting them as their party members and proclaiming their achievements as the achievements of the party. The media has been sensitized on the women issues and as a result the media has given wide coverage to the activities of the Women's Federation. Elected women representatives have learnt the art of managing bureaucracy. They have picked up communication skills. They have developed bargaining power. Moving with higher officials has become a routine affair and the fear to meet the District Collector and other higher officials has gone. A large number of new leaders are drawn from self-help groups towards the Panchayats. Sharing the struggles and achievements in the regional and annual conventions has motivated other women leaders to emulate them. The fear syndrome and the dependency syndrome have gone. The group activities have developed a positive attitude among the women leaders to strive for achievements.

NOTES

1. S. Raju, P.J. Aakkins, N. Kumar and J.G. Jownsend, *Atlas of Women and Mass in India,* New Delhi: Kali for Women, 1999.
2. Ranjani K. Murthy (ed) *Building Women's Capacities,* New Delhi: Sage Publications, 2001, p.18.
3. G. Palanithurai, *New Panchayati Raj System as Prosperity Movement,* New Delhi: Kanishka Publishers and Distributors, 2001.

4. G. Palanithurai, *Empowerment of Women: Problems Faced by the Elected Women Representatives in Tamil Nadu,* Gandhigram: Rajiv Gnadhi Chair for Panchayati Raj Studies, 2001.
5. S. Wieringa, "Women's Interests and Empowerment: Gender Planning Reconsidered" *Development and Change,* 25 (1994) pp. 829-848.
6. Rajiv Gandhi Chair for Panchayati Raj Studies has been recognised by the Government of Tamil Nadu as a nodel centre for training and hence series of training programmes had been organised with the financial support of CAPART, Government of India, Social Welfare Board, Government of India, Population Foundation of India, DANIDA and DRDA, District Administration. For more details about the training programme see the following reports.

List of Reports on Activities brought out by the Rajiv Gandhi Chair

Sl. No	Year	Title of the Report	Sponsoring Agency
1.	1997	Report of the training programme conducted for District Panchayat Council Members on Social Development	Population Foundation of India
2.	1998	Report of the training programme conducted for Women Presidents of Gram Panchayats in Five Districts of Tamil Nadu	Social Welfare Board, Government of Tamil Nadu, Chennai
3.	1999	Report of the training programme conducted for Gram Panchayat Presidents and Vice-presidents on Panchayati Raj Administration with special reference to Water Supply and Sanitation in Villupuram District – Phase I	DANIDA Villupuram
4.	1999	Training for Gram Panchayati Presidents and Vice-Presidents on Panchayati Raj Administration with special reference to Water Supply and Sanitation in Villupuram District – Phase II	DANIDA Villupuram
5.	1999	A report on training on Improvement of Panchayat Administration and Total Rural Sanitation Programme in Cuddalore District – Phase I	DRDA Cuddalore
6.	2000	A report on training on Improvement of Panchayat Administration and Total Rural Sanitation Programme in Cuddalore District – Phase II	DRDA Cuddalore

Sl. No	Year	Title of the Report	Sponsoring Agency
7.	2000	Report of the training programme conducted for Gram Panchayati Women Presidents of Madurai, Ramanathapuram and Pudukottai Districts	CAPART Hyderabad
8.	2000	Report of the training programme conducted for Gram Panchayati Presidents	CAPART Hyderabad
9.	2000	Report on the Training of Trainers on Multi Level Planning	State Planning Commission, Government of Tamil Nadu
10.	2001	A report of the training programme on Testing of Training Module for Training of Panchayati Raj Functionaries	Rajiv Gandhi Foundation, New Delhi

7. The problems faced by the women Panchayati Presidents have been documented. For more details refer to Rajiv Gandhi Chair, *Empowerment of Women: Problems Faced by the Elected Women Representatives in Local Bodies in Tamil Nadu,* Gandhigram: Rajiv Gandhi Chair for Panchayati Raj Studies, 2001.
8. K. Veeramani, *Periyar on Women's Rights,* Madras: Emerald Publishers, 1994.
9. Detailed proceedings are reported in the document. For more details, see Rajiv Gandhi Chair, *State Level Consultation on Feminist Perspective in Associating Women Representatives in Local Bodies: A Report*, Gandhigram: Rajiv Gandhi Chair for Panchayati Raj Studies, 2000.
10. For more details about the discussion, see Rajiv Gandhi Chair, *A Report on State Level NGOs' Network Meet on Associating Women Reprsentatives in Local Bodies*, Gandhigram: Rajiv Gandhi Chair for Panchayati Raj Studies, 2000.
11. The entire discussions and deliberations have been documented. For details refer to the following documents: Rajiv Gandhi Chair, *A Report on Regional Level Meet on Associating Women Representatives in Local Bodies – I*, Gandhigram: Rajiv Gandhi Chair for Panchayati Raj Studies, 2000.

    Rajiv Gandhi Chair, *A Report on Regional Level Meet on Associating Women Representatives in Local Bodies – II,* Gandhigram: Rajiv Gandhi Chair for Panchayati Raj Studies, 2001.

    Rajiv Gandhi Chair, *A Report on Regional Level Meet on Associating Women Representatives in Local Bodies – III,* Gandhigram: Rajiv Gandhi Chair for Panchayati Raj Studies, 2001.

    Rajiv Gandhi Chair, *A Report on Regional Level Meet on Associating Women Representatives in Local Bodies – IV,* Gandhigram: Rajiv Gandhi Chair for Panchayati Raj Studies, 2001.

12. Rajiv Gandhi Chair, *The Annual Convention of the Elected Women Representatives in Tamil Nadu: A Report*, Gandhigram: Rajiv Gandhi Chair for Panchayati Raj Studies, 2001.
13. Rajiv Gandhi Chair, *A Report on First Networking Meeting and Interface Programme*, Gandhigram: Rajiv Gandhi Chair for Panchayati Raj Studies, 2002.

    Rajiv Gandhi Chair, *A Report on Second Networking Meeting and Interface Programme,* Gandhigram: Rajiv Gandhi Chair for Panchayati Raj Studies, 2002.
14. Rajiv Gandhi Chair, *A Report on Women Panchayat Leaders Meet on 20.02.02*, Gandhigram: Rajiv Gandhi Chair for Panchayati Raj Studies, 2002.

    The following constitute the 15-point programme of the Government of Tamil Nadu.

    Rajiv Gandhi Chair, *Role of Local Bodies in the Process of Implication of 15-Point Programme* Gandhigram: Rajiv Gandhi Chair, 2002.

    The Honourable Chief Minister, Selvi. J. Jayalalitha, has announced her commitment to make Tamil Nadu the best State in the country in every sphere. "To provide opportunities for a healthy and productive life for all" will be the goal of this Government. This vision will be realized through the implementation of the Chief Minister's 15-point programme which will encompass the following:

    (i) *Evergreen Revolution :* Raising farm productivity in perpetuity; Saving every drop of rain; More crop per drop.

    (ii) *Food Security :* Physical, economic and social access to balanced diets to every child, woman and man.

    (iii) *Livestock Security :* Upgradation of livestock, better veterinary care; Supplementing farm income; Improving fish diversity and increasing fish density.

    (iv) *Water Security :* Safe drinking water and adequate water for agriculture, industry and ecosystem maintenance.

    (v) *Health Security :* Control of all preventable diseases including leprosy, tuberculosis, preventable blindness, and eradication of diseases for which effective vaccines are available; reduction in birth and death rates and increase in average life span; Reduction of Infant Mortality Rate (IMR), Maternal Mortality Rate (MMR) and incidence of low birth weight children; Adoption of a maternal and child care code; Fight against HIV/AIDS; Special attention to physically and mentally handicapped children, women and men.

    (vi) *Livelihood Security :* "Work for all" and transition from unskilled to skilled work; Integrated attention to rural on-farm and non-farm employment as well as to micro-enterprises supported by micro-credit; A New Deal to the self-employed through technology, training, techno-infrastructure and domestic and external trade.

    (vii) *Shelter Security :* Promotion of housing activities designed to harvest sun and rain so that solar energy capture and rainwater harvesting become everybody's business.

(viii) *Ecological Security* : Conservation and enhancement of life support system like land, water, forests, bio-diversity, ocean and the atmosphere; Recycling of solid and liquid wastes and composting of all organic wastes. Safe disposal of hospital wastes; Bio-environmental control of malaria.

(ix) *Energy Security* : Building sustainable energy systems with concurrent attention to thermal, hydro, nuclear and renewable forms of energy like wind, solar, biogas and biomass; Energy self-sufficiency for the farm, industrial and domestic sectors.

(x) *Infrastructure for Development* : Provision of basic amenities in rural and urban areas; Connectivity to all habitation with population above 500; Bridging the rural-urban divide.

(xi) *Literacy and Technicracy* : Attention to quality improvement in education ranging from the pre-school to University; Special attention to the technological and skill empowerment of illiterate or semi-literate women and men; Eradication of child labour.

(xii) *Folk, Classical and Modern Arts, Culture and Drama* : Generation of awareness and appreciation of the cultural heritage of Tamil Nadu and revitalization of cultural traditions, including the street theatre.

(xiii) *Gender Equity* : Removal of gender bias, elimination of adverse sex ratio, and support services to working women, taking into account the multiple burden on a woman's day-to-day life.

(xiv) *New Deal for the Oppressed Classes* : Educational and economic empowerment of the Adi-Dravidas, Scheduled Tribes, Backward Classes, Most Backward Classes Denotified Tribes.

(xv) *Technological Leapfrogging* : Promotion of research and development in frontier areas of science and technology like biotechnology and information technology, coordination of efforts between academic know how and field level do how. Launching a movement for fostering greater public understanding of science and promoting a new social contact between scientists and society; providing equal attention to connectivity and content in efforts to bridge the digital divide; including access to appropriate technologies in the basic minimum needs programme.

The Chief Minister's 15-point programme outlined here will be the road map for this Government in the next four years. It will be the endeavour of this Government to realize this vision by March 2006.

15. Rajiv Gandhi Chair, *Report of the Second Annual Meet of Elected Women Representatives*, Gandhigram: Rajiv Gandhi Chair for Panchayati Raj Studies, 2002.
16. Letter received from the Director Rural Development, Government of Tamil Nadu dated 20.05.02.
17. Rajiv Gandhi Chair, *Report of the Special Meet of the Elected Women Representatives of Local Bodies at Gandhigram*, Gandhigram: Rajiv Gandhi Chair for Panchayati Raj Studies, 2002.

18. Their activities are covered in the press. The details are:

New Indian Express 06.05.2002	Panchayat Chiefs favour Govt. programmes. Women leaders keen on development activities of panchayats
Dinamalar 12.01.2002	Nanillam Union – Panchayat Leaders meet
Dinamani 13.01.2002	Network meeting of SSF-Thiruvarur Cheap liquor Scheme / Hitting below the belt
Dinamalar 10.05.2002	Second Annual Meet of SSF Director of Rural Development – Suggest?
Dinamani 29.04.2002	Annual Conference of Women Leaders at State Level
Dina Thanthi 01.05.2002	Annual Conference of Women Leaders at State Level
The Hindu 02.05.2002	Elected Women Representatives Meet
Dina Thanthi 04.05.2002	Elected Women Representatives Meet
The Hindu 04.05.2002	Information kiosks coming up for SHGs in 10 districts
The Hindu 08.12.2001	Cheap Liquor Scheme/Hitting below the belt. Women feel let down by a woman
Theekkathir 21.12.2001	Funds to Local Bodies plan to file PIL
Dinamalar 05.03.2002	A modified Family Card – Leader did – Minister encouraged
Dina Thanthi 04.12.2001	Satisfying the basic needs – Funds to Local Bodies – A request
The Financial Express 19.12.2001	Tamil Nadu Panchayats plan to fild PIL for release of statutory grants
News Today 20.12.2001	Funds to Local Bodies 'Relent or face a stir' Women Panchayat chiefs on warpath
Dinamani 20.12.2001	Funds to Local Bodies 'Relent or face a stir' Women Panchayat chiefs on warpath
Dina Thanthi 20.12.2001	Funds to Local Bodies 'Relent or face a stir' Women Panchayat chiefs on warpath
Dinamalar 20.12.2001	Allot 20 per cent of MLA and MP fund to Panchayats – leaders wish
Dinakaran 20.12.2001	EWRs meet at Chennai — a crisis on implementing activities — struggle on cheap liquor scheme
The Hindu 03.04.2002	No nomination for wards, polls went empower *dalits*
The Hindu 19.03.2002	Spell out stand on devolution: Tamil Nadu Panchayat

Dinamani 06.11.2001	Fulfil the responsibilities and commit your needy Dr. Pankajam, Vice-Chancellor, GRI – suggest
The Hindu 08.11.2001	Village Panchayats told to concentrate on tax collection
New Indian Express 22.02.2002	Centre fixes target of 14 lakh SHG – M. Vengaiah Naidu, Rural Development Minister, Government of India at GRI
The Hindu 16.02.2002	Participatory development key to Panchayat Raj
Dinamalar 16.02.2002	From Education to Family Planning – Need for a change in training the leaders
Dinamani 15.02.2002	New method of training to the president – Suggest
The Hindu 13.01.2002	Panchayat chiefs play key role in Primary Education
Dinamani 12.01.2002	Panchayat chiefs play key role in Primary Education
The Hindu 20.12.2001	Women Panchayat chiefs threaten stir
New Indian Express 18.12.2001	Bureaucrats treat women Panchayat president as servants
Dina Thanthi 07.10.2001	Women Panchayat chiefs threaten stir. Say 'No' to corruption in Panchayat
The Hindu 06.10.2001	Women Panchayat chiefs threaten stir. Say 'No' to corruption in Panchayat
Dinakaran 06.10.2001	Women Panchayat chiefs threaten stir. Say 'No' to corruption in Panchayat

8

CAPACITY BUILDING OF GRASSROOTS LEADERS

Capacity building is an imperative for the elected representatives of the people at all levels from grassroots to National Parliament. Capacity building for the elected representatives is not perceived in perspective and hence it is the most neglected area in governance. For the establishment of the three-tier governance at grassroots as an institution of self-government, conscientisation and capacity building are needed exercises to be done on a war footing. It not only builds the skills and managerial capacity of the elected representatives but also builds a movement for prosperity at the grassroots as the system has been created in such a way that the performance of the Panchayats can be evaluated and monitored constantly by the people. Cleansing operations for the establishment of good governance must start from the bottom. The present article highlights the capacity building exercises conducted in Tamil Nadu against the backdrop of the prevailing negative setting and its implications. The experience brings to light the emergence of the grassroots movement to utilize power and authority to decide on issues which affect the life of the people. It also indicates what is further needed to strengthen the grassroots democracy.

Introduction

'Capacity Building' is the most urgent and imperative step in every sector to cope with the pace of development at present. In market driven development activities enhancement of capacity plays an important role in placing individuals, organizations and associations in competition. Development sectors take conscious decisions to enhance the capacity of the professionals and personnel working in organizations and institutions. New technologies and institutional mechanics require conscious steps to enhance the capability of individuals who are handling technologies and new organizational mechanisms to use the full potential of the technologies and institutional structures to bring out the maximum competence.

The 73rd Amendment to the Constitution of India has created a structure at the grassroots for governance. It has come with a set of promises and assurances to the people[1]. Compelling global, national and regional contexts make everyone look at the new system contextually. The new system has its own roles and responsibilities and, to perform the assigned roles and responsibilities, the leaders who are managing the new system should build up their skill and capacity[2]. The new system has been created to break new ground in governance and to tackle the problems and issues which are unmet and unsolved through the policy options of the governments at the State and the Central level. It should be clearly noted that the new institutions have to perform a variety of activities at the grassroots for which the grassroots leaders should have a clear-cut perception of the roles and responsibilities that are to be discharged and the skills needed to manage these institutions which are under the purview of the elected Panchayat leaders[3].

It is unfortunate that, in India, capacity building is not a serious issue for the representatives of the people who determine the fate of millions of people[4]. The elected representatives of the people do not feel that it is an imperative as it is considered in other sectors. In all sectors capacity building is a much valued exercise for the enhancement of their activities in their respective domains. But in politics it is not so and, as a result, one can notice a retrograde trend in politics.

However, in the Panchayati Raj scenario, it has been felt that, to manage the Panchayats, training is essential even though there is no training policy and no conscious steps have been taken by the Government to build the capacity of the elected representatives of the people in the grassroots institutions. It has been argued time and again that training is an imperative and needs to be undertaken on a war footing. Yet only a few states have taken conscious steps and in many places it is only the voluntary organizations who have imparted training to local body leaders despite several constraints, like the absence of well developed training centres, training material and well equipped trainers.[5]

In Tamil Nadu it is the demand of the Panchayat leaders that training should be given to Panchayat leaders and Panchayat functionaries to manage the institutions efficiently[6]. To cater to the needs of the local body leaders, there are enough training centres in Tamil Nadu. The Government of Tamil Nadu has established Rural Extension Training Centres in different regions and, at the state level, the State Institute of Rural Development. It is unfortunate that the Government sends unwanted employees to these training centres. As a result the training centres have lost their importance and value. They are mostly defunct. Further there is no training manual to train the Panchayat leaders and functionaries[7]. Realising the problems involved in training, the Rajiv Gandhi Chair for Panchayati Raj Studies took a conscious decision that it has to train Gram Panchayat Presidents for which a training manual has to be prepared.

Training in the First Phase

When the decision was taken to train Gram Panchayat leaders, what powers were going to be devolved, how much of fiscal devolution was going to be effected and what functionaries were going to be part of the Panchayats had not been spelt out. The Government of Tamil Nadu had allowed the Panchayats to perform the old civic functions along with agency functions to carry out the schemes and programmes of the Central and State Governments. Based on these activities a training module was prepared and training programmes were conducted. It was just a conscientization programme to change the mindset of the leaders by indicating the spirit of the 73rd Constitutional Amendment Act and the basic details about the Panchayati Raj Act of Tamil Nadu and its implications in the socio-economic and political transformation of the rural society. Gradually the sensitization programme was extended to other tiers with the financial support of various agencies.

Table 8.1 : Training Programmes Organised in Gandhigram Rural Institute

Sl. No	Title	Sponsored Agency	Total No.of Leaders Trained
1.	Empowering Panchayati Raj Institutions on Issues of Population, Health and Social Development	Population Foundation of India	6834
2.	Capacity Building for Gram Panchayat Presidents	CAPART	1369
3.	Training of Presidents and Vice-Presidents in Panchayat Administration with Special Reference to Water and Sanitation	DANIDA	814
4.	Training of Women Presidents of Gram Panchayats	Social Welfare Board	825
5.	Training of Trainers in Multi-Level Planning	State Planning Commission	71
6.	Capacity Building for Weaker Sections in New Panchayati Raj System	CAPART	271
7.	Capacity Building Exercise for Gram Panchayat Women Leaders	The Hunger Project	390

Source : Computed.

Capacity Building Programmes

Total number of elected local body leaders trained	:	10,584
Total number of Panchayats covered	:	4,426
Districts covered	:	11

In the whole process of training what was achieved was that the Panchayat leaders were sensitized on the issues of democratic decentralization of powers and the bases of the 73rd Amendment to the Constitution of India and the issues of social development.

In the meanwhile the First State Finance Commission submitted its recommendations and they were placed before the Legislative Assembly[8]. Subsequently, the L.C. Jain Committee[9] constituted for making recommendations on entrusting responsibilities to the three-tier Panchayati Raj Institutions submitted its report. Based on the report, decisions were taken and the action taken report[10] was placed before the Legislative Assembly. Political parties, Panchayat leaders, academics and NGOs criticized the Government for not devolving needed powers to the local bodies and, as a result, yet another committee was constituted, with the Local Administration Minister[11] as the Chairperson and representatives of the major political parties as members, to look into the devolution process and to make recommendations. This Committee also submitted its recommendations to the Government and action has been taken on the recommendations[12]. As a result many changes have been effected in the Act and several Government Orders have been passed. Thus the first period from 1996 to 2001 marked a transition period wherein steps were taken to transfer power to the local bodies in Tamil Nadu. For the Panchayat leaders, it was a period of guessing and the officials were also in the same predicament. Virtually all the three tiers Panchayat shared the Government schemes and implemented the same and, as a result, the Panchayats became agents of the State Government. Leaders elected to Panchayats became contractors.

Initiatives of Rajiv Gandhi Chair

During this period the Rajiv Gandhi Chair for Panchayati Raj Studies took a series of steps to prepare a training manual to train the Panchayat leaders with the support of the Ford Foundation. The manual was tested and published for the benefit of the NGOs who are interested in organizing training programmes for Panchayat leaders[13]. Following the preparation of the training manual, steps were taken to collect the needed information, namely, the amendments introduced on the Act, orders passed by the Government as well as rules and schemes and programmes of the Government of India and the Government of Tamil Nadu relating to rural development. They were collected and compiled as a basic referable document and published for wider circulation and for distribution in the training programmes for Panchayat leaders[14]. Even today the Government offices do not have the updated Panchayat Act. So far the Government has passed eighty-four orders for Gram Panchayat administration alone. But not even a single Government Order has been sent to the Gram Panchayats. Yet Panchayat Presidents have been taken to task by the District Collectors as they have not followed the GOs. Panchayat Presidents ask how the Panchayat can follow the GOs in the absence of the GOs. So, with the help of retired staff, all Government Orders were colletced from various departments along with the updated Acts and rules. It took about a year to do this.

With the training module and the information package ready, the Rajiv Gandhi Chair identified a band of retired officials at the level of Additional Director for Rural Development based on their commitment, honesty and sincerity, as resource persons to impart training along with the Rajiv Gandhi Chair team. The Rajiv Gandhi Chair team has been already oriented on social development issues besides Panchayat administration. Along with the retired officials and the Rajiv Gandhi Chair team a few resource persons were drawn from NGOs as they run organizations for specific problems in the rural society such as environment, health care of child and women, RCH, child labour, human rights and natural resources management. Thus a comprehensive team was developed.

Apart from these arrangements, a specific initiative was taken to prepare a separate module for women as they require special leadership training. The Hunger Project, New Delhi, helped the Rajiv Gandhi Chair to prepare the training module on leadership and the same was published[15].

Along with the training modules, training materials to be used in the classroom were prepared. Because the educational background of the trainees varies from illiteracy to post-graduation, training aids were prepared in the form of charts. An artist was inducted in the team of resource persons, as his services were needed in the vision building class. Trainees would be asked to portray the existing conditions of the villages and to project their vision of how to develop the village. The entire vision was to be brought out in a chart.

With these preparations, the Rajiv Gandhi Chair approached the CAPART (Government of India) and the Hunger Project (New Delhi) for financial support to conduct training programmes for Gram Panchayat leaders of eight districts. The two agencies extended their support to conduct the programme. With the financial support of the CAPART, men leaders were trained and with the financial support of the Hunger Project women leaders were trained.

Table 8.2 : Training Programmes Organised in Gandhigram Rural Institute

Sl. No.	Name of the District	Total No.of Presidents			No.of Presidents attended the Training			Percentage of Panchayat Presidents		
		Men	Women	Total	Men	Women	Total	Men	Women	Total
1	Pudukkottai	326	172	498	275	140	415	84	81	83
2	Dindigul	200	105	305	191	100	291	96	95	95
3	Tiruchirappalli	275	132	407	255	131	386	93	99	95
4	Sivagangai	292	153	445	242	112	354	83	73	80
5	Ramanathapuram	282	147	429	229	116	345	81	79	80
6	Theni	82	48	130	66	43	109	80	90	84
7	Karur	109	49	158	91	49	140	83	100	89
8	Virudhunagar	303	144	447	245	103	348	81	72	78
	Total	1869	950	2819	1594	794	2388	85	84	85

Source: Computed.

Collaboration

Before starting the training programme, a conscious decision was taken that the training programme should be conducted in collaboration with the Government of Tamil Nadu for two reasons. Gandhigram Rural Institute should be recognized as a nodal centre for training and officials should recognize the training programme which should not be duplicated by any other agencies. Secondly Panchayat Presidents have to be brought to the training centre by the officials. It was very difficult to bring the Panchayat Presidents to training programmes in previous exercises. Further it was decided to have at least three officials dealing with Panchayats at the Block level from every Block in the training programme. To ensure attendance in the training programme Gandhigram Rural Institute needed the support of the Government. The training had to be made official. In this regard the Government issued an order[16]. As a result it is fully a Government recognized programme.

It was a fully residential programme. The Panchayat Presidents had to stay for five days in the campus of Gandhigram Rural Institute. Of the five days, three days would be devoted to Panchayat administration and two days to social development issues. Subjects such as the bases of decentralization of powers in the context of the globalization of the economy, Panchayat administration, Panchayat finance, common property resources management, people's participation, micro level planning, economic development, accounting and auditing procedures, Gram Sabha and its implications, social justice, and the implications of reservation of seats for women and *Dalits* were covered in three days. Social development issues such as sanitation, water supply, gender bias, child care, pre- and post-natal care, school environment, child labour, RCH and other issues were covered in the remaining two days of the five-day programme. In each one and half hour lecture, half an hour was set aside for a question and answer session. Men and women had separate training classes. Special sessions were arranged in the night both for men and women and all their doubts were cleared. Local and specific problems of the Gram Panchayats were discussed with the resource persons individually in the Gandhigram Rural Institute Guest House. It was an advantage that the entire team of resource persons stayed in the Gandhigram Rural Institute Guest House.

A special session was devoted to eliciting the Panchayat Presidents' problems in Panchayat administration. On the last day of the training programme the trainees were taken to the field and finally, they were asked to give their feedback.

Feedback from the Training

Before starting the training programme a questionnaire was circulated among the participants. This was done with the aim of assessing their level of understanding of Panchayat administration. It was noticed that excepting the Panchayat leaders elected for a second term, all the trainees knew only that the Panchayat provides an opportunity to serve people better and deliver services and were aware of a few schemes of the state and Central Governments. It was observed that the Panchayat Presidents were virtually under the control of the Panchayat clerks and lower level officials working in the Block Development Offices. After imparting training their feedback was recorded. The Panchayat leaders had now learnt the details of their powers, duties and responsibilities, sources of income to the Panchayats, Panchayat management, common property resource management, removal of encroachments and accounting and auditing procedures. They further insisted that they need periodical refresher courses at least for a day every year and that, apart from the refresher courses, they need help, information and counselling regularly for which the Rajiv Gandhi Chair has to work as a nodal centre for Panchayats[17]. From the experience of the Panchayati leaders, suggestions were made for appropriate followup. The following are their suggestions:

Acts which contradict the provisions of the Tamil Nadu Panchayati Raj Act of 1994 have to be identified and suitable amendments have to be made. All officials have to be trained and sensitized on the New Panchayati Raj System. Many officials at lower levels do not understand the Act and the rules and, as a result, Panchayats land themselves in trouble. For proper Panchayat administration, an administrative manual has to be prepared and published. All Government Orders pertinent to Panchayat administration have to be compiled and kept in all the Panchayat offices as it has been done in Pudukkottai District. A review has to be undertaken of the actions taken by the District Collectors on Panchayat leaders by using provision 205 of the Tamil Nadu Panchayat Act of 1994. This suggestion was made because 80 per cent of the dismissals and suspensions have been stayed by courts. It means that the officials have erred somewhere.

No proper handing over and taking over takes place in Gram Panchayat administration after the election to the Panchayats. Records created by the previous Panchayat administration are not handed over to the newly elected Presidents. A sizeable area of common properties encroached upon by influential individuals are to be recovered. It can be done by the revenue department as a special drive. Though a Government Order has been passed, no Village Administrative Officer has handed over village maps to the Gram Panchayat Presidents and the properties of the Gram Panchayats have not been shown to the Gram Panchayat Presidents. The higher officials of the Revenue Department, preferably the Secretary for Revenue, has to instruct the Village Administrative Officers through an order that all poramboke lands of the Panchayats have to be identified and shown to the Gram Panchayat Presidents and that village maps have to be given to the Panchayats. House tax collection has to be made rigorous and revision has to be enforced. In most of the places the Panchayats want a direction from the State Government to enhance the house tax as the Panchayat is seen as leader centric. Minor minerals revenue should go to Gram Panchayats. But now it is in court. Nobody takes action in this regard. As a result minor minerals are being lifted for the advantage of the mafia. The State Government has to take the initiative to expedite the case in the court.

Drinking water supply is going to become a difficult task in the years to come in the rural areas. There is no proper water management system, no regularization of illegal tap connections. All these problems have to be solved. Water policy and water regulation rules have to be evolved. Panchayats have to take the initiative for micro level plan which would turn the activities from a supply driven mode to a demand driven one. Huge sums have been spent in the villages by different agencies but the demands of the people projected in the Gram Sabha meeting remain unmet. Departments and representatives of the people have spent the money at their disposal in the rural areas as per their wish and perception. To avoid this kind of wastage, micro planning has to be initiated and thereby planned activities have to be carried out by pooling the resources of all the departments and representatives of the people. Panchayat leaders have to be sensitized on social development issues. Awareness has to be created among the leaders about the status of rural areas in terms of social development. Panchayats have to keep the Electricity Board cards in the Panchayat office. Panchayat leaders have to monitor the electricity consumption and meter reading. In many Panchayats, the cards are not available in the Panchayat office and the Panchayat Presidents are not aware of the expenditure on electricity, because the cards are in the EB office. Wherever the Panchayat leaders are sensitized and conscious about the expenditure, they take action to reduce electricity consumption by fitting tubelights for streetlights, removing sodium vapour lights and regulating the water supply.

It should be made mandatory that all development works, whether sponsored by sectoral departments or the Central or the State Government, should be carried out in the Panchayat area with the approval of the Gram Sabha. Panchayat Presidents are being criticized for not convening Gram Sabha meetings seriously as the Gram Sabha attendance is poor. When the proceedings, resolutions and demands of the Gram Sabha are not seriously considered by the officials, MLAs and MPs, how can one expect people to participate in the Gram Sabha meetings? People know that the Collector is powerful, the Project Officer, DRDA, is powerful, the MLA has Rs.77 lakhs and the MP two crore rupees at his/her disposal every year and hence people meet all these representatives and the Collector. Issue of birth, death and community certificates should be entrusted to the Panchayat administration. Certificates issued by the Panchayat should be provided for public verification. Funds earmarked for Panchayat activities should be directly given to Panchayats. The District Planning Committee has to take the initiative for evolving a perspective development plan for the district. The District Planning Committee has been constituted but there is no work assignment for the committee. A District Panchayat Secretary has been appointed planning officer but no planning work has been entrusted to him. Manuals have been prepared for planning, training has been conducted for officials in multi-level planning and yet there is no systematic planning at the grassroots.

Officials should not allow the husbands of the women Panchayat Presidents either to participate in the official meetings or to sign any of the papers which are to be signed by the elected women representatives. In many of the districts, lower level officials encourage the male family members of the women leaders either to attend meetings to carry out activities. If officials are very strict in this regard either genuine women will emerge as leaders or the men of the women leaders' families will change their attitude. Most of the women leaders insist that a very strict order has to be issued to the officials not to encourage the husbands of the women leaders to participate in the official meetings.

For each Panchayat an untied fund up to a maximum of Rs.5,00,000 could be given with an instruction that the amount should be spent only for economic activities, particularly employment generation and social development, as it has been done in Kerala. For women and *Dalits* a special development component plan could be developed. Panchayati Raj Institutions require a State level Director to look after the functioning of Panchayati Institutions as per the recommendations of the Swaminathan Committee. At present there is no State level authority to monitor the functioning of the Panchayati institutions. All officials, top to bottom, are interested in monitoring the implementation of schemes though they are not legally authorized to intervene in Panchayati affairs. As a result the Panchayat administration is not properly monitored and helped. To make the Panchayati institutions from District Panchayat to Gram Sabha institutions of self-government, their functioning has to be monitored and corrective steps have to be taken then and there, for which a State level officer has to be given charge of these institutions. Revenue from forestry has to come to Panchayats. But no effort has been made in this regard. Panchayat leaders have repeatedly pleaded in vain for the dues to Panchayats. Appropriate initiatives have to be taken by the district administration in this regard.

Village Panchayats which are very near to industrial estates can get a lot of revenue by way of house tax, building tax, layout approval fee and plan approval fee. But now it does not happen so in many of the cases because the Panchayat Presidents are not aware of the rules. In certain cases the rules are misused for the advantage of some leaders. In many of the cases house tax assessment is very poor or sometimes it is wrong. Proper assessment has to be made. In many places, huge amounts of revenue are being lost due to improper assessment. This has to be rectified. Cheque transactions could be avoided and the entire amount could be sent to the bank account of the Panchayats for all activities by which corruption could be eliminated since all

Panchayats maintain bank accounts. This suggestion is made because of the demands made by officials whenever they issue cheques to Panchayats. Unless the Panchayat President pays a sum, cheques will not be released. Still a major portion of the common properties are vested with traditional Panchayats. They get huge amounts of revenue from common properties but they pay very little to the Gram Panchayats. In many places auctions of commons are taken by the traditional Panchayats at a nominal rate and the same commons are re-auctioned for a huge sum. The traditional Panchayats keep the lion's share after remitting the meagre dues to the Panchayats. In many places the traditional Panchayats work in tandem with formal Panchayats. In some places they are at loggerheads. This is to be studied seriously and appropriate action has to be taken.

All sectoral departments have to inform the Panchayat Presidents about the schemes and programmes they are going to carry out in the Panchayat area. The Panchayats are given powers, not to decide about the works to be carried out but to help the sectoral departments to implement and carry out the activities. But, at present, the sectoral departments do not even consult or inform the Panchayats about the programmes being carried out in the Panchayat areas. If the annual plan preparation is done in every Panchayat, the sectoral departments' activities could be integrated with the plans of the Panchayats. Whenever a licence is issued for quarrying, a copy of the licence should be sent to the Panchayats.

Panchayat leaders at Gram Panchayat level feel that the District Collectors have to convene a meeting of Gram Panchayat leaders once in a while and help the Panchayat administration by eliminating hurdles created by lower level officials. It would help not only the Panchayat administration but also the district administration for speedy implementation of schemes and programmes. Wherever the District Collector establishes direct contact with Gram Panchayat leaders, the Panchayat administration is streamlined and strengthened and innovative practices are developed while implementing the schemes and programmes. The best innovative practices have to be documented properly and scientifically and disseminated through the media[18].

At present Panchayat institutions are not functioning as a system but discretely and individually in a leader centric or officer centric manner. Both officials and leaders perceive Panchayat affairs as their affairs. Both leaders and officials are not well versed in the rules of the game. To make the Panchayat an institution of real self-government a series of steps have to be taken[19].

Table 8.3 : Overall Feedback of the Participants about the Training Programme

Sl. No.	Training Details	Fully Satisfied	To some Extent	Not Satis-fied	Total
1.	Materials Supplied	2124	149	115	2388
2.	Classes Handled	2218	112	58	2388
3.	Quality of Resource Persons	2220	118	50	2388
4.	Accommodation	1922	321	145	2388
5.	Food	2015	330	43	2388
6.	Classroom and Training Facilities	2119	218	51	2388
7.	Programme Coordinator's Role	2301	40	47	2388
8.	Cooperation of Officials	1880	322	186	2388
9.	Duration of Training Programme	2010	248	130	2388

Source: Computed.

Integrated Analysis

Of the two-phase training, the second phase was scientific as it was conducted with the guidelines of the manual and by a good training team. The participants, namely the Panchayat Presidents, attended the programme with a volley of questions. The precise roles and responsibilities to be performed by the Panchayat leaders and the resources and grants which are due to Panchayats were clear. Information to be supplied to the leaders were compiled and distributed to them. In the training programme they were briefed about their destination and where they are now and how they have to reach their destination. In the first phase the Panchayat leaders were groping in the dark but now they were enlightened leaders with a sense of commitment. Finding the environment not positive towards devolution of powers to Panchayats, the Panchayat leaders had formed their own associations regionwise and integrated them in to a federation. Women leaders had formed their own federation and *Dalit* Panchayat leaders had formed their own outfit[20]. These associations and federations demanded powers. Further, to clarify day-to-day administrative problems, Gandhigram Rural Institute with the collaboration of a popular vernacular (Tamil) daily, namely, *Dinamalar* had started a weekly supplement (every Monday) under the caption 'Panchayat Malar' which carries Panchayat news and information. For the 'Panchayat Malar' the Rajiv Gandhi Chair does all the work for the entire page, recording the struggles and the successes of Panchayats, providing useful information for effective Panchayat administration, and, giving answers to the questions of the public and Panchayat leaders on the affairs of Panchayats[21]. Gandhigram Rural Institute, with the support of the Hunger Project, New Delhi, conducted a workshop for journalists and sensitized them on the issues of Panchayati Raj and development. Now the media is focusing attention on the successes and struggles of the Panchayats[22]. Gradually the grassroots movement is emerging as a popular movement, gaining momentum from the people, wherein training plays a major role.

Conclusion

Capacity building and information dissemination are the two prerequisites for the effective functioning of local bodies at present. But it is unfortunate that serious thought has not been given to training since there is no policy on training. Conducting training programmes is not easy as it requires several facilities and a well trained team of trainers. Further it requires a volley of information pertinent to Panchayati administration. By imparting training, the skills and the capacity of the Panchayati leaders have been enhanced. The existing conditions and the way in which Panchayats are being administered have been identified only through the training programmes. Steps which are to be taken to put the Panchayats on the proper track have been identified. From the experience of Gandhigram Rural Institute it is perceived that by building the capacity of the leaders of grassroots institutions, a movement can be generated with the active participation of the people for the establishment of the Panchayati system as an institution of self-government. One need not wait for the initiative of the Government either for the preparation of a manual and a module for training and for conducting capacity building exercises. If a few NGOs join together the right kind of leadership can be developed at the grassroots and through them the people could be mobilized for the establishment of grassroots institutions. Through the capacity building exercise, the leaders can be sensitised as to where they are now in terms of devolution of powers and where they have to go in consonance with the spirit of the Constitutional Amendment for devolution of powers and a strong people's movement can be mobilized with the initiative of the grassroots leaders. As a result Panchayats can move to the right track to reach the destination.

NOTES

1. Rajiv Gandhi Foundation (1998), *Charter of Panchayats*, New Delhi: Rajiv Gandhi Foundation.
2. Government of Tamil Nadu (1999), *Democratic Decentralization: Powers Entrusted to Panchayat Raj Institutions*, Chennai: Rural Development Department.
3. Bandyopadhyay, D., Amitava Mukerjee and Mitali Sen Gavani, (2003), *Empowering Panchayats: Handbook for Master Trainers using Participatory Approach*, New Delhi: Concept Publishing Company.
4. Palanithurai, G., (1991), *Role Perceptions of Legislations: A Case Study of Tamil Nadu*, New Delhi: Konarak Publishers.
5. Aslam, M. (2001), *Directory of Panchayati Raj Training Institutions in India*, New Delhi: Rajiv Gandhi Foundation.
6. Panchayat Leaders have made such demands in their federation meetings and while submitting petitions to the Government.
7. In the month of June 2003, the Government of Tamil Nadu released the training module along with a G.O. 14440/2003 dated 28.4.2003. It is stated in the G.O. that wherever Gandhigram Rural Institute conducts training for Local Body Leaders the Government should not conduct similar training.
8. State Finance Commission (1995), *First State Finance Commission Report*, Chennai: State First Finance Commission.
9. State Planning Commission (1997), *Report on Entrustment of Responsibilities to Three Tier Panchayats*, Chennai: State Planning Commission.
10. Government of Tamil Nadu (1998), *Action Taken Report on the Entrustment of Responsibilities to Three-Tier Panchayats*, Chennai: Department of Rural Development.

11. Government of Tamil Nadu (1998), *Report on Roles, Responsibilities and Powers Devolved to Panchayats,* Chennai: Government of Tamil Nadu.
12. Government of Tamil Nadu (1999), *Action Taken Report on the Entrustment of Responsibilities to Three-Tier Panchayats,* Chennai: Government of Tamil Nadu.
13. Rajiv Gandhi Chair (2002), *Training Module for Panchayat Training Progress,* Gandhigram: Rajiv Gandhi Chair for Panchayati Raj Studies.
14. Palanithurai, G. (2002), *Tamil Nadu Panchayati Government Act, Rules and Schemes (in Tamil),* Chennai: South Vision.
15. The Hunger Project (2002), *Training Module for Leadership Training for Women in Panchayat,* Gandhigram: Rajiv Gandhi Chair for Panchayati Raj Studies.
16. Letter from the Director of Rural Development, Government of Tamil Nadu Rc.No.85678/2002/Training dated 17.9.2003.
17. Since the participants demanded a service and support centre to provide information to the Panchayat leaders, the Rajiv Gandhi Chair decided to launch an on-line service and the Panchayat leaders have been asked to contact the phone number 0451-2451775 for any help.
18. All the points drawn from the Panchayat Presidents were submitted to the Secretary to Government, Department of Rural Development and Director of Rural Development, Government of Tamil Nadu on 30th June, 2003.
19. In the meanwhile an interface meeting between the higher officials and women representatives of Gram Panchayats was arranged and facilitated by the Rajiv Gandhi Chair on 11th July, 2003 at Chennai.
20. Gram Panchayat Presidents have formed a Federation which is called the Federation of Gram Panchayat Leaders of Tamil Nadu. Women Gram Panchayat Leaders have formed their own federation called the Tamil Nadu Federation of Women Panchayati leaders. *Dalit* leaders in Panchayats have for their federation. These three federations periodically meet and discuss their problems. They are drawing the support of NGOs. These federations are independent and not politically affiliated. District Panchayat leaders have their own associations but they are not effective.
21. This newspaper has a readership of 5 lakhs. The entire exercise is being done with the support of The Hunger Project.
22. The media has not developed an appropriate perspective to look at Panchayats and as a result it has only projected the official versions of the Government on local bodies. After the media workshop was conducted, the media has started covering the struggles, successes and innovations of the Panchayats and the media has started helping the Panchayats.

9

DALIT LEADERSHIP IN PANCHAYATS

Introduction

The New Panchayati Raj System has started penetrating into the socio-political institutions at the micro level in an organised way with power, authority and resources. It moves deeper into the society with the objective of deepening democracy by accommodating all sections of the society in the institutions of governance. Before the enactment of the 73rd and 74th Constitutional Amendment Acts, there were about 4700 people's representatives to represent the people and to articulate the grievances of the 100 million population in the State Legislative Assemblies and National Parliament. After 53 years of democratic governance it could not be stated that the state in India had either provided basic entitlements to all citizens of the country or satisfied the political aspirations of the masses, as Indian polity has its own limitations in terms of structure and functions. The Indian political system has neither the structure to accommodate the aspiring social segments nor the capacity to address the issues and redress the grievances of the people.[1] To overcome the inherent weaknesses in the political system, a new institutional mechanism has been found as a consequence of the reform process initiated in the world in the domain of economy.[2]

In the new dispensation in India, about 32 million representatives are positioned constitutionally through elections in different offices from Gram Panchayats to District Panchayats with earmarked roles and responsibilities.[3] While expanding the political space, the scope for accommodating the hitherto marginalised and depressed social groups has been increased. Yet, care has been taken to see that the people hailing from the last rung of the social ladder are accommodated in the power structure in the grassroots institutions at all levels through reservation of seats for all the positions proportionate to their population. As a result, all sections of the society are finding enough opportunity to manage their affairs on their own.

Now the representatives hailing from the marginalised communities have to manage the institutions to administer economic development and social justice.[4] The basic question is to what extent the representatives from the marginalised sections are able to discharge their functions effectively in a caste-ridden and caste-conscious society with the domination of the higher caste groups through their traditional Panchayats?[5] It is also true that the marginalised caste groups are at present vociferous in voicing their grievances and aggressive in asserting their claims and positions through organisations. It does not mean that they are allowed to function independently as leaders of the institutions without barriers and hurdles. Even after 53 years of state intervention in social reconstruction, micro social structures could not be altered much as institutional roots are very deep in terms of the values and symbols in Indian society.[6] Social institutions are so powerful at the micro level that even after the intervention of the state they have not capitulated to the political institutions. At the micro level, the social institutions have the power to resist any change. That is why power has now been accorded to the political institutions constitutionally and reservation of seats has been provided for the deprived and marginalised sections mandatorily. The influence and the power of social institutions vary from place to place depending on the process of deconstruction and reconstruction of the society by the involvement of political institutions with the support of social reconstructionists and their movements. Hence, one finds variations in the operation of the political institutions.

In Tamil Nadu, nearly 24 per cent of the seats in all positions from Gram Panchayat ward members to District Panchayat presidents have been reserved for SC and ST. They are in position and discharging their roles and responsibility as per the functions and powers assigned to them legally through laws and notifications of the Government. Tamil Nadu is known for its social reformation and women's emancipation through the concerted efforts of the social movements broadly under the label of the Dravidian Movements.[7] Tamil Nadu, at present, is equally known for caste conflicts and formation of caste identity and caste mobilization. This trend is drawing the attention of all as a paradox being exhibited in both the polity and the society. Against this background, the newly elected leaders hailing from SC and ST community have to convene the Gram Sabha meeting and manage the crowd and manage the Panchayat council and perform the assigned functions. Discharging the responsibilities in the grassroots institutions by the leaders hailing from SC and ST community is not so easy as the caste groups are powerful in the rural areas. It is the general assumption that the conflicts cannot be so intense as in North India because of the influence of the Dravidian Movement.

It is true that except in a few places, elections had been conducted and 28,149 representatives hailing from SC and ST communities occupy positions in Panchayat institutions in Tamil Nadu. As on date, they are in power and position. Yet, it would be begging the question to argue that the representatives belonging to SC and ST communities enjoy equality and freedom in the rural society to perform their duties.[8] Available records amply provide evidences to construct the proposition that when powers are being decentralised in an organised way and constitutionally, attempts are made by the social segments to capture power in an organised way. In the process, conflict becomes inevitable as the communities have been sensitised and conscientized by the reconstructionist movement through the media over a period of time in Tamil Nadu. The conscientization process has further deepened the cleavages so as to form separate identities and to mobilise the people with the object of claiming stakes in the benefits of services and power. Hence the conflict is intense to maximise the benefits from authorised allocations by keeping the power structure under the hold of the dominant caste and class either explicitly or implicitly.

Statement of the Problem

The present study makes an attempt to analyse the perception of *Dalit* leaders about the new opportunity provided them to ameliorate the conditions of the *Dalits*, problems faced by the *Dalit* leaders in handling power in Panchayat administration, perception of the people about the performance of the *Dalit* leaders and the steps to be taken to overcome all the barriers. In this study, the relationship between the marginalised and the dominant groups in handling power at the grassroots will be evaluated. This analysis does not confine itself to the relationship between the legally created institutions under the marginalised leaders and the dominant communities holding control over the people through traditional Panchayats. It moves beyond the political institutions to pinpoint some of the key issues which are being faced by the leaders belonging to SC and ST communities. This analysis does not end with either confirming and testing the theoretical propositions of inter-relationship among the social groups of the grassroots institutions for sharing and shaping of power or to evolving new propositions to construct new theories in political sociology. It will be suggest measures to reconstruct the rural society and polity to maintain equity and justice in administering development.

Backdrop of the Statement

Proper historical understanding of the issues will help the researchers to gain insights into the issues for a meaningful academic exercise and theorization. The concept of decentralization of power from the federal Government to the village had been a subject of debate ever since India won independence. Three statements generated a great deal of debate among the intellectuals and politicians of this country. These are the statements of Gandhiji, Ambedkar and Rajiv Gandhi on decentralization of power. When the Constituent Assembly was in session, Gandhiji made an observation that "I must confess that I have not been able to follow the proceedings of the Constituent Assembly [the correspondent] says that there is no mention or direction about village Panchayats and decentralization in the foreshadowed Constitution. It is certainly an omission calling for immediate attention if our independence is to reflect the people's voice. The greater the power of the Panchayats, the better for the people."[9]

While expressing his opinion to shape Indian polity, Gandhiji made a statement that "the Centre of Power is in New Delhi or Calcutta or Bombay in the big cities. I would have it distributed among the seven hundred thousand villages of India."[10]

Yet another point of view, expressed by Ambedkar, was quite opposite to the opinion expressed by Gandhiji in the same tenor. Ambedkar started his argument by picking a statement from Metcalfe. Ambedkar observed: "What is the village but a sink of localism, a den of ignorance, narrow-mindedness and communalism? I am glad that the Draft Constitution has discarded the village and adopted the individual as its unit."[11]

These observations of Gandhiji and Ambedkar generated a volume of debate in the Constituent Assembly and speaker after speaker referred to the statements made by the two leaders. No one was in a position to disprove the reality projected by Ambedkar and so the members had to come to the conclusion that it should be enshrined in Article 40 of the Constitution of India. After forty years, a rethinking was advocated by Rajiv Gandhi on the assumption that society had changed drastically. With caution and care he proposed to empower the marginalised. Rajiv Gandhi observed: "We trust the people, we have faith in the people. It is the people who must determine their own destinies and the destiny of the nation. To the people of India, let us ensure maximum democracy and maximum devolution. Let the people be empowered."[12]

Rajiv Gandhi took the individuals as units as observed by Ambedkar. But individuals cannot use power unless they are organised. Power can be utilised only through institutions and the institutions can be handled only by organisations. The question here is to what extent the social situation had changed between the era of Mahatma Gandhi and that of Rajiv Gandhi. Against this historical background, the interface between communities has to be analysed in terms of decentralization of powers. To look at the issues posited above an appropriate theory has to be evolved and the problem can be clearly visualised only against such a theoretical background.

Theoretical Considerations

For a meaningful discourse on caste, one has to look upon the contributions of anthropologists and sociologists. Caste is an

Indian phenomenon which has been extensively studied and researched by western anthropologists and sociologists who developed a variety of theories. Of course, Indian scholars have also contributed but a substantial quantum of literature has been developed by western scholars. Various approaches have been developed by anthropologists and sociologists and they have been widely adopted to study the problems of continuity and change in the operation of the concept of caste. Till date, hard core academics have found it difficulty to construct a corpus of knowledge of the role of caste in society against the backdrop of change because there are differences between the book-view and the field-view. The book-view is based on the scriptures and the field-view is based on the implications and the impact of the social reconstruction movement.[13] A variety of theories have been developed over this issue on the basis of the dialects among the scholars. A number of schools have developed based on their contributions. Initially, Dumont conceptualized his idea holistically and presented the admirable characteristics of the caste system in India. But this has been disputed by Andre Beteille.[14] Following the criticisms levelled against Dumont, an array of documents have been prepared and published by a host of scholars.[15] The contributions center round the sociological implications of the institution of caste. Over the years, one finds major arguments in eulogy as well as condemnation of the caste system perpetuated in Indian society. Fifty years have gone by and much water has flown under the bridge but the position and the role of caste in society does not find any significant change since the structure of the caste is very strong in the society. There will not be much change in the position of the caste in the Indian society. Studies were carried out in tiny villages long back and recorded and they are being compared with recent studies undertaken in the same villages after forty years. Significant changes have not been observed.

Scores of theories have been developed and several theoretical approaches have been evolved by the ethnographers, anthropologists, sociologists, socio-biologists and historians on the subject of caste. Pure anthropological studies, cultural anthropological studies, pure sociological studies, ethnosociological studies, ethnobiological studies and historical studies have been carried out. In all these studies the characteristics of the caste system, the implications of the caste system in the broader functioning of the social system, major distinctions of the sub-caste systems, attempts to construct new systems by deconstructing and reconstruct the existing system have been extensively studied and propositions have been made by classifying the scholars as constructionist, deconstructionist, reconstructionist, reformist, classical, neo-classical and so on. All these studies have extensively analysed the linkages between the collectivities and the resources. The linkages between the collectivities and the resources are determined by the established hierarchy in the social system. But the whole of the relationship started losing its grip over the system during the period of the colonial administration. Subsequently, the concept of state system gained currency and it tried to alter the position to the advantage of the colonial administration. From the colonial period to the present, the concept of power or authority has been playing an important role in determining the interrelationship among the communities.

Since our concern is to trace the linkages between the social structures and the political system, it is necessary to consider the approaches of modern political sociologists. The well known political scientist Rajni Kothari also done commendable work in this area.[16] He has analysed the transformative process of the caste structure and politics in India over a period of time. As per the propositions of sociologists on modernization, social structures are moving from one stage of activities to another, with changing and distinctive characteristics and so do the political institutions. The question is to what extent the changes take place and to what extent they have an impact on the society. Against this background, Rajni Kothari looked at the Indian social system. Every province and every region of every province is distinct in terms of keeping the characteristics of the local social sub-system. Considering the wide variations among the regions it has been decided that, for this study, Andre Beteille's analytical framework will be adopted. The reason for selecting Andre Beteille's framework for this study is that his contributions are mostly drawn from Tamil Nadu experience.

Andre Beteille's argument stems from a basic premise that power starts moving from one dominant community to another at the micro level for which macro level politics is responsible in many ways. It starts from Panchayats and the change is exhibited through elections periodically. The flow of events and activities creates changes in the structures of the social system. Caste enters politics in a number of ways. It enters through appeals for mobilization, creating a network of interpersonal relationships during election time and, at other times, for mobilising the people into caste associations by articulating the interests of the caste.

The whole process could be seen against the backdrop of the nature of the caste system prevailing in Tamil Nadu. The caste system in Tamil Nadu is both elaborate and deeply segmented. It is characterized by several levels of differentiations. There are several larger units and the same are divided into smaller ones and these are sub-divided on the basis of fairly enduring cleavages. These segments are differentiated by themselves or by others. The caste groups are characterised on the one hand by certain diacritical distinctions and on the other by a set of syncretic values. Diacritical values incite the process of maintaining the unity of the segment by differentiating itself from others. Syncretic values incite the unity moves the groups or segments in terms of internal solidarity. The diacritical differences are elaborate in Tamil Nadu.

The caste structure in Tamil Nadu is different from that in other states. Hence, it is necessary to present a picture of the caste structure in Tamil Nadu. The Tamil population can be broadly divided into three major groups, *viz.*, Brahmins, Non-Brahmins, and the Harijans (Adi-Dravidas). All the three groups have distinct dwelling units. Of the three major groups, the non-Brahmins represent a broader spectrum of cultural variations and appear to be, on the whole, less cohesive than the other two segments. Each segment has its own sub-divisions for social and cultural relationships.

When caste enters politics, it works in a different pattern. As of now, there are two propositions that castes can successfully enter state politics only when they combine into fairly large aggregates and too much segmentation tends to work in grassroots politics. Groups tend to align with other sets of groups to oppose any targeted group on specific issues. Hence, there is constant movement from one alignment to another and this practice is normal in Tamil Nadu. One can find fissions and fusions in caste groups which are the common features of caste polities in Tamil Nadu. For the purpose of sociological analysis, it is necessary that a distinction has to be made between caste at the political level and at cultural level.

From the foregoing arguments, it is concluded that caste may be significant to the political process at every level and organisations are rigid at the lowest level and that they tend to exhibit flexibility when they move towards higher level. Thus, for this study, the three-fold division of society into Brahmin, Non-Brahmin and Harijan provides broad basis for the study of communal politics in Tamil Nadu. This division also provides the basic framework for the analysis of the functioning of the Panchayats in Tamil Nadu.

Panchayats in Tamil Nadu: Historical Context

It is obvious from history that Tamil Brahmins enjoyed a favourable position in the traditional economic system. A considerable section of the Brahmins owned land. Subsequently, during the period of the British, the distance between the Brahmins and the non-Brahmins increased structurally because of the westernization of the Brahmin community. In the first quarter of the century, they utilised all the opportunities to place themselves in distinct positions and distanced themselves from the non-Brahmins. They formed a clique and everywhere left no space for the non-Brahmins.

To counter the expansion of the Brahmins' hold over the political structures and economic institutions, a non-Brahmin movement was organsied. It could not succeed initially. Even in the Panchayat institutions at the micro level, Brahmins began to dominate during the British Raj. In the past, the Brahmins enjoyed the highest positions in the hierarchies of status, class and power. Even today, they enjoy ritual and economic dominance but political power has shifted to the non-Brahmins.

The shift in political power has been hastened by the introduction of the Panchayat system.

At the dawn of independence and a little earlier, the non-Brahmins, with the help of the movement, began to capture Panchayats and brought the power centre from the agraharam to the streets of non-Brahmin settlements. Panchayat halls were the centres of political gatherings of the villages and automatically the Brahmins were excluded. Simultaneously the Brahmins moved over to towns and cities to take up positions.[17]

Though it was articulated that the non-Brahmin movement included all castes other than Brahmins, including Muslims and Harijans who speak South Indian languages, the lingual groups and the social groups never treated themselves as non-Brahmins, because the dominant caste group dominated at the micro level and a few dominant caste groups jointly dominated the power structure above the micro units. The non-Brahmin ascendancy reached its peak in the mid-fifties. In wake of the consolidation of non-Brahmin power, internal cleavages developed within it. With the introduction of the Panchayat system the rift among the sub-caste groups was widened.

Among the dominant caste groups, competition arose to share and shape power. In the early Panchayat system, there was no reservation for the marginalized. So there was competition among the dominant caste groups to capture the power structure. In the whole process of socio-political transformation, many of the caste groups moved away from the broader organisation called non-Brahmins and formed their own segments. It is significant that the Adi-Dravidars have totally kept away from the non-Brahmin movement and called themselves *Dalits* and developed a movement for their upliftment. Widespread agitations against the non-Brahmin movement were conducted, the failures of the non-Brahmin movement were highlighted the genuine demands of the *Dalits* were voiced.

New System at Work

Now, the New Panchayati Raj System has come to stay as an institution of self-government with earmarked roles and responsibilities through a constitutional amendment. The new

Framework for the Analysis of the Transformation of Caste Groups

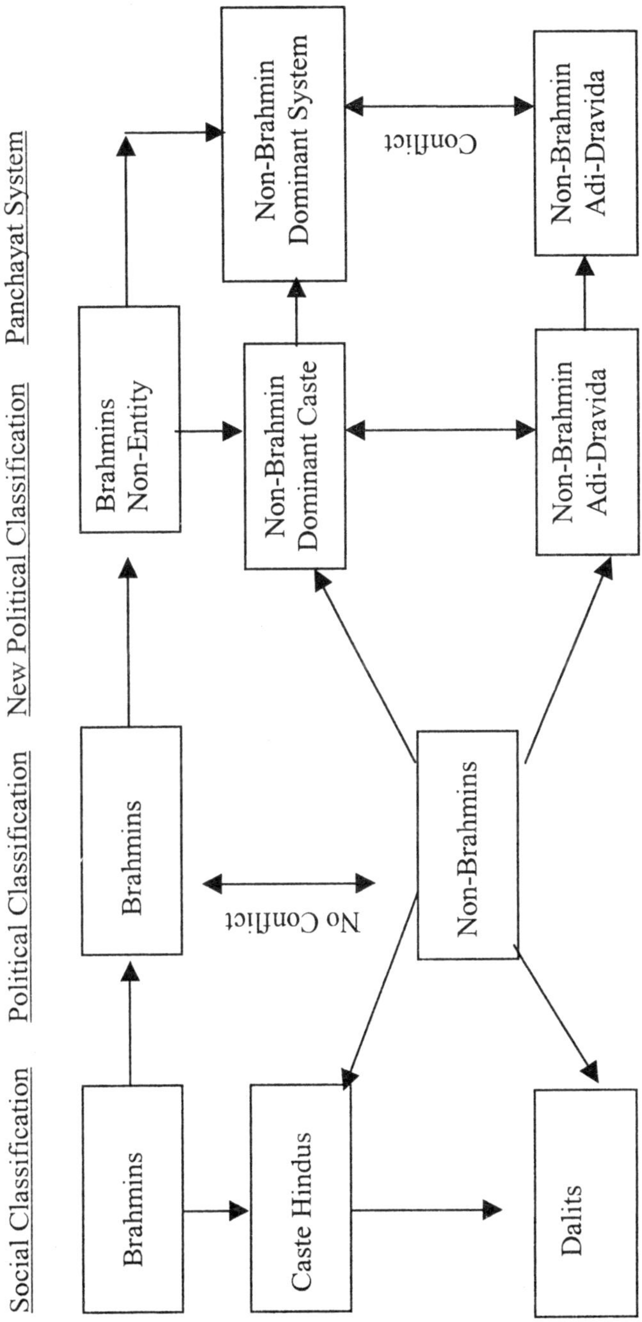

task assigned to the institution is to administer economic development and social justice. This new dispensation came in with the basic objective of deepening democracy by ensuring opportunities to all the social segments hitherto marginalised in order to take part in the development activities of the community. To ensure this objective, reservation has been provided for the *Dalits* in the Panchayat structure from the lowest level to the highest at the district level. This is a mandatory provision and the quantum of seats has been fixed in proportion to their population. This kind of reservation will create a critical mass for the process of empowerment of the marginalised and the underprivileged.

This new dispensation has come into operation in a context where in the *Dalit* collectivities have taken an aggressive stance to negotiate with the power structure at the state and central level to get their legitimate socio-economic demands settled. When this provision is put into practice, naturally the *Dalits* have an opportunity to move into over the power centre in large numbers and carry out programmes and schemes for the development of the *Dalits*. But the process is not smooth. One has to remember that the social change the Indian society has witnessed is a rather slow process when compared to the political transformation. Social structures remained unchanged for long. The competition to capture power was between the dominant castes and not among all the caste groups. When the competition was between two or three social segments of the non-Brahmins excluding the *Dalits*, it never took an aggressive form. Even during the period of power shift from the Brahmins to the non-Brahmins it was not so aggressive as we witness when power shifts from non-Brahmin dominant castes to *Dalits* a per the reservation of seats in the Panchayat system.

One has to analyse how the power shift took place from the cohesive Brahmin community to the non-cohesive non-Brahmin dominant caste groups and in the same way, how the power shift now takes place from the non-cohesive non-Brahmin caste groups to the cohesive *Dalit* group. The two power shifts have thrown up several propositions for further validation.The first power shift was from the westernised, socially, economically, and culturally highly placed cohesive Brahmin community to the non-cohesive, socially and economically disadvantaged dominant non-Brahmin caste groups. The Brahmin lost power at the grassroots but retained their economic and social power through several institutional structures. Further, they were westernised in understanding the transformation process. Hence it was not an aggressive development.

The second power shift that is taking place now is an aggressive one as the incohesive social groups are not in an advantageous position socially and economically or enjoy the power to distribute the benefits from the Government. The existing social structure has not changed much and hence there is no orientation for the dominant non-Brahmin caste groups to digest the power shift from them to the *Dalits* as they still treat them as untouchables. The incohesive non-Brahmin dominant communities have developed an antipathy towards the *Dalits* as they are enjoying more benefits from the Government, even though the economic condition of certain sections of the non-Brahmin communities and the *Dalits* are the same. However, the non-Brahmin communities are incohesive, though they are functionally cohesive due to their distinct functional responsibilities their resource base. The groups in the non-Brahmin category, who have developed themselves in the process of transformation that took place in Tamil Nadu in the past thirty years because of the policy interventions of the non-Brahmin movement, have now started migrating from the rural areas to urban centres to enhance their economic and political status.

As a consequence of the reservation of seats made for the *Dalits*, the transformation process has started but it is painful, because it is passing through a stage of conflict. Wherever the population of the *Dalits* outnumbers the non-Brahmin communities, they take an aggressive posture and in, other places too, they entered into conflicts with the other caste groups. These attempts often meet with resistance from the dominant castes. These conflicts have been particularly a significant feature of the relations between the non-Brahmins and the *Dalits* throughout the state.[18]

Now, the *Dalits* enjoy power legitimately in the hierarchy power structure at the grassroots level. Nearly 24 per cent of the positions have been occupied by *Dalit* representatives. At present, they have formed a critical mass for socio-political and economic action. But this power is not being actualised because many factors stand in their way. There is yet another interesting development that, wherever the *Dalits* are a minority, their leaders are brought under the control of the dominant caste groups. The dominant caste group leaders ensure that their own nominees from the *Dalit* community are elected to Panchayat positions and thereby they have established their sway over the society.

The *Dalits* have to carry out their struggle with in-built weaknesses. On one side, the elders of the community are not able to assert themselves and their rights due to a long tradition of servility. But, the younger elements of the *Dalit* community are developing a spirit of challenge and conflict with the other communities to establish their position on par with the other communities. Even in the case of the younger elements, lack of education and contact with the outside the world and poor economic conditions block their way to enhance their skills to cope with the challenges of organised politics. The problems are multi-dimensional in nature. The *Dalits* are being oriented by certain organisations of the civil society to develop perspectives of their own to look at their issues. They are being conscientised as to how their issues are to be sorted out. The *Dalit* leaders who have come to power and look at the basic issues which have been affecting their life in the rural areas are to be conscientised.

For the poor and landless non-Brahmins, the concessions extended by the Government to the *Dalits* by law are a thorn in the flesh. The land owners of the dominant caste have become jittery over the demand of the *Dalits* on land and other resources and they feel that the *Dalits* are the real threat to their social and economic position. Therefore, they are also very aggressive. The non-Brahmins have their own traditional Panchayats looking after the community affairs and they are dominant in the rural areas. These traditional organisations have established control over the resource bases. When the *Dalits* take over the reins of the formal Panchayats, the traditional Panchayats, with their resource base, powerfully challenge the formal Panchayats headed by the *Dalits*. The resultant social conflict is intensive in many parts of the state and it has been violent forms in both South and North Tamil Nadu. In the southern regions, *Dalits vs.* Kallars conflicts and in the Northern districts *Dalits vs.* Vanniars conflicts have been erupting frequently. There are victims are from both the camps.

It is an irony that in the past six to seven decades, it has been argued that steps should be taken to bring about unity among the non-Brahmins of South India under the concept of Dravidian Nationalism and later among, non-Brahmins of Tamil Nadu under Tamil Nationalism and yet, no such unity or identity has been achieved. For the past 30 years, the Tamil ethnic political parties are in power and both in urban and rural areas, people are said to have been oriented in Dravidian ideology. But, in reality, the non-Brahmin dominant caste groups have not reconciled themselves to the concept of social equity and justice as enunciated by the state authorities. The struggle is still on.

Methodology

To analyse the condition of the *Dalit* leadership and the performance of the *Dalit* leaders in the New Panchayati Raj System an in-depth study has been conducted in Nilakkottai Block. Different categories of respondents have been interviewed and records have been consulted. The respondents are Gram Panchayat leaders both *Dalits* and non-*Dalits*, Gram Panchayat Ward Members, Self-Help Group Leaders, Panchayat Clerks, Block Development Officials and traditional Panchayat leaders and community leaders. Questions related to their perceptions, social justice, economic empowerment and obstacles faced by the Panchayat leaders in implementing development programmes have been posted to them to elicit their views. Case studies have been conducted with a *Dalit* woman Gram Panchayat President, a *Dalit* official working in the Block Development Office and an NGO working for the empowerment of *Dalits*. This study has not attempted to make any evaluation on the impact of the schemes and programmes in the rural society.

Responses of the Respondents

SECTION I

In this section the socio-economic background of the respondents and the activities carried out by the Gram Panchayats are given in Tables 9.1 to 9.18.

Table 9.1 : Category of Respondents (Panchayat-wise)

Sl. No.	Village	Name of the President	Sex	Comm-unity	Clerk	Ward Member (men)	Ward Member (women)	SHG	Village key person	Total
1.	Noothulapuram	Ms. Kala	Female	SC	*	1	-	1	1	4
2.	Kodanginaickenpatti	Ms. Pichayam-mal	Female	SC	1	1	-	-	1	4
3.	Pachamalaiyankottai	Mr. Muthukalai	Male	SC	1	1	-	1	1	5
4.	Sivagnanapuram	Mr. Mottayandi	Male	SC	1	-	1	1	1	5
5.	Silukkuvarpatti	Ms. Amutha	Female	BC	*	-	1	1	1	4
6.	Kullichettipatti	Ms. Kamala	Female	BC	1	-	-	1	1	4
7.	Mettupatti	Mr. Paraman	Male	BC	1	-	1	1	1	5
8.	Pallapatti	Mr. Gunasekaran	Male	BC	*	1	-	1	1	4
	Total				5	4	3	7	8	27

* The clerks of Noothulapuram, Silukkuvarpatti Village Panchayats were not available during the visits made by the investigator. In Pallapatti Panchayat the clerk resigned last year and the vacancy is yet to be filled.

Source: Computed.

Table 9.2 : Profile of the Gram Panchayat Presidents

Sl. No.	Panchayat Name	Name of the Panchayat President	Sex	Age	Commu-nity	Education	Occupation	Land Holding	Annual Income	Party Affiliation	Remarks
1.	Noothulapuram	Ms. M.Kala	F	38	SC	10th Standard	Agriculture	2 acres	Rs.30,000	Congress	ASSFFA activities
2.	Kodangi naickenpatti	Ms. Pichaiyammal	F	36	SC	10th Standard	Agriculture (Husband Bank staff)	4 acres	Rs.1,00,000	No party affiliation	Husband bank staff
3.	Pachamalayan-kottai	Mr. Muthukalai	M	41	SC	9th Standard	Agriculture+ Dairy	5 acres	Rs.75,000	Congress	Ex-Ward member
4.	Sivagnanapuram	Mr. Mottayandi	M	51	SC	5th Standard	Agriculture	3 acres	Rs.60,000	AIADMK	Ex-President
5.	Silukkuvarpatti	Ms. Amutha	F	46	BC	10th Standard	(Husband is a vessel merchant)	Nil	Rs.80,000	DMK	Husband DMK unit secretary
6.	Kullichettipatti	Ms. Kamala	F	52	BC	10th Standard	Agriculture	5 acres	Rs.75,000	Congress	Social Worker
7.	Mettupati	Mr. Paraman	M	41	BC	5th Standard	Agriculture	3 acres	Rs.30,000	AIADMK	Social Worker
8.	Pallapatti	Ms. Gunasekaran	M	45	BC	10th Standard	Agriculture	10 acres	Rs.1,00,000	DMK	Social worker

Source: Computed.

Table 9.3 : Profile of the Panchayat Clerks

Sl. No.	Panchayat Name	Name of the Clerk	Sex	Age	Community	Education	Land Holding	Annual Income	Party Affiliation	Remarks
1.	Kodanginaickenpatti	Mr. N. Sivakumar	M	34	SC	ITI	Nil	Rs.15,000	Nil	-
2.	Kullichettipatti	Mr. Ramanathan	M	28	BC	10th Standard	Nil	Rs.12,000	Nil	-
3.	Mettupatti	Mr. M. Sinnan	M	27	BC	10th Standard	Nil	Rs.12,000	Nil	Physically disabled
4.	Sivagnanapuram	Mr. Selvam	M	40	SC	10th Standard	Nil	Rs.12,000	Nil	Involved in youth activities
5.	Pachamalayankottai	Mr. Jeyaganesh	M	30	BC	B.Com	Nil	Rs.12,000	Nil	Involved in youth activities

Source: Computed.

Table 9.4 : Profile of the Panchayat Ward Members

Sl. No.	Panchayat Name	Name of the Ward Member	Sex	Age	Community	Education	Occupation	Land Holding	Annual Income	Party Affiliation	Remarks
1.	Pachamalayan-kottai	Mr. Francis Xavier	M	44	BC	10th Standard	Agriculture	10 acres	Rs.75,000	DMK	Social worker
2.	Kondanginaica-kenpatti	Mr. Ibrahim	M	40	Muslim	B.A	Agriculture	2 acres	Rs.15,000	No	Member in Par. Tr. Association
3.	Mettupatti	Ms. Subbuthai	F	34	SC	3rd Standard	Pettyshop	Nil	Rs.10,000	No	Involved in SHGs
4.	Sivagnanapuram	Ms.Sumathi	F	35	BC	8th Standard	Housewife and Coolie	Nil	Rs.10,000	No	Involved in SHGs
5.	Silukkuvarpatti	Ms. Palaniammal	F	45	SC	3rd Standard	Coolie	Nil	Rs.10,000	No	Husband vegetable vendor
6.	Pallapatti	Mr. P. Laksh-manan	M	43	SC	5th Standard	Coolie	Nil	Rs.10,000	Congress	Social worker

Source: Computed.

Table 9.5 : Profile of the SHG Leaders

Sl. No.	Panchayat Name	Name of the SHG Leader	Sex	Age	Comm-unity	Education	Occupation	Land Holding	Annual Income	Party Affiliation	Remakrs
1.	Pachamalayan-kottai	Ms. Mary	F	35	BC	9th Standard	Petty shop	Nil	Rs.25,000	AIADMK	Social worker
2.	Kullichettipatti	Ms. Sasikala	F	30	BC	9th Standard	Coolie work	Nil	Below Rs.10,000	No	President of SHG
3.	Panchavarnam–Mettupatti	Ms. Panchavarnam	F	30	SC	10th Standard	Coolie work	Nil	Below Rs.10,000	No	President of SHG
4.	Sivagnanapuram	Ms. Muthulakshmi	F	52	BC	5th Standard	Coolie work	Nil	Below Rs.10,000	No	President of SHG
5.	Pallapatti	Ms. Chinnammal	F	60	BC	8th Standard	Housewife	Nil	Above Rs.10,000	No	Broken family
6.	Silukkuvarpatti	Ms. Maniammal	F	47	BC	10th Standard	Flower Vending	Nil	Above Rs.10,000	No	Keen interest in forming SHGs
7.	Noothulapuram	Ms. Savithiri	F	33	BC	10th Standard	Housewife	2 acres	Rs.25,000	No	Husband is a contractor

Source: Computed.

Table 9.6 : Profile of Traditional Leader

Sl. No.	Panchayat Name	Name of the Traditional Leader	Sex	Age	Comm-unity	Education	Occupation	Land Holding	Annual Income	Party Affiliation	Remarks
1.	Pachamalayankottai	Mr. Muniandi	M	70	SC	2nd Standard	Agriculture	6 acres	Rs.40,000	Congress	Volunteer in Panchayat activity
2.	Kondanginaickenpátti	Mr. Falardin	M	53	Muslim	5th Standard	Agriculture	2 acres	Rs.25,000	AIADMK	–
3.	Kullichettipatti	Mr. Angathevar	M	70	BC	5th Standard	-	Nil	Rs.12,000	No	Community guard
4.	Mettupatti	Mr. Kamatchi	M	70	SC	3rd Standard	-	Nil	Rs.12,000	Congress	Volunteer during temple celebration
5.	Sivagnanapuram	Mr. Pitchaimani	M	45	SC	10th Standard	Coolie work	Nil	Rs.15,000	No	Literacy activities
6.	Pallapatti	Mr. K. Raja	M	55	BC	8th Standard	Agriculture	10 acres	Rs.1,00,000	AIADMK	Money lender
7.	Noothulapuram	Mr. Murugan	M	50	BC	10th Standard	Driver	2 acres	Rs.30,000	Congress	*Dalit* related activities
8.	Silukkuvarpatti	Mr. Chockan	M	51	BC	10th Standard	Vessel–merchant	Nil	Rs.80,000	DMK	Ex-President

Source: Computed.

Table 9.7 : Profile of the Officials

Sl. No.	Name of the Official	Sex	Age	Community	Education	Occupation	Land Holding	Annual Income	Party Affiliation
1.	Balasubramanian	M	58	BC	10th	BDO	-	Rs.1,00,000	No
2.	Shanmugavelu	M	58	BC	10th	BDO	-	Rs.1,00,000	No
3.	Ilaya Raja	M	27	BC	B. Com.	RWO	-	Rs.75,000	No
4.	Pitchaikannan	M	52	BC	10th	EOP	-	Rs.75,000	No
5.	O. Kannan	M	49	BC	10th	EO (AD)	-	Rs.75,000	No
6.	Manickam	M	30	SC	B. Com.	RWO	-	Rs.75,000	No
7.	Ms. Parameswari	F	38	BC	B.Sc., B.Ed.	RWO	-	Rs.75,000	No

Source: Computed.

Table 9.8 : Profile of the Villages

Sl. No.	No. of hamlets	Panchayat Name	Population -- 1991 Census				Ward Members						Major Community	Dominant Community	SHGs		Remarks
			Total	Male	Female	SC Population Only	Total	Male	Female	SC					BC	SC	
										Male	Female	Total					
1	10	Silukkuvarpatti	9815	4929	4886	3198	12	8	4	2	1	3	Christian-Vanniar, Vellalar, Chettiar, Asari, Pallar, Sakkiliyar	No Idea	4	7	Flower production Infant Jesus Church
2.	2	Kullichettipatti	1472	729	743	487	6	4	2	1	-	1	Chettiar, Goundar, Vellalar, Naidu, Parayar	Chettiar, Goundar	3	2	Poor bus facility (only 3 times per day)
3.	19	Pachamalaiyan kottai	7169	4002	3167	2782	12	9	3	4	2	6	Thevar, Pillai Nadar, Naicker, Muslim, SC	SC	5	10	Sempatti bus stand available flowers, vegetable, . production
4.	7	Kodanginaicken patti	3325	1702	1623	1187	9	6	3	3	2	5	Naicker, Asari, Muslim, SC, Weaver, Nadar	SC	12	3	Differences of opinion between Pallar, Parayar, Sakkiliyar

(Contd.)

Table 9.8 *(Contd.)*

5.	1	S. Mettupatti	1052	546	506	128	6	4	2	-	1	1	Thevar, Nadar, Naicker, Mooper, Maniar, Asari, Pillai, Parayar	Thevar	1	1	Two Tumbler system, famous Hanuman temple
6.	11	Noothulapuram	4685	2365	2320	2639	9	6	3	4	2	6	Chettiyar, Pillai, Naicker, Thevar, SC	Naicker	3	4	SC population is high, Makkal Mayyam, Wasteland development programme
7.	7	Pallapatti	7694	3890	3804	2063	12	8	4	3	4	7	Thevar, Gounder, Pillaimar, Konar, Servai, Mooper, Asari	Thevar, Gounder	3	10	Mavoor Dam is available
8.	4	Sivagnanapuram	2366	1226	1140	924	9	6	3	3	1	4	Pillai, Thevar, Chettiar, SC, Maniar, Servai, Asari, Naicker	SC – Pl	2	3	Bus facility is poor, Flower production

Source: Computed.

Table 9.9 : Status of Major NGO's in Nilakkottai Block

Sl. No.	Details of NGO	Programmes
1.	CENTREEDA Functioning since 1988	SHG, NF, Child Labour and Watershed programmes, Target: all poor Chief Functionary: BC
2.	Kalanchiyam For the past three years	DHAN Foundation, Regional Office (Madurai), SHG activities Target: all poor
3.	ASSEFA – Association for Sarva Seva Farms Since 20 years back	Gandhian Institution SHG, IGP activities Target: all poor
4.	TAPWA* Since 1988	Housing, pre-school, SHG & IGP activities Chief Executive: BC Target: SC community in particular
5.	MMSS* – Madurai Multipurpose Service Society For the past 15 years	Church based NGO, SHG, IGP, awareness activities Target: Both SC & BC More focus on SC
6.	SEDWIN** For the past 6 years	Awareness programme SC Chief

Source: Computed.

Notes :

* TAPWA & MMSS fielded their SHG members in the Panchayat election and helped them. Some of them won in the election.

** SEDWIN encourages the SC youth to participate effectively in Panchayati Raj Institutions and activities.

Table 9.10 : Noothulapuram Panchayat 2001-2002

Income Sources		Expenditure	
Categories	Amount in Rs.	Categories	Amount in Rs.
House tax	16721	Salary for staff	41755
Library tax	1672	TA for President	7525
Professional tax	14640	TA for clerk	2943
Licence fees	260	Sitting fees	5225
Funeral grant	10500	TV maintenance	885
House tax matching grant	25820	Office equipment	9862
Other tax sources	10549	Newspaper	4173
Stamp duty	41136	Sanitation	19392

(Contd.)

Table 9.10 (*Contd.*)

Income Sources	Expenditure	Income Sources	Expenditure
SFC grant	382293	Street light maintenance	27001
Income from Union level	50000	Borewell maintenance	23670
		Funeral grant	95000
		Bank commission	2654
		Insurance	7175
		Purchasing electric motor	18755
		Cement road	37123
		Pipeline maintenance	98859
		Motor maintenance	38025
		Advance amount for festival	3400
		Pongal bonus	1800
		Construction of motor room	73538
		Other expenses	18081
Scheme Fund		Expenditure	
SGRY	57,000	Maintenance of hut houses	80,000
For new motor	1,00,00	Desilting work	57,000
	1,57,100		1,37,100

Source: Computed from Panchayat records.

Table 9.11 : Kodanginaickenpatti Panchayat 2001-2002

Income Sources		Expenditure	
Categories	Amount in Rs.	Categories	Amount in Rs.
House tax	15479.00	Salary for staff	34320.00
Library tax	1547.90	TA for President	17680.00
Professional tax	6000.00	Electricity material	10187.00
Blueprint approval	380.00	Recovery from Union level	45000.00
Licence for shop	250.00	Administrative expenses	1140.00
House tax matching grant	26869.00	Funeral grant	10500.00
SFC grant	197283.00	Insurance	9075.00
Funeral grant	8500.00	TV maintenance	2657.00
Stamp duty	12674.00	Street maintenance	5584.00

(Contd.)

Table 9.11 (*Contd.*)

Income Sources		Expenditure	
Categories	Amount in Rs.	Categories	Amount in Rs.
2-C patta	126.00	Pipeline work	46419.00
Bank interest	108.60	Pumpset work	16699.00
Local cess	2031.00	Drinking water material	5150.00
Auction of trees	45.00	Office equipment	780.00
Auction of wastage	60.00	Recovery by bank	70.00
Other sources	352.10	Recovery by AD Panchayat's office	47.50
Total	**2,71,716.00**	Graveyard road work	4400.00
		Library tax paid	2466.00
		Hand pump work	9250.00
		Electricity charges	5128.00
		Recovery by bank	11810.00
		Balance amount	16861.00
		Total	**2,88578.50**
Scheme Fund		*Expenditure*	
JGSY	1,62,800	Pipeline work	68451
IAY	90,000	IAY	76277
Bank interest	2333.50	**Total**	**1,44,728**
Other sources	5,320.00		
Total	**2,690,453.50**		

Source: Computed from Panchayat records.

Table 9.12 : Pachaimalayankottai Panchayat from 2001-2002

Income Sources		Expenditure	
Categories	Amount in Rs.	Categories	Amount in Rs.
House tax	1,01,675	Salary for staff	48,496
Library tax	10,182	TA for President	2,900
Professional tax	28,270	TA for Panchayat clerk	1,520
Other sources	35,192	Office equipment	4,021
House tax matching grant	18,710	Electricity charges	8,640
Other sources	2,286	Electricity for building	3,300
Deposit amount for water	17,000	OHT maintenance	76,520
Rent from toilet	51,000	Newspaper	390

(*Contd.*)

Table 9.12 (*Contd.*)

Income Sources		Expenditure	
Categories	Amount in Rs.	Categories	Amount in Rs.
Other sources	530	Hand pump maintenance	18,948
Cable TV tax	150	Bank commission	394
Blueprint approval	319	Funeral grant	8,000
Auction of wastage	614	Drinking water material	10,000
Rent from shops	24,516	Maintenance of burial ground	1,450
Other taxes	6,640	Maintenance of TV	8,042
Auction of trees	3,739	Maintenance of roads	3,948
Entertainment tax	2,286	Electricity material	7,085
Other sources	185	Sitting fees	700
Auction of trees	3,739	Sanitation	2,746
Initial amount	1,19,546	Stationery items	766
Total	**4,29,276**	Festival advance	8,500
		IAY	1,50,00
		Other maintenance	11,004
		Maintenance of pipeline	4,863
		Drainage construction	24,346
		Rent for vehicle	1,760
		Administrative expenses	2,440
		Festival advance	4,950
		Balance amount	13,607
		Total	**4,29,276**

Source: Computed from Panchayat records.

Table 9.13 : Pachamalayankottai Panchayat 2001-2002 (Scheme Fund)

Income Sources		Expenditure	
Categories	Amount in Rs.	Categories	Amount in Rs.
JGSY	3,72,700	Drinking water work	3,16,723
IAY	4,27,500	Bank commission	1,496
Initial amount	4,409	JGSY	70
Total	**8,06,205**	Maintenance charges	40

(*Contd.*)

Table 9.13 (*Contd.*)

Income Sources		Expenditure	
Categories	Amount in Rs.	Categories	Amount in Rs.
		20 group houses	3,14,694
		Bank commission	240
		Cement expenses	79,200
		Balance amount	93,742
		Total	**8,06,205**

Source: Computed from Panchayat records.

Table 9.14 : Sivagnanapuram Panchayat 2001-2002

Income Sources		Expenditure	
Categories	Amount in Rs.	Categories	Amount in Rs.
House tax	10,056	Salary for staff	39,560
Library tax	1,013	TA for President	5,400
Professional tax	4,200	Office equipment	11,257
Other taxes	920	Electricity charges	44,513
Licence fees	400	Hand pump maintenance	3,653
Stamp duty	99,623	Street light maintenance	27,900
Local cess	13,690	TV maintenance	31,465
2-C patta	238	Sanitation	11,810
SFC grant	1,45,866	Festival expenses	1,500
House tax matching grant	4,550	Road work	7,500
Funeral grant	4,500	Library tax paid	1,679
Other sources	73,500	Advance amount to staff	2,400
Initial amount	1,274	Other expenses	5,197
Total	**3,59,830**	Cement road	13,197
		Pipeline work	50,000
		Funeral expense	2,000
		Bank interest	2,252
		Extension of pipeline	91,500
		Total	**3,52,763**

Source: Computed from Panchayat records.

Table 9.15 : Silukkuvarpatti Panchayat 2001-2002

Income Sources		Expenditure	
Categories	Amount in Rs.	Categories	Amount in Rs.
House tax	84,614	Salary for Staff	33,630
Library tax	8,463	TA for President	5,030
Professional tax	21,540	Sitting fees	1,950
License fees	6,983	Office equipment	6,620
Plan approval	1,940	Electricity charges	22,041
Building rent	250	Hand pump maintenance	16,693
Marketing sources	13,243	OHT maintenance	40,708
Auction of trees	1,249	Street light maintenance	16,693
Stamp duty	7,655	TV maintenance	945
Entertainment tax	646	Advance amount	12,200
Local cess	5,831	Other expenses	4,242
SFC grant	1,87,039	Auction from trees	832
Other grants	22,930	Pipeline extension	84,000
Funeral grant	4,000	Recovery from survey Dept.	8,318
Bank interest	365	Insurance	10,800
Total	**3,66,748**	Recovery from Union	35,000
		Funeral grant	7,500
		Other sources	140
		Total	**3,20,308**
Scheme Fund			
JGSY	2,99,715	Borewell work	64,157
Bank interest	1,083	Road formation	1,99,801
Total	**3,00,798**	Bank commission	408
		Total	**2,64,366**

Source: Computed from Panchayat Records.

Table 9.16 : Kullichettipatti Panchayat 2001-2002

Income Sources		Expenditure	
Categories	Amount in Rs.	Categories	Amount in Rs.
House tax	21,141	Salary for staff	22,800
Library tax	2,120	TA for President	10,160
Professional tax	9,360	Office equipments	9,823
Water deposit	2,600	Electricity charges	10,639
License fees	190	Well maintenance	800
SFC grant	1,12,888	OHT maintenance	1,700
Stamp duty	13,956	Street light maintenance	13,556

(Contd.)

Table 9.16 (*Contd.*)

Income Sources		Expenditure	
Categories	Amount in Rs.	Categories	Amount in Rs.
Local cess	4,778	Sanitation	16,238
House tax matching grant	4,684	Road maintenance	7,800
Funeral grant	3,000	Pre-amount paid	2,100
Building plan approval	380	Pipe line maintenance	2,260
Auction of wastage	100	Hand pump maintenance	600
Other sources	54	Funeral grant	2,500
Initial amount	33,747	Newspapers	2,000
Total	**2,08,998**	Photocopying	2,490
		Bank commission	830
		Gram Sabha meeting expense	850
		Drinking water charges	32,030
		Others	250
		Recovery by Union	28,000 (*Contd.*)
		Hand pump material	3,293
		Recovery for survey	536
		Playground maintenance	12,370
		TV maintenance	695
		Graveyard road maintenance	1,175
		Balance amount	29,503
		Total	**2,08,998**
Scheme Fund			
JGSY for cement work	266	Cement road	35,710
JGSY for cement work	68,400	Drainage water	3,441
Initial amount	33,342	Bank commission	402
Total	**1,02,008**	Balance amount	62,455
		Total	**1,02,008**

Source: Computed from Panchayat Records.

Table 9.17 : Pallapatti Panchayat 2001-2002

Income Sources		Expenditure	
Categories	Amount in Rs.	Categories	Amount in Rs.
House tax	40,914	Salary for staff	1,04,975
Library tax	3,429	TA	13,060
Professional tax	22,262	Electricity charges	1,39,642
Licence fees	1,750	Hand pump maintenance	14,000
Building licence	2,945	Pipeline/OHT maintenance	1,33,215
Other sources	950	Street light maintenance	28,966
Auction of trees	5,245	TV maintenance	2,660
Other sources	750	Sanitation	20,778
Stamp duty	50,456	Bank commission	726
Entertainment tax	2,582	Gram Sabha expenses	1,000
Local cess	14,790	Funeral grant	19,000
House tax matching grant	12,641	Drainage work	18,370
SFC grant	2,57,896	Road work	5,100
Initial amount	94,139	Auction of trees	375
Total	**5,10,760**	Street maintenance	2,000
		Festival advance	8,000
		Others	4,746
		Balance amount	2,14,650
		Total	**5,10,760**
Scheme Fund			
JGSY	3,41,900	Bank commission	1,623
Group houses	1,91,000	Cement expense	39,600
Hut houses	58,500	Group houses	1,39,262
Initial amount	52,231	Ground level tank	1,38,374
Total	**6,43,631**	Hand pump work	22,860
		New motor fixed	53,111
		Hut houses	90,000
		Balance	1,58,801
		Total	**6,43,631**

Source: Computed from Panchayat records.

Table 9.18 : S. Mettupatti Panchayat 2001-2002

Income Sources		Expenditure	
Categories	Amount in Rs.	Categories	Amount in Rs.
House tax	5,707	Salary for staff	16,630
Library tax	565	Traveling allowance	6,420
Professional tax	750	Sitting fees	3,150
Stamp duty	13,618	TA	2,555
Auction of trees	5,571	Office equipment	7,001
SFC grant	44,352	Newspapers	2,030
House tax matching grant	5,751	Insurance	2,700
Funeral grant	1,000	Maintenance of street lights	14,420
Other sources	1,723	Maintenance of drainage	950
Licence fees for shop	240	Sanitation	5,685
2-C patta	376	TV maintenance	2,420
Licence fees for rice-mill	100	Uniform dress	539
Initial amount	1,607	Stationery	475
Total	**81,360**	Library tax	946
		Other expenditure	11,435
		Total	**77,910**
		Balance amount	3,450
		Total	**81,360**
Scheme fund			
JGSY	27,500	Cement thalam	26,844
IAY	2,47,500	Group houses construction	2,37,508
Balance amount	2,244	CRSP	2,000
Total	**2,77,244**	Balance amount	9,777
		Total	**2,77,244**

Source: Computed from Panchayat records.

Block Profile

S.No.	Details	Denominations
1.	District	Dindigul
2.	Block	Nilakottai
3.	Total population (1991 census)	1,01,851
	Male	51,500
	Female	50,351
	SC category	31,203
	SC – Male	15,847
	SC – Female	15,356
4.	Total Village Panchayats	23
	Town Panchayats	2
	Total hamlets	161
5.	(i) Union Councillors	
	Male	12
	Female	8
	Total	20
	(ii) District Councillors	2
	(iii) Total Ward Members	210
	SC – Men	34
	SC – Women	20
	General – Men	106
	General – Women	50
	Total	210
6.	Primary Health Centres	6
	Health sub-centres	6
	Veterinary Health Centres	2
7.	Total street lights	2143
8.	Total Hand pumps	427
9.	Total power pumps	143
10.	Total television sets	230
11.	Educational Institutions	
	(i) Primary Schools	84
	(ii) Middle Schools	18
	(iii) High Schools	7
	(iv) Higher Secondary Schools	4
	(v) Women's College	1
	(vi)Total	114

Source : Computed from the Records of Nilakkottai Panchayat Union.

Dalit Related Activities Carried out by Panchayats

I. *Pachamalayankottai Panchayat*

1. Drainage systems were completed from village Panchayat fund at a cost of Rs.25,000
2. From 11th Finance Commission funds the following items were carried out:
   (a) Pipeline work - Rs. 50,000
   (b) Pipeline work - Rs. 24,000
   (c) Extension work - Rs. 25,000
   (d) Colony work - Rs. 25,000
   (e) Maintenance work - Rs. 34,000
3. From SGRY funds the following items of work were carried out:
   (a) Drainage system - Rs. 35,000
   (b) Metal road work - Rs. 41,000
   (c) Graveyard work - Rs. 50,000
4. From DPAP funds the following items of work were carried out:
   (a) Extension of pipeline - Rs. 2,00,000
   (b) Hand pump work - Rs. 45,000
5. From Panchayat Union fund, the following items of work were carried out:
   (a) New borewell work - Rs. 1,50,000
   (b) Toilets for schools - Rs. 2,00,000
   (c) Metal road work - Rs. 50,000

II. *Pallapatti Panchayat*

The following items of work were executed for the *Dalit* people.

1. Group houses were constructed for 16 persons at a cost of Rs. 32,000 under IAY.
2. From the 11th Finance Commission scheme, a submersible motor was installed at a cost of Rs. 50,000.

3. From SGRY funds cement thalam work was completed in different places.
4. *Katcha* houses were sanctioned to 10 persons.

III. *Sivagnanapuram Panchayat*

Cement roads have been completed in 3 hamlets at a cost Rs.1,36,000. Under the 11th Finance Commission scheme, maintenance of street was completed. From SGRY funds cement roads have been completed for SC/BC people at a cost of Rs. 2,05,100.

IV. *Silukkuvarpatti Panchayat*

Particulars	*Amount in Rs.*
Seeragampatti road	1,96,000
Mannavarathi group houses construction for 5 persons	1,60,000
Mannavarathi cement road	73,000
Road at Kariampatti	50,000
Metal road at Kariampatti	25,000
Group houses at Kariampatti	1,60,000
Threshing floor in Silukkuvarpatti	60,000
Sanitary latrines in Ellaichamipuram	2,00,000
Borewell works in Kariampatti	4,30,000
Group houses in Kuppalapalanipatti(3)	96,000
Pipeline in Kuppapalanipatti	1,25,000
Group houses in Sillukkuvarpatti (3)	96,000

These items of work were executed for the SC people.

V. *Kodanginaickenpatti Panchayat*

1. Group houses in Kokkupatty under IAY. (5 nos.)
2. Cement road work is going on in Kokkupatty.
3. Group houses have been extended to 10 persons
4. For 10 *katcha* houses, work is going on.
5. Bridges and small culverts were constructed.
6. Cement road work was completed in Kodanginaickenpatti.

The cost-wise details of the above work were not given by the clerk as it were not available in the Panchayat office.

VI. *Kullichettipatti Panchayat*

1. From Panchayat funds, new pipeline works was completed.
2. From JGSY fund, cement road was completed.
3. Group houses have been constructed under IAY (20 nos.)
4. From SGRY funds, cement road was completed.

The cost-wise details of the above work were not given by the clerk as they were not available in the Panchayat office.

VII. *Mettupatti Panchayat*

1. From Union Councillor's fund, cement road work was completed.
2. From MLA fund, a Drama theatre was completed.
3. From Union fund and MLA fund, 2 borewells have been sunk.

The cost-wise details of the above work were not given by the clerk as they were not available in the Panchayat office.

SECTION II

Respondent's Feedback

(i) Dalit Men

With regard to reservation for *Dalits*, the Pachamalayankottai President an SC male, pointed out that, before 1996, the Thevar community influenced all the decisions and there was no sympathy for the *Dalit* community. After 1996, *Dalit* people were selected for Panchayat positions due to reservation. Further reservation for *Dalits* is very useful to the *Dalit* community, because various basic facilities have been provided to the *Dalit* community, since 1996 by making use of this opportunity. In order to get the cooperation of the other communities the traditional leaders are given due respect by the President. Gandhigram Rural Institute's training has developed leadership qualities among the leaders of the *Dalit* community in various ways to cope with the situations arising in a multicaste society.

The people of the BC do not cooperate in the Panchayat development activities. For instance, even in conducting Gram Sabha meetings. This could be seen in many Gram Panchayats wherever *Dalits* are Presidents. Besides, there is no cordial relationship among the Pallar, Parayar and Sakkiliyar caste groups. There are three castes, though all of them are SC, do not inter-marry. Cleavages are very deep among the sub-groups of *Dalits*. This is being effectively exploited by the non-*Dalits*.

Because of the reservation of seats for *Dalit*, the *Dalits* are provided with an opportunity to make use of all the schemes meant for the upliftment of the *Dalits*. It requires enormous skill and capacity to manage the non-*Dalits* and the officials.

(ii) Dalit Women

The water problems of the *Dalit* people have been solved due to reservation for *Dalits*. Since *Dalits* have occupied positions in the Panchayat, members of the community now involve themselves in Panchayat activities. Drinking water is a major problem for them and it is solved by the *Dalit* leaders.

Real poor people from *Dalit* families could be included in the BPL list. *Dalits* have to be oriented on development. In fifty-five years of democratic governance the basic facilities are provided to *Dalits* only now. In any village one can notice that 90 per cent of the *Dalits* are leading a life of sub-human conditions. The *Dalits* have been made to believe for generations that it is their lifestyle and that these are the conditions in which *Dalits* should live. They are not aware of decent human living conditions. Efforts have to be made to sensitise the *Dalits* to development.

(iii) Non-Dalit Women

Generally people do not like to keep *Dalits* in high positions in the rural local bodies. The case of Keeripatti and Nattarpatti

Village Panchayats in Madurai district where in the *Dalits* were not permitted to contest was referred to. Even if they are elected, they are not allowed to continue in office. They are forced to step down from office. This is the practice prevalent in these Gram Panchayats. To prevent such practices, the Government should take strong action against those who are responsible for this kind of activities.

Wherever people are aware of the importance of Panchayats they participate in the development activities without any caste bias. It is also proved that wherever *Dalits* are Presidents, people of the *Dalit* community get water supply without much difficulty.

Even though adequate grants and credit facilities are available for the development of *Dalits*, they are not being used as the other communities oppose such a move. Moreover even the *Dalits* are not aware of the method by which they can get these facilities.

Wherever educated *Dalits* are occupying positions, they work well in the Panchayats for the *Dalits*. Till *Dalits* entered the Panchayat system nobody bothered about the road connectivity to SC hamlets. Now this problem has been solved. THATCO is a scheme meant for the development of the *Dalits*, but the *Dalits* are not aware of. But now after *Dalits* assumed responsibilities some of the programmes have been implemented and *Dalits* have got the benefits.

(iv) Non-Dalit Men

The *Dalit's* first demand in the Gram Sabha is free group houses for their community and, next to it, drinking water supply to their settlement their third demand is road connectivity. The fourth is graveyard for the *Dalits*. Wherever they are the majority, the *Dalits* participate in the Gram Sabha on their own. If they are a minority, they have to be coaxed to Gram Sabha meetings. Wherever *Dalits* are Presidents, people from the same community freely participate in the meeting and in other places they are only spectators. It is also true that the non-*Dalits* are bringing pressure on the Presidents of the Gram Panchayats that unless all the economically poor communities get facilities and assistance from the Government, the schemes meant for the *Dalits* should not be implemented.

(v) Panchayat Clerks

- Reservation is an opportunity for the *Dalits* to participate in social activities along with other communities.
- Non-*Dalit* Presidents easily mobilize non-*Dalit* communities for the Gram Sabha meetings. But *Dalit* Presidents are not able to do so. Non-*Dalit* communities do not take the *Dalit* leadership seriously. *Dalit* leaders find it very difficult to mobilize even their own community to attend the Gram Sabha meetings.
- Non-*Dalits* organize festivals and celebrations successfully. The members of non-*Dalit* communities take part and contribute whereas among *Dalits*, that much of unity cannot be expected. Employed individuals among the *Dalit* do not come forward to enable the community to get their entitlements. Due to this, the development of *Dalits* is delayed.

The economic conditions of the *Dalit* leaders prevent them from acting individually and they have necessarily to rely on others. If a *Dalit* is made clerk in a Panchayat headed by a *Dalit* leader, problems are few. Wherever non-*Dalits* are made clerks in Panchayats headed by *Dalit* leaders, the problems are many. The clerks dominate over the Panchayat leaders. Yet another problem they have been facing in the Panchayat in the non-*Dalit* Vice-President developing a non-cooperative attitude towards the *Dalit* President of the Gram Panchayat.

(vi) Panchayat Ward Members

The reservation of seats for non-*Dalits* and *Dalit* should be determined based on their percentage in the population. Poverty alleviation and income generation activities should be extended in the non-*Dalit* poor also. Ward Members group themselves on community basis. There is no common sharing among them. *Dalit* Presidents do not give much importance to non-*Dalit* members if their community enjoys majority. Presidents are the main actors in the Panchayat and they only enjoy the fruits of the position. Hence the members do not take the Panchayat affairs seriously. Non-*Dalit* Presidents do not immediately attend to the basic needs demanded by the *Dalit* members. Ward Members who are in political parties can influence the Presidents. But a political members' voice is not heard by the Presidents. Higher level representative like Union Councillor, District Panchayat Councillor, MLA and MP must maintain official relationship with the Panchayat. All categories of Ward Members demand more facilities in their wards. The *Dalit* Ward Members in addition to basic facilities, demand loan facilities for the *Dalit* poor. As the majority of the encroachers are non-*Dalits* the *Dalits* are interested in evicting them.

The Ward Members do not know the details and position of common property resources as they are not told anything about it. If Ward Members are encouraged to involve themselves in Panchayat activities and opportunities are provided to them to contribute to the success of the Panchayat, they will come forward to serve better than now. NGOs are not really targeting the poor in all communities. Creamy layers of both *Dalit* and non-*Dalit* communities get more benefits from the NGOs than the really poor. Illiterate Ward Members are not properly informed of the Panchayat's financial transactions. The general statement is not clear in this regard. Detailed information is necessary during the Gram Sabha and Panchayat Council Meetings. The Gram Sabha have not yet to become a common people's forum. Ordinary people are not evincing interest. Rich and well settled families do not participate in the Gram Sabha meetings. The elite do not attend the Gram Sabha meeting. They could share their ideas and experiences if they attend. As they are self-supported they do not depend on the Panchayat. The priority of work is not adhered to. Instead of need based activity, less important items of work are being carried out in the rural areas. The Ward Members are left in the dark. Training to Ward Members would improve the relationship and the Members could function effectively.

(vii) Self-Help Group Members

Reservation is a boon to *Dalits* and women as it creates importance to these marginalized sections. The *Dalit* community leaders encourage SHGs to participate in Gram Sabha meetings. It is good to learn that new things for the improvement of their life are taking shape. A special concientization programme is needed for *Dalit* SHG members. Maintaining unity and morale among the group members is a very tough task. Some NGOs are seriously working with the people but some others are not performing well. With much expectation the SHG members attend the Gram Sabha meeting, but their demands are not met by the Panchayats. The plan components should include employment generation activities for poor families particularly for women and more specifically *Dalit* women. The Panchayats could develop gardens of medicinal plants where women could get employment. The rural youth are wasting their energy. Sometimes they involve in eve-teasing. They need proper guidance. The Panchayat should work for their development. The Panchayat should help and assist the SHGs to establish proper rapport with various sectoral departments of the State Government. Educated Presidents are performing better than illiterate and semi-illiterate Presidents.

There is no sharing among the SHGs of the same village in general. In some villages if NGOs are serious, there is interface between *Dalit* SHGs and non-*Dalit* SHGs. Women Presidents give comparatively more attention to SHG members than men Presidents. One *Dalit* woman president herself formed a trust to serve independently to the *Dalit* community. A few non-*Dalit* families residing near this *Dalit* community were also targeted by her.

(viii) Village Traditional Panchayat Leaders

Reservation brings welfare to the *Dalit* community. Representation in Panchayati Raj Institutions has come to the Village Panchayat for their development. Before 1996, no significant work in the sector of water supply, street lights, street improvement, road facilities was carried out in the hamlets of the *Dalit* community. Interface with officials has now improved as the *Dalits* try to directly contact officials in connection with Panchayat affairs. Through the mass media, the public come to know much about Panchayats and demand Presidents to provide more facilities.

Employed *Dalits* provide assistance to the *Dalit* poor to avail of government programmes and schemes. Inter-caste marriage among the sub-castes of *Dalits* is in general discouraged, whereas such marriages between between non-*Dalits* and *Dalit* is encouraged. With its limited resources the Panchayat cannot function effectively. Resources to Panchayats have to be enhanced. Transparency is yet to be developed in Panchayat affairs of Ward Members consult the village elders, they might come to their assistance and participate in the Panchayat activities. The counsel of elderly persons is not properly harnessed by the Panchayat. Literacy is the key factor to *Dalits* by which they empower themselves. NGOs concentrate more on *Dalits*, since they get money from funding agencies for that. There are poor people among non-*Dalits* also. Their problems are not yet solved. Non-*Dalits* expect respectful treatment from the *Dalits*.

Of late both *Dalits* and non-*Dalits* are discriminating against each other in teashops, bus stands, and political activities. *Dalits* and non-*Dalits* are forced into close proximity. In general non-*Dalits* are not happy with this development. Non-*Dalits* need not feel envious of the development of *Dalits*. *Dalits* demand that their entitlements should be properly implemented, say *Dalit* traditional leaders. *Dalit* based organizations like SHGs and youth groups are coming forward to work for the public cause but they need guidance. The Government must plan new loan schemes with more subsidy for the economic development of the *Dalits*. Public telephone facility colony areas is essential.

Improvement of roads and bridges is necessary for *Dalit* habitations. Otherwise during the rainy season their condition becomes very difficult. Community halls for *Dalits* will help immensely.

(ix) Union Chairpersons (Non-Dalit)

The *Dalits* are now getting orientation in holding responsible positions due to the reservation. The *Dalits* may establish close contact with *Dalit* leaders and avail of more benefits from

Panchayati Raj Institutions. Some *Dalit* candidates are also spending a lot of money during the election. Poor *Dalits* who are addicts to liquor used to keep close to non-*Dalits* during any dispute as a private army. More number of rival groups are active against *Dalit* Presidents than in the case of non-*Dalit* Presidents. The *Dalits* do not function independently and they are in the hands of non-*Dalits*. The poorest among poor are not getting any benefits properly. Officials refer to rules, regulations and procedures. Field realities are not taken into consideration by the officials. *Dalit* leaders do not have any vision regarding community development activities. Community institutions of *Dalits* are not strong enough to assist the *Dalits* whereas the Backward Castes community institutions are functioning effectively. Transport facilities are still not adequately provided to *Dalit* hamlets. Agriculture can not provide adequate employment opportunity and hence non-*Dalits* have migrated to other districts and states but the *Dalit* youth are living in poverty in the villages.

(x) Officials

Reservation gives leadership qualities to *Dalits* and they get orientation in moving with higher officials and in office procedures. The Panchayat Presidents do not maintain transparency. They involve in corrupt practices. The *Dalit* leaders are always in the hands of others. Water supply scheme activities are carried out in those Panchayats whose Presidents come frequently and pressurise the officials. Group rivalry very often ends in submitting written complaints against the Presidents on petty issues like replacement of streetlights. Selection of beneficiaries for group houses is not an easy task. Many factors influence to the selection process. Block officials find it very difficult. Political interference is at a high rate. Selecting individuals who live below the poverty line is not so easy in the rural areas as there is always political interference. Village Presidents have joined together and formed an association. The office bearers cut across castes and function unitedly. They establish direct contact with district officials bypassing block officials. In this process the *Dalit* Presidents are also benefited. This is a unique phenomenon in this Union. Women Presidents function independently. They get encouragement from the women Presidents who won a second time. Out of 8 women Presidents two, that too *Dalit* women, have won a second time and they have constructively oriented the other women Presidents. The *Dalit* women Presidents are gender-sensitized and function together. Delay in fund allocation to Panchayats disturb the process of strengthening the Panchayat. Functional knowledge has to be imparted to the public in the aspects of Panchayati Raj Institutions. The Gram Panchayat as a unit of administration has to be strengthened further. The President, Vice-President, Ward Members and staff do not perceive about Panchayati Raj properly and find fault with one another and disturb the Panchayat administration. The role and the functions of the NGOs are not known to the Block officials. The NGOs work in villages through the PO (Women's Development). Interface between NGOs and Block officials is necessary.

(xi) NGOs on Dalit Leadership

In general the *Dalit* community accepts the dominant caste's leadership. Many welfare activities are carried out through Panchayats for the *Dalits*. Roads, streetlights and drinking water facilities are provided to *Dalit* hamlets also. There is a tug of war between *Dalit* President and non-*Dalit* Members. Non-*Dalit* leaders spend money to denigrate the *Dalit* leadership and to create groupism against the *Dalit* Presidents. Communal clash do not occur where the *Dalit* community is in the majority. *Dalit* leaders and Ward Members need training and support for their effective representation in Panchayati Raj Institutions. NGOs in general should not openly involve themselves in Panchayat election activities as many other ulterior motives count during Panchayat elections.

(xii) Expectations of the Dalit Presidents

More allocation of resources to Panchayats and more allocation for the welfare of the *Dalits* should be provided. Training/

capacity building are imperative needs for the Panchayat leaders to improve their performance. Special attention must be paid to improving sanitation facilities to all communities, particularly the *Dalit*s. There should not be any delay in fund allocation to attend to the basic needs of the people.

The leaders need to have access to other Government offices. Officials should avoid getting commission from the *Dalit* leaders. Complaints given by the *Dalit* Presidents should be given due attention by the Police and Revenue officials as the issue of social harmony is involved in their dealings. Special projects should be formulated for generating employment opportunities for *Dalit* community members. More loan facilities could be created for self-employment opportunities.

(xiii) Enabling Factors for Dalit Leadership

Dalit leaders need continuous flow of information and support structure to face the problems in the villages. Government Departments have to respond quickly to the representations from the *Dalit* leaders. Periodical training is needed for them to improve their skills. NGO linkages are essential for their functioning effectively in the Panchayats.

SECTION III

A. Noothulapuram Panchayat President – Case Study

Ms. M. Kala, the Noothulapuram Panchayat President, is a daughter of an inter-caste married couple. Though she was educated up to the 10th standard, she worked as a coolie. With the help of an NGO, namely ASSEFA, she received training in health education and served in villages in and around Nilakottai. She also served as a promoting agent for the small savings scheme. Her husband runs a travel agency after getting a bank loan. When the Panchayat elections were declared in the year 1996, Noothulapuram Village Panchayat President's position was reserved for *Dalit* women. The villagers of Noothulapuram encouraged Kala to contest and her husband also did so. Hence she contested and won in the election. She is associated with the Tamil Manila Congress (now it has merged with the Tamil Nadu Congress Party).

Kala's candidature under *Dalit* reservation was challenged in court. But the case was dismissed and her candidature under *Dalit* reservation was upheld because even though her father belongs to a non-*Dalit* community her mother is a *Dalit*.

In Noothulapuram Village, there are 11 hamlets and the total population is 5000. The *Dalit* community is more in number than the caste Hindu communities.

Communal Dispute and Intervention of the President

Goddess Chelliamman shrine is the village temple and both *Dalits* and Thevars jointly celebrate the 3-day festival. The Thevar community enjoys the right to the sanctum sanctorum. This is the traditional practice. During the recent festival the *Dalit* youth got into the sanctum sanctorum. It became a communal dispute. Government officials intervened and it was settled peacefully through negotiation. The *Dalits* and the Thevars were to celebrate the festival separately. The first day was reserved meant for the Thevar and the second day for the *Dalit* community.

Recently, in the year 2001, when the celebration was declared, anticipating communal clash police officials did not permit the celebration. Kala met the police officials and explained the practice earlier adhered to. The representatives of the non-*Dalits* who were present during this meeting appreciated Kala's the leadership as she took a neutral position and explained the truth. She assured the police that no dispute would arise during the celebration. The Police as well as the leaders of non-*Dalits* accepted this assurance and permission was granted for the celebration and it was completed without any dispute.

The youth of the *Dalits* felt very much upset about the unfolding of the truth in the Police station by Kala as she referred to the earlier practice of privilege to the Thevar community. But President Kala convinced the youth that during the celebration this practice could be removed in the presence of the police and the *Dalit*s can also enjoy the privilege of going into the shrine. Since any further difference created would disturb the communal harmony most of the youth agreed to Kala's advice but a few radical youngsters did not agree. Yet Kala conducted the celebration successfully.

When Kala contested for a second term, she felt that the *Dalit* youth particularly men, entertaining enmity for caste Hindus, would work against her. But the village women has got socialized through SHGs. Women of *Dalit* and non-*Dalit* communities joined together through SHG activities and eliminated the differences between these two communities. The power pump of the drinking water system is being operated by women of both communities through an SHG. There is no dispute between these groups on any aspects. Wherever necessary, the women of both communities work jointly for the common cause. Being a woman hailing from the *Dalit* community occupying the post of Gram Panchayat President, Kala encourages understanding among the womenfolk in Noothulapuram.

Kala contested in the election again as the Government of Tamil Nadu ordered that the reservation of seats for women continue for a second tenure also. Though huge amounts of money were spent by the other candidates in the election, Kala projected the activities carried out by her, cutting across castes and won the election by a margin of 380 votes. Kala said that she served fairly, treating all communities alike, and so she won in the election.

Panchayat Activities

The scheme fund earmarked for the welfare of *Dalits* is more than the fund earmarked for non-*Dalits* and so a large number of terms of work have been carried out in the hamlets of *Dalits*. During the Gram Sabha meeting she explained the fact that since more *Dalits* live in the Panchayat, the Panchayat gets more for the *Dalit* community. To provide necessary basic facilities for the habitations of non-*Dalits*, Kala mobilized funds from other sources like the MLA fund, the District Councillor's fund, the MP fund and the Union fund. In this way she is able to retain the support of all the communities.

People's Expectations

Irrespective of caste, lower middle class and poor families demand loan facilities for economic activities, patta for house sites, group houses and improvement of facilities in their streets. In the Gram Sabha there is good participation by the non-*Dalit* community. Available funds position and priorities of work are properly deliberated upon the Gram Sabha meeting. It is only through the Gram Sabha she has proved herself a genuine and sincere President.

Disunity among Dalit

Kala feels that the people of the *Dalit* communities do not function as a unified force. The families of the *Dalit* are divided in the name of clan and traditional positions followed by their forefathers. Recently the *Dalit* community representatives brought about a change in these systems and selected responsible individuals from other non-traditional *Dalit* families who did not hold any traditional positions. In reaction against this unexpected decision a few people encouraged an individual who had encroached upon Panchayat land and prevented the formation of a road through that site.

Relationship with Officials

Kala says that officials in general encourage the women Presidents when they shed their inhibitions. She herself never feels inferior to men and her husband used to visit the block office to question any unwarranted reactions of the officials in respect of her Panchayat activities.

Reservation of Seats for Dalits

According to Kala, reservation of seats for *Dalit*s and women is the right approach to empower them. Through the position of elected representatives, individuals belonging to the so called marginalized sectors have got exposure and established contacts with officials by which they have enhance their leadership qualities.

Only those women Presidents who are able to get the support of their own families and womenfolk in general could sustain their leadership. The socio-economic conditions of *Dalit*s could be improved only if they are oriented in many activities other than farm sector activities, as the scope for employment in agriculture is shrinking now-a-days. Economic background, group support, caste association support, encouragement given by family, educational background and patronage from the general public are the enabling factors determining the upward mobility of *Dalit* leadership emerging through reservation. The NGOs are not fully involved in the election campaign even though they support their own SHG members. Political parties in general do not work seriously in Village Panchayat elections whereas in the case of the other two positions, namely Union Councillor and District Ward Member the candidates depend mostly on the political parties. When the Presidents of Village Panchayats gain popularity political parties try to draw them into their party and encourage them to contest for higher positions. Through the Panchayats, *Dalits* have come to understand the system of governance and avail of their entitlements and now psychologically they feel better. The community will be benefited by interlinking Panchayat with the sectoral department particularly the *Dalit* community for whom plenty of schemes and programmes are available.

B. A Case Study of an Officer

Mr. Manickam, aged 30, is a graduate working as Rural Welfare Officer (RWO) in Nilakkottai Panchayat Union. He entered service as Junior Assistant and is now serving as RWO. After this service he could get promotion as Assistant. He belongs to the SC community.

His Observation

Village Panchayat Presidents in general do not have any perception of the office procedures and the administrative system. They regard the Union office as an office for transacting scheme funds or as an office for obtaining administrative sanction. They depute the Panchayat clerk for other transactions with the Panchayat Union. As there is no authority vested with her union officials to control the Panchayat Presidents, the Union Office cannot spare time to educate them in administrative procedures. The training given to the Presidents is not effective, as no attitudinal and behavioural change has been observed among the trained leaders. For any procedural lapse, the staff are held responsible but the Presidents do not get any punishment. Of course, for any misdeed found in Panchayat management the Presidents are booked.

Education and experience in public life count in the performance of the Presidents. Those who wish to gain upward leadership to visit the Union office and learn a lot through interaction and with the guidance of the officials. In general most of the Presidents do not know the functioning of other departments where programmes to develop Panchayats are available. Presidents need a lot of seriousness, innovation and creativity in their leadership as the village community has several issues. Still the traditional institutions play a vital role in Panchayat elections. Equality between *Dalits* and non-*Dalit* is slowly emerging. Caste feelings are not openly expressed. However, it is still in the hearts of caste Hindus, deeply rooted change of mindset is the only wayout.

The Government should encourage a change of mindset among the caste Hindus. Exclusive subsidies and assistance to *Dalits* is necessary but they are being questioned by the non-*Dalits*. Those who function constructively as Presidents can emerge as good leaders. Presidents do not demand big schemes. They were insist on fulfilling the basic needs. The family plays a vital role in shaping the *Dalit* leaders. *Dalit* leaders in the Panchayats do not understand the power and authority vested in them. Reservation for women (in general) is a need as they have also been under subjugation for long. People have not yet got the needed awareness of social transformation. The climate in Tamil Nadu is generally threatening as the caste Hindus openly mobilize their communities caste-wise. To bring about harmony between the two groups the Government must come forward with special assistance to the marginalized group. Democracy is being strengthened through the Panchayat. By contesting in the general category, the non-*Dalit* communities could have the opportunity to understand the *Dalit* community and leadership.

General Observation

- During the tenure of *Dalit* leadership social harmony has improved.
- There is no proper rapport between NGOs and the Panchayats at present.
- The NGOs socio-economic activities should help the ultra poor but they are not yet doing that work.
- The Police try to run away from the disputes between the *Dalit* and the non-*Dalit* communities. They encourage them to settle the issue between themselves.
- Villagers compare the other nearby Panchayats' development work and demand the same in their Panchayats also.
- During the Gram Sabha meetings, the attendance of people from the *Dalit* community is poor in general. Only SHG women attend and the other women do not attend.
- Both *Dalit* and non-*Dalit* Presidents felt that transparency is not an easy task. People cannot understand when they explain their transactions.
- The clerks who are functioning under *Dalit* Presidents believe that the Presidents spend heavily for winning the election and then some of them expect the clerk to help them in getting back the money.
- The clerks feel harassed when both the Block officials and the Presidents demand their services at the same time.
- Some clerks reported that a few Presidents, particularly non-*Dalit* Presidents, look after their clerks well by giving extra money to them.
- People expect more doles and schemes from the Government.
- The less educated Presidents do not have faith in their clerks and they always suspect them.

Major Findings

- Reservation is very much useful for bringing about socio-economic transformation of the *Dalit* community through the Panchayat.
- Earlier, the schemes and programmes of the Government were not known to the *Dalits*. Now reservation has been provided for according to the percentage of the Scheduled Caste population in the total population. Through this arrangement now more number of *Dalits* become Ward Members. In a few places even in the general category *Dalits* have contested and won the election. The reservation of seats in Panchayati Raj Institutions has created a new confidence in the minds of the *Dalits*.
- As Ward Members and Presidents are elected from *Dalits* developmental activities for *Dalit* are properly executed. Their entitlements are realized.
- Provision of basic facilities like drinking water, street light, street improvement, improvement to burial ground and its approach road have been carried out for *Dalit* habitations.
- Implementation of group house scheme has been properly done under the leadership of *Dalit* Presidents. Right beneficiaries have been selected for the Government schemes.
- *Dalit* Presidents used to visit various development departments and collect the details of schemes pertaining to *Dalits* available with these departments and try their best to make use of the same.
- Non-*Dalit* Presidents are not serious about in these activities as they are preoccupied with other activities. Moreover they are not sensitive to the issues of social justice. Very few non-*Dalit* leaders are sensitive to the issues of *Dalits*.
- During the *Dalit* leadership, the youth, volunteers, traditional leaders and women belonging to the *Dalit* community freely visit the Panchayat office and have

interaction with the President and make effective use of the institution.

- *Dalit* Presidents, with the support of the *Dalit* community, enhance their leadership. In the case of *Dalit* women Presidents, *Dalit* women get easy access to the Panchayat. The SHGs of *Dalit* women move freely with the *Dalit* women Presidents. They utilize the services of the President for their development efforts.
- *Dalit* Presidents consider their leadership as an opportunity to do more welfare work to their community. They take this opportunity as a challenge also. They try their level best to do whatever work is possible for the poor *Dalit* families.
- *Dalit* Presidents get recognition in Police stations. They are able to influence the Police officials in handling the cases of *Dalit* community members. Earlier they had to depend on the caste Hindus or the political party leaders in this regard.
- *Dalit* Presidents have an opportunity to meet various officials of the Government and get to understand the functioning of the Government. They get good orientation in Government affairs.
- Non-*Dalit* Presidents feel that the *Dalit* community members demand group houses and cement road which are costly whereas the allocation of funds under in these heads is very limited.
- The *Dalit* community members demand employment opportunities during the Gram Sabha meetings. *Dalit* Presidents feel that the non-*Dalit* Presidents are not considering the demands of the *Dalits*. They simply inform that there is no provision in the Panchayat for employment opportunities.
- Non-*Dalit* Presidents claim that due attention has been to improving the facilities in the burial grounds belonging to *Dalits*.
- *Dalit* Presidents complain that the officials give respect and recognition to all non-*Dalit* presidents. At the same time, if *Dalit* Presidents are very bold and courageous, the officials deal softly with them. On many occasions

Dalit Presidents are not respected or treated on par with non-*Dalit* Presidents.

- Those *Dalit* Presidents who can communicate well who have a sound economic background receive recognition and respect from the officials. Others, who are less educated, economically poor and weak personalities, are not able to influence the officials.
- *Dalit* Presidents of remote Village Panchayats suffer a handicap in communication. Officials do not show any interest in meeting them. *Dalit* Presidents who have easy access to officials get more acquaintance with the officials and get more benefits through them.
- *Dalit* Presidents who won for the second time receive recognition and respect from the officials. They maintain their relationship with the officials and through them they establish good rapport with the new officials also.
- Both *Dalit* and non-*Dalit* Presidents felt that training is very much needed to *Dalit* men and women Presidents.
- Both *Dalit* and non-*Dalit* Presidents among the respondents stated that the training given by Gandhigram Rural Institute was very useful. The training gave them confidence and guidance to function effectively. Powers, responsibilities, functions and roles are realized through training according to them.
- The Presidents reported that, in general, Block officials do not spare their time to orient the Presidents. Some officials seen determined to let the Presidents make mistakes by which they could be booked so as to make them to act as per the wishes of the officials.
- *Dalit* men Presidents have easy access to officials than the *Dalit* women Presidents. The *Dalit* men Presidents understand the officials better and so they move easily with them.
- Some officials in general avoid eating with *Dalit* Presidents at public functions.
- Officials are of the opinion that clerks belonging to the *Dalit* community are not functioning efficiently.

- The inter and intra group rivalry among the *Dalit* community is considered a big hurdle to development according to both *Dalit* and non-*Dalit* Presidents.
- In general the officials feel that the *Dalit* Presidents have not yet established a grip over the Panchayat administration. The field officials do not spend adequate time to go through the records and registers maintained in the Panchayats. They just glance through a few transactions and immediately complain against the Panchayat to the higher officials.

Constraints

- Those who have been defeated harbour enmity even after the elections, which causes a lot of problems for the *Dalit* leaders and prevents them from concentrating on development activities.
- Former Presidents have developed groupism in the community and encouraged the malcontents disturb the Panchayat administration.
- Vice-Presidents of non-*Dalit* castes form their own groups and harass the *Dalit* Presidents.
- Clerks in general do not report regularly to the Presidents.
- The Vice-Presidents harbour the wrong notion that *Dalit* women Presidents do not have the needed capacity to administer development.
- Non-*Dalits* generally feel that by way of reserving seats for *Dalit* women, the existing social arrangement has been disturbed.

Analysis and Observation

It is unequivocal that the social structure has not changed fast enough despite the efforts of various social reform movements though faster changes are witnessed in other sectors. The on-going debate among the academics about the large scale exodus of members from the Dravidian Movement to form casteist organisations is whether the Dravidian Movement has failed to deliver the goods to the deprived masses. Forming caste based associations and organisations is an indicator of the failure of the Dravidian Movement. Secondly, the caste based associations which predominantly belonging to the poorer segments indicate that the policies pursued by the ethnic political parties who had been in power were not helpful to the poorest sections and, as a consequence, they moved out of the ethnic political parties and formed different organisations indicating the Dravidian political parties in the process. Primarily they could not find equity at the political level. At the social level, dominant caste groups are powerful and hence their control and sway over the society could not be eliminated even with the intervention of the State. The moment the Panchayat institutions became constitutional entities, they were captured in an organised manner. But the reservation of seats for the *Dalits* has been given in proportion to their population. Hence, 24 per cent of the seats have been allotted to the SC and ST communities in all positions. The newly enthroned *Dalit* representatives could not do anything in favour of the *Dalits* against the wishes of the dominant community. In a few places, dominant caste groups have not allowed people to contest in the elections despite the concerted attempts of the State Government. Even those who have contested and won the election, have to rely on the support of the caste panchayat leaders. *Dalit* women who have come to power have to adjust with the community Panchayat. They seek the help of the traditional leaders even to run the administration. When this is the situation, how could the *Dalit* leaders administer social justice? So many of the *Dalit* leaders, who have established contact with state level *Dalit* leaders, have taken a confrontationist posture and started waging a struggle against oppression. Thus, the Panchayati institutions are in a conflict ridden phase of their evolution.

The nature and the intensity of the problems of *Dalit*s vary from place to place. *Dalit* leaders who live in a place where *Dalits* are a minority have to succumb to the pressures of the traditional Panchayats and the activities are to be designed as per the direction of the traditional Panchayat leaders. Even in such areas, there are *Dalit* leaders who defy such directions and are determined to carry out the Panchayat activities without the influence of the traditional Panchayats and such Presidents and leaders are facing plenty of problems in their administration. Some of the Presidents of Panchayats have touched upon the encroachment of the Panchayat lands by influential individuals who are non-Brahmins caste Hindus. This problem calls for the support of the State Government. It is unfortunate that the State Government has not come to the rescue of the *Dalit* leaders such in Panchayats. *Dalit* leaders are leading a struggle for social justice. When they organise Gram Sabha meetings, they are either boycotted by the caste Hindus or the caste Hindus create chaos and confusion with the purpose of creating the impression that the *Dalits* do not have the capacity to manage the Panchayats. Moreover, pressure has been built around the *Dalit* leaders from all quarters, while officials, the Police, party leaders, and even their own caste leaders do not extend their support to them.

Dalit leaders are being exploited by the others as their skill, capacity and education is poor. Of course, a large number of *Dalit* leaders are waging a relentless fight to secure or carve out a niche for themselves legitimately. *Dalit* women leaders are being ill-treated by all sections of the society. Wherever the dominant caste groups are powerful, *Dalit* women leaders are brought under the control of the traditional Panchayat leaders. Their economic condition forces them to hand over responsibility to the caste Hindu leaders. Thus, the micro institutions under the leadership of *Dalit* leaders are virtually embattled.

Conclusion

Caste associations have been formed and activated vigorously for establishing the rights and rightful position of the respective castes in the socio-political system. The marginalised communities have started moving away from the Dravidian Movement and started asserting their position in polity and society. At the same time, the dominant caste groups also tread in the same path and hence one witnesses the struggle between the *Dalits* and the dominant caste in Panchayats. Of course, in certain places there is perfect understanding between the *Dalit* leaders and the dominant caste group leaders. But, in many of the places, conflict is being witnessed. Hence, the role of the Government in empowering *Dalits* is a major issue to be analysed seriously at this juncture. In the light of the large scale exodus from the Dravidian Movement for separate caste outfits, the existing theories and approaches on formation of caste identity and mobilisation have to be re-evaluated. Further, the currents and undercurrents of the influx and exodus of members from organisation to organisation have to be examined. The analysis made in this paper with the limited experience from the field and the available data indicates the emergence of new propositions in the social transformation process of Tamil society which needs further investigation and validation for evolving a meaningful theoretical framework.

NOTES

1. The conditions and state of affairs have been adequately explained in recently published articles and books. For more details see Atul Kohli, (1990), *Democracy and Discontent*, Cambridge: Cambridge University Press, pp. 3-32; Kothari, Rajni, 1988, *State Against Democracy*, Delhi : Ajanta Publications, James Manor, 1981, "Party Decay and Political Crisis in India," *The Washington Quarterly*, pp. 25-40.
2. Manor, James, (1999), *The Political Economy of Democratic Decentralisation*, Washington D.C.: The World Bank.
3. For details of statistics pertaining to the Indian Panchayati Raj System, refer to George Mathew (ed.), (2000), *Status of Panchayati Raj in the States and Union Territories of India 2000*, New Delhi: Concept Publishing Company.
4. The 73rd Constitutional Amendment Act makes as per the governing clause of the Amendment 243(G), mandatorily requires Panchayats to administer economic development and social justice through the planning exercise done at the bottom with the participation of the people. Government of India, *73rd Constitutional Amendment Act*, 1993, New Delhi : Government of India.
5. Banu, Zenab., "Modernity and Tradition: An Analysis of Traditional Panchayat *versus* Democratic Panchayat," in R.P. Joshi (ed.), (1998), *Constitutionalisation of Panchayati Raj : A Reassessment*, Jaipur: Rawat Publications, pp. 26-36.
6. Fuller, C.J., (1997), *Caste Today*, Delhi: Oxford University Press.
7. Hardgrave, R.L., (1965), *The Dravidian Movement*, Bombay: Popular Prakashan.
8. Legal Resources for Social Action (LRSA), a voluntary organisation working for the development of the *Dalits*, has initiated steps to federate

the small organisations of *Dalit* Panchayat leaders to represent their grievances in an organised way to the Government. A. Ganesan, the President, G. Sikamani, the Secretary and M.V. Sikamani, the Treasurer of the Federation of *Dalit* Panchayat Leaders held several sittings in different parts of the Tamil Nadu and prepared a document on the problems faced by the *Dalit* Panchayat Presidents. For more details refer to the documents prepared by them. Also see *Problems of Dalit Panchayat Leaders*, 2000, Chenglepet: LRSA.

9. M.K. Gandhi, (1947), *Harijan*, 21 December.
10. Jawaharlal Nehru quoted the speech of M.K. Gandhi in the Constituent Assembly, (1962), *Panchayati Raj as the Basis of Indian Polity: An Exploration into the Proceedings of the Constituent Assembly*, New Delhi: AVARD.
11. Dr. B.R. Ambedkar, in his speech in the Constituent Assembly, mentioned about the Panchayats. For more details see, AVARD, *op.cit.*, p. 25.
12. Rajiv Gandhi explained in a detailed why power should be decentralised in India, while presenting the 64th Constitutional Amendment Bill in Parliament. The bases of decentralisation of power has been explained in *A Charter for the Panchayats*, 1996, by Rajiv Gandhi Foundation, New Delhi: Task Force on Panchayati Raj.
13. C.J. Fuller, *op.cit.* pp.4-5.
14. Dummont, Louis, 1970, *Homo Hierarchius,* Chicago : Chicago University Press.
15. Marriot, M., Srinivas, M.N., Dube, S.C., Kathaleen Gough, E., Cohn, B.S., Beals, A.R., Steel, G.P., Stein, B., and Fuller, C.J., have contributed substantially to this field.
16. Kothari, Rajni, (ed.), 1970, *Caste in Indian Politics*, New Delhi: Orient Longman.
17. Beteille, Andre, "Caste and Political Group Formation in Tamil Nadu," in Sudipta Kariraj (ed.), 1977, *Politics in India*, New Delhi: Oxford University Press, pp.71-93.
18. For more details, refer to the documents prepared by Human Rights Research Foundation, Chennai, and Legal Resources for Social Action at Chenglepet. Detailed narratives are from in the Special Number on Local Bodies by Theekathir, 1999.

10

CONCLUSION

In Tamil Nadu, State politics and the State Government are not positive towards decentralisation of powers. It is a well known fact that the ethnic political parties, both the DMK and the AIADMK, openly opposed to the three-tier system of Panchayati Raj. To fulfil the Constitutional obligation the AIADMK Government enacted a conformity legislation conforming to the basic structure of the 73rd Amendment to the Constitution of India. It is unequivocally true that the spirit of the 73rd Amendment is missing in the Tamil Nadu Panchayati Act of 1994. The Tamil Nadu Panchayati Act of 1994 has given overriding powers to the bureaucracy to control the Panchayats and provided a retrograde provision (Article 205), empowering the District Collector to dismiss and suspend the elected representatives. There are no organic linkages among the three-tiers of Panchayats. Powers have not been given to the Panchayats on 29 subjects through law. All the powers which have been given to the Panchayats are only by notifications. All the powers are supervisory in nature and advisory in character. The District Planning Committee has to play a vital role in preparing a perspective development plan for the entire district. But the District Planning Committee is not activated and it is only a showpiece. The State Government has not moved 8 per cent of the total resources to the Panchayats. Sectoral departments are not brought under the purview of Panchayat institutions. All the functionaries are with the Government. The Panchayat institutions are functioning with all these limitations. The Panchayat leaders, in the initial stages, demanded powers continuously. But they have started functioning and discharging their roles and responsibilities in the *status quo*. The Panchayati leaders, during the first period, were provided with neither needed information nor needed training. As a result the Panchayat leaders managed the Panchayats according to their own perception and the direction of the officials. The officials closely working with the people established their sway over the elected representatives as the knowledge of the Panchayati leaders on Panchayati Raj was poor. It does not mean that the officials are thorough with the rules and procedures of the new Panchayati Raj System. Since they speak from the position of an office whatever they directs has got a value. In the first period from 1996 to 2001 the elected leaders were turned into contractors as they were given the responsibility of carrying out the programmes and schemes of the Government. Local Body elections in Tamil Nadu are being conducted at one stroke to all the tiers of rural Local Bodies and for urban Local Bodies. In the electoral process one always finds the expression of community will. Communities determined the candidates through various means and the selected candidates were allowed to take part in the electoral process. It is true that of all the three elections, namely election to the Lok Sabha, election to the State Legislative Assembly and election to the Local Bodies, the highest turn out will be for the Local Bodies. Communities adopted different practices, namely selecting the candidate by lot, choosing the candidate by nomination of the chief of the clan, selecting the candidate on the basis of bidding, and a few other modalities. The communities have very strong roots and people have faith in the communities and, as a result, it was difficult for the State Election Commission and the State Government to tackle this. These cases were reported in the newspapers but not registered as cases. Both the Election Commission and the State Government were interested in conducting the election and not in tackling this kind of problems. No doubt, these are all aberrations of democracy, yet they do occur regularly.

To overcome this kind of problems a Voters Awareness Campaign was conducted throughout the State and, as a result, a large number of candidates from women SHGs contested in the election and won the election also. The Voters Awareness Campaign yielded good results in terms of participation of the people in the election and the induction of good individuals into local bodies from various organizations.

Panchayat institutions are political institutions and they need the support of communities to carry out any programme or scheme in the society. Depending on the rapport with the communities, the Panchayat will succeed in administering development. Social development is an important area which is a left out by all political institutions in their discourses. Non-issues are being focused upon in politics. The Panchayat cannot ignore these issues of social development. But to achieve success the Panchayat needs the support of the communities. An action research was conducted in ten Gram Panchayats by fixing social development indicators. After the end of the project period, the Panchayats performance was evaluated and found to be positive. It proved that, with small incentives, the Panchayats can be motivated to work on social development issues.

Yet another action research in the area of planning for development at micro level warrants discussion. The development role provided to the Government has been given back to the people by taking a conscious stand that the Government is not a provider but a facilitator. Gram Panchayat Presidents of selected villages have taken up the responsibility of developing a perspective plan for the development of the Gram Panchayat and thereby initiatives had been taken by the Panchayat and the people and it will go a long way in yielding results. But the process has been started and it is the first step needed at this juncture.

In the fast changing scenario in the society, the role of the traditional Panchayats has been questioned by the formal Panchayats. The conflict is visible in many areas in Tamil Nadu. But, in many places, there is a close linkage between the two and both work together to achieve development. A micro study has brought to light the changes the traditional Panchayats are undergoing to integrate themselves with the formal Panchayats.

The Panchayat leaders have been facing a volley of problems in managing the Panchayats and administering development. The women Panchayat leaders' problems, are more acute and they are prevented from using power to administer development. Having perceived the barriers and problems, the women Panchayat leaders have formed their own associations to tackle their problems on their own collectively. It is a documentation of two years' experience. Women leaders have come to a stage to negotiate with the higher level officials. The demands projected by them have been addressed and the issues of women had been brought to the centre stage in all the discussions.

Capacity building is an imperative for the effective functioning of any organization. Hence it has been emphasized that the Local Body leaders have to be trained and they have to be concientized on social development issues. For about five years efforts were made to prepare the training manual and module. Gandhigram Rural Institute developed a manual and module to conduct a training programme for elected leaders of Local Bodies. Based on the module, training was imparted. The training programme enabled them to visualize the gap between the intent and what is actually going on in the Panchayati Raj System. It dispelled many of the doubts of the Panchayat Presidents. It proved that the training is the key to empowerment.

Yet another major question repeatedly asked is whether the *Dalit* leaders have performed their role properly with the notion that they cannot perform as they face several barriers and obstacles in the process. To evaluate the performance and the problems a study was undertaken by which it was brought to the limelight that the *Dalit* Panchayat leaders have performed their role and responsibilities very effectively by overcoming all the barriers and obstacles. They have picked up several methodological nuances to manage the Panchayats. Thus the myth has been broken.

Panchayati Raj Institutions have taken different routes to reach the goals fixed by the 73rd Amendment to the Constitution of India. Many dimensions are emerging in the Panchayati Raj System in Tamil Nadu as it integrates with the local community system. Though limited power, finance and functionaries have been given to the Local Bodies, the institutions have excelled in terms of performance. It is the result of devolution but takes place in the form of evolution.

BIBLIOGRAPHY

Aslam, M., (2001), *Directory of Panchayati Raj Training Institutions in India*, New Delhi: Rajiv Gandhi Foundation.

Bandhopadhyay, D., *Empowering Panchayats: Handbook for Master Trainers Using Participatory Approach*, New Delhi: Concept Publishing Company.

Basu, Amrita and Kohli, Atul (1998) *Community Conflicts and the State in India*, Delhi: Oxford University Press.

Beteille, A. (1965), *Caste, Class and Power: Changing Patterns of Stratification in a Tanjure Village*, Berkeley: University of California Press.

Chinnammal, C. (2002), *Perspective Plan for Development of Urathupatti*, Thirupathur: Grama Iyakkam.

Common Wealth Foundation, 1999, *Citizens and Governance: Civil Society in the New Millennium*, London: The Common Wealth Foundation.

Dumment, Louis, (1970), *Homo Hierarchies*, Chicago: Chicago University Press.

Fulter, C.J., 1997, *Caste To-Day*, Delhi: Oxford University Press.

Gomathy, S., (2002), *Perspective Plan for Development of Manalur*, Thirupathur, Grama Iyakkam.

Government of India (1993), *73rd Constitutional Amendment Act*, New Delhi: Government of India.

Government of Tamil Nadu (1998), *Action Taken Report on the Entrustment of Responsibilities to Three-Tier Panchayats*, Chennai: Department of Rural Development.

Government of Tamil Nadu (1998), *Report on Roles, Responsibilities and Powers Devolved to Panchayats*, Chennai: Government of Tamil Nadu.

Government of Tamil Nadu (1999), *Action Taken Report on the Entrustment of Responsibilities to Three-Tier Panchayats*, Chennai: Government of Tamil Nadu.

Government of Tamil Nadu (1999), *Democratic Decentralization: Powers Entrusted to Panchayati Raj Institutions*, Chennai: Rural Development Department.

Hardgrave, R.L. (1965), *The Dravidian Movement*, Bombay: Popular Prakashan.

Issac, T.M. Thomas and Franke Richard W. (2002), *Local Democracy and Development*, New Delhi: Left Word Books.

Joshi, R.P. (ed) (1998), *Constitution of Panchayati Raj: A Reassessment*, Jaipur: Rawat Publications.

Kaviraj, Sudipta (ed) (1977), *Politics in India*, New Delhi: Oxford University Press.

Kohli, Atul (1990), *Democracy and Discontent,* Cambridge: Cambridge University Press.

Kothari, Rajni (ed) (1970), *Caste in Indian Politics*, New Delhi: Orient Longman.

Kothari, Rajni (1998), *State Against Democracy*, Delhi: Ajanta Publications.

Lele, M.K., (2001), "Local Government: Conflict of Interests and Issues of Legitimization", *Economic and Political Weekly,* Vol. No. XXXVI: 51 (Dec. 22).

Manor, James (1999), *The Political Economy of Democratic Decentralization,* Washington D.C.: The World Bank.

Mathew, George (ed), (2000), *Status of Panchayati Raj in the States and Union Territories of India 2000,* New Delhi: Concept Publishing Company.

Nagajothi, Y. (2002), *Perspective Plan for Development of Kozhikudipatti,* Thirupathur: Grama Iyakkam.

Narayanasamy, N., Boraian, M.P. and Jeyaraju, M.A. (eds) (2000) *Corruption at the Grassroots: The Shades and Shadows*, New Delhi: Concept Publishing Company.

Palanithurai, G. (2001), *Problems faced by the leaders of Gram Panchayat*, Gandhigram: Rajiv Gandhi Chair for Panchayati Raj Studies.

Palanithurai, G. (2002), *Report of the Pre-Election Voters Awareness,* Gandhigram: Rajiv Gandhi Chair for Panchayati Raj Studies.

Palanithurai, G. (2002), *Report of the Training on Multi-Level Planning,* Gandhigram: Tamil Nadu Council for Sustainable Livelihood.

Palanithurai, G. (2002), *Report of the Workshop on Multi-Level Planning*, Gandhigram: Tamil Nadu Council for Sustainable Livelihood.

Palanithurai, G. (2002), *Tamil Nadu Panchayati Government Act, Rules and Schemes (in Tamil)*, Chennai: South Vision.

Pushpam, A. (2002), *Perspective Plan for Development of P.Nerpugapatti,* Thirupathur: Grama Iyakkam.

Rajagopal, Indhu, (1985), *The Tyranny of Caste*, New Delhi: Vikas.

Rajiv Gandhi Chair (2002), *Training Module for Panchayat Training Process*, Gandhigram: Rajiv Gandhi Chair for Panchayati Raj Studies.

Rajiv Gandhi Foundation (1998), *Charter of Panchayats*, New Delhi: Rajiv Gandhi Foundation.

Rakku, K. (2002), *Perspective Plan for Development of Vadavanpatti*, Thirupathur: Gram Iyakkam.

State Finance Commission (1995), *First State Finance Commission Report*, Chennai: State Finance Commission.

State Planning Commission (1997), *Report on Entrustment of Responsibilities to Three-Tier Panchayats*, Chennai: State Planning Commission.

Sundaram, K.V. (1997), *Decentralized Multi-Level Planning: Principle and Practice*, New Delhi: Concept Publishing Company.

The Hunger Project (2002), *Training for Women in Panchayat,* Gandhigram: Rajiv Gandhi Chair for Panchayati Raj Studies.

Veerakalaiarasi (2002), *Perspective Plan for Development of Veppankulam*, Thirupathur: Grama Iyakkam.

INDEX